McGRAW-HILL

Brief Version

COMPUTING ESSENTIALS

Annual Edition
1996-1997

D1315583

McGRAW-HILL

Brief Version

COMPUTING
ESSENTIALS

Annual Edition
1996-1997

Timothy J. O'Leary
Arizona State University

Linda I. O'Leary

The McGraw-Hill Companies, Inc.
New York St. Louis San Francisco Auckland Bogota Caracas Lisbon
London Madrid Mexico City Milan Montreal New Delhi San Juan Singapore
Sydney Tokyo Toronto

About the Authors

Timothy J. O'Leary is a professor in the Department of Decision and Information Systems at Arizona State University. He has written several books and articles on computers and information systems.

Linda I. O'Leary is a professional trainer in the area of computers. She has developed computer training manuals for corporations and presented seminars on a wide variety of application programs.

Dedication

To Roger Howell, editor and friend. Thanks for all your support and all the good times—Tim and Linda

McGraw-Hill

A Division of The McGraw·Hill Companies

McGraw-Hill Computing Essentials Annual Edition
1996–1997—Brief Version

1 2 3 4 5 6 7 8 9 0 BAN BAN 9 0 9 8 7 6

ISBN 0-07-049090-2

Sponsoring editor: *Frank Ruggirello*

Editorial assistant: *Kyle Thomes*

Production supervisor: *Richard DeVitto*

Project manager: *Greg Hubit, Bookworks*

Cover design: *Christy Butterfield*

Interior design: *Christy Butterfield*

Compositor: *GTS Graphics, Inc.*

Photo researcher: *Sarah Evertson/Image Quest*

Printer and binder: *Banta Co.*

Library of Congress Catalog Card Number 95-77497

Contents in Brief

Contents

2

Application Software: Basic Tools

3

Application Software: Power Tools

6 *Input and Output* *114*

7 *Secondary Storage* *136*

NEW!

The Internet Guide: How to Surf the Net

IG1

The Buyer's Guide: How to Buy Your Own Microcomputer System

BG1

Preface to the Instructor

This book is designed for students in an introductory computer or microcomputer course. It assumes no prerequisites.

Objective: Creating Computer Competency

This book is intended to give students competency in computer-related knowledge and skills to support their academic pursuits and be of immediate value to their employers. Our goal is to prepare students to be:

- **Microcomputer-literate**—able to employ microcomputers to increase their productivity and effectiveness.

- **Familiar with commercial software**—especially word processing, spreadsheet, and database management packages.

- **Grounded in fundamental concepts**—a basic working vocabulary and knowledge of computing and information concepts.

Distinguishing Features

Flexibility The Microcomputing Annual Edition system allows instructors to choose exactly what they want to teach.

- **McGraw-Hill Computing Essentials: Annual Edition 1996–1997** in 14 brief chapters describes basic computer and information concepts.

- **Brief Version Computing Essentials: Annual Edition 1996–1997** contains Chapters 1 through 9, featuring the hardware and software concepts.

- **More than 40 Lab Modules** offer hands-on, beginning-skill-level, easy-to-use software application tutorials. A case study in each tutorial provides a problem-solving approach to using the software.

- **Custom-Bound Version.** With this option, you can build your own book by choosing either version of *Computing Essentials* and/or 2 to 5 *Lab Modules.* You can choose exactly what you want to teach and provide your students with an affordable, easy-to-use spiral-bound textbook. The following can be custombound.

Essentials
Brief Essentials
Microsoft Office for Windows 95
    (with and without PowerPoint)
Microsoft Office for Windows 3.1
    (with and without PowerPoint)

Internet
Windows 95
Windows 3.1
DOS 3.3–6.0
DOS 5.0
DOS 6.0

Word 7.0 for Windows 95
Word 6.0 for Windows
WordPerfect 6.1 for Windows
WordPerfect 6.0 for Windows
WordPerfect (5.1/5.2) for Windows
WordPerfect 6.0 for DOS
WordPerfect 5.1

Excel 7.0 for Windows 95
Excel 5.0 for Windows
Lotus 1-2-3 for Windows Release 5.0

Lotus 1-2-3 for Windows Release 4.0
Lotus 1-2-3 for Windows Release 1.0
Lotus 1-2-3 Release 2.4
Lotus 1-2-3 Release 2.3
Lotus 1-2-3 Release 2.2 Revised
Quattro Pro 5.0 for Windows
Quattro Pro 5.0 for DOS

Access 7.0 for Windows 95
Access 2.0 for Windows
Paradox 5.0 for Windows
Paradox for Windows
Paradox 4.5 for DOS
Paradox 4.0
dBASE for Windows
dBASE IV 1.1/2.0
dBASE III PLUS

PowerPoint 7.0 for Windows 95
PowerPoint 4.0 for Windows

Microsoft Office Integration
LAN
Works for Windows 95
Works 3.0 for DOS
Works 3.0 for Windows

Consult with your McGraw-Hill sales representative to put together the best "customized" package for your course.

Revised Annually Annual revisions allow us—and our readers—to keep pace in this dynamic field.

New to the 1996–1997 edition:

- **Update of Technology and Issues.** New coverage includes National Information Highway, the Internet, World Wide Web, Windows 95, plug and play, CD-R drives, P6 chip, multimedia, virtual reality, and much more.

- **Updated Graphics.** Over 50% of the illustrations are new, reflecting the rapid changes in technology and applications.

- **New Lab Modules.** New labs on the Internet, Windows 95, and other new software applications have been added (see listing above). These new labs have been designed to emphasize concepts and critical thinking by including visual concept summaries and new problems with varying levels of difficulty.

The Internet The 1996–1997 Annual Edition has Internet topics woven throughout.

- **The Internet Guide: How to Surf the Net** is included with each version of *Computing Essentials Annual Edition 1996–1997*. This comprehensive guide presents a conceptual model of the Internet and presents details on e-mail, discussion groups, Telnet, FTD, gophers, World Wide Web, and much more.

  NEW!

- **Projects.** Each chapter of *Computing Essentials* concludes with a short project requiring students to use the Internet to research selected topics. Special software, derived from McGraw-Hill's *Every Student's Internet Resource Guide,* is provided to help students navigate the World Wide Web and access information.

  NEW!

- **Lab Modules: The Internet** consists of four modules. Students learn hands-on from a beginning-skill-level how to send and receive e-mail, join and participate in discussion groups, find resources using gophers, and navigate the Net using the World Wide Web.

  NEW!

Visual Orientation We believe that students learn visually. Accordingly, *Computing Essentials* balances text with color graphics. Our Visual Summaries capture in a nutshell the key concepts covered in each chapter. The text contains numerous color illustrations, photos, and charts. Adopters tell us that our visual orientation enhances their students' interest and comprehension.

"Learn-by-Doing" Approach Each chapter in *Computing Essentials* concludes with Review Questions and Discussion Questions and Projects. These pedagogical aids are designed to reinforce learning and encourage students to apply the concepts covered in each chapter to solve actual problems.

The lab modules also follow the "learn-by-doing" approach. An ongoing case study based on real-world use of the software leads the student step by step from problem to solution. Each lab module includes the following additional learning aids:

- Conceptual Overview
- Competencies
- Case Study
- Numerous Screen Displays
- Summary of Key Terms and Commands
- Lab Review (Matching and Fill-in Questions)
- Hands-on Practice Exercises
- Case Project
- Glossary of Key Terms
- Summary of Commands
- Index

The Support Package

Comprehensive teaching material sets are available for *Computing Essentials* as well as for each of the lab modules. Each set includes:

- Objectives
- Schedule
- Procedural Requirements
- Teaching Tips
- Answers to End-of-Chapter Problems
- Command Summary
- Answers to Practice Exercises
- Transparency Masters
- Printed Test Bank
- 3½-inch Student Data Disk and Test Questions

Additional support materials:

- Color Transparencies
- Multimedia—A CD-ROM Presentation Device—Updated annually
- Electronic Transparencies for Microsoft Office lab modules
- Software Assistance Program—Updated
- Documentary-Style Videotape Series

If you would like information on how to obtain the supplements described above, please contact your McGraw-Hill sales representative.

Acknowledgments

We are grateful for the helpful comments from our reviewers: David Anderson, Fort Peck Community College; Bill Barth, Cayuga Community College; Janice Burke, South Suburban College; C. T. Cadenhead, Richland College; Earline Cocke, Northwest Mississippi Community College; Barbara Comfort, J. Sergeant Reynolds Community College; Terry Cooper, Medicine Hat College; Sharon Cotman, Thomas Nelson Community College; Frank Coyle, Southern Methodist University; Jack Cundiff, Horry-Georgetown Tech; Jim Davies, DeAnza College; Michael Dixon, Sacramento City College; Paul Duchow, Pasadena City College; Orlynn R. Evans, Stephen F. Austin State University; William Ferns, Baruch College; Eleanor Flanigan, Montclair State University; Tanya Goette, Kennesaw State College; Usha Jindal, Washtenaw Community College; N. Jurkovich, Palo Alto College; Tom Kane, Centennial College; Debbie Kramer, Rowan College; Linda Kridelbaugh, Southwestern Oregon Community College; Albert Leary, St. Charles County Community College; Martha Long, North Essex County Community College; Donna Matherly, Tallahassee Community College; Curtis Meadow, University of Maine; Josephine Mendoza, California State University—San Bernardino; Pam Milstead, Louisiana Tech University; Jeff Mock, Diablo Valley College; Oven Murphy, California State University—San Bernardino; Sonia Nayle, Los Angeles City College; Pamela Nelson, Panhandle State University; Brenda Nielson, Mesa Community College; Paul Northrup, University of Colorado; Carl Penzuil, Corning Community College; Scott

Persky, McHenry County College; Winfred Pikelis, United States Military Academy; Lisa Rosner, Stockton State College; Marion Sackson, Pace University; Joe Sallis, University of Mississippi; Peg Saragina, Santa Rosa Junior College; Judith Scheeren, Westmoreland Community College; Faye Simmons, SUNY Canton; Daniel Simon, Northampton Community College; Elizabeth Swope, Louisiana State University; Danver S. Tomer, University of Central Arkansas; Barbara Wertz, Clackamas Community College; Mark Workman, Frank Phillips College; and James Worley, East Tennessee University.

In addition, we are very appreciative of all the efforts of the McGraw-Hill staff and others who worked on this book: Roger Howell, Frank Ruggirello, Rhonda Sands, Kyle Thomes, Alan Sachs, and Gary Burke for their support of this edition; Richard DeVitto for production supervision; Kris Johnson and Jeff Rydman for their marketing support; Karen Jackson, Eric Munson, Erika Berg, and Steve Mitchell for their past editorial, marketing, and managerial support.

We are also grateful for the contributions of those outside McGraw-Hill: Colleen Hayes for her creativity, hard work, and continued dedication to the project; Susan DeMar, Susan Lanier-Graham, and William Graham for their developmental support; Carol Dean for her creative new practice exercises; Greg Hubit for his excellent project management; Christy Butterfield for her innovative design work; Sarah Evertson for photo research; Peg Sallade for permission to use parts of her research on "Aquatic Fitness"; Marianne Virgili of Glenwood Springs Chamber of Commerce and Jim Price of the Sports Authority for their contributions toward the development of case materials; GTS Graphics for line illustrations and composition; Elaine Brett for production supervision; Pat Rogondino and Beth Bevans for design and format; Susan Defosset, Carol Dondrea, Cathy Baehler, Catherine Lindberg, and Jane Granoff for their continued excellent production support.

Write to Us

We welcome your reactions to this book, for we would like it to be as useful to you as possible. Write to us in care of: Microcomputer Applications Editor The McGraw-Hill Companies, Inc. 55 Francisco St, Suite 200 San Francisco, CA 94133

Timothy J. O'Leary
Linda I. O'Leary

You and Computer Competency

Computer competency: This notion may not be familiar to you, but it's easy to understand. The purpose of this book is to help you become *competent* in computer-related skills. Specifically, we want to help you walk into a job and immediately be valuable to an employer. In this chapter, we first describe why learning about the computer is important to your future. We then present an *overview* of what makes up an information system: people, procedures, software, hardware, and data. In subsequent chapters, we will describe these parts in detail.

COMPETENCIES

After you have read this chapter, you should be able to:

1. Explain computer competency.
2. Distinguish four kinds of computers: microcomputer, minicomputer, mainframe, and supercomputer.
3. Explain the five parts of an information system: people, procedures, software, hardware, and data.
4. Distinguish application software from system software.
5. Describe hardware devices for input, processing, storage, output, and communications.
6. Describe document, worksheet, and database files.
7. Explain computer connectivity and the Internet.

Fifteen years ago, most people had little to do with computers, at least directly. Of course, they filled out computerized forms, took computerized tests, and paid computerized bills. But the real work with computers was handled by specialists—programmers, data-entry clerks, and computer operators.

Then microcomputers came along and changed everything. Today it is easy for nearly everybody to use a computer. People who use microcomputers today are called "end users." (See Figure 1-1.) Today:

- Microcomputers are common tools in all areas of life. Writers write, artists draw, engineers and scientists calculate—all on microcomputers. Businesspeople do all three.

- New forms of learning have developed. People who are homebound, who work odd hours, or who travel frequently may take courses by telephone-linked home computers. A college course need not fit within the usual time of a quarter or a semester.

- New ways to communicate and to find people with similar interests are available. All kinds of people are using electronic mail and the Internet to meet and to share ideas.

What about you? How can microcomputers enhance *your* life?

End Users and Computer Competency

By gaining computer competency, end users can use microcomputers to improve their productivity and their value in the workplace.

End users are people who use microcomputers or have access to larger computers. If you are not an end user already, you will probably become one in the near future. That is, you will learn to use packaged computer programs to meet your unique needs for information. Let us point out two things here.

■ By "packaged programs," we mean programs that you can buy rather than those you have to write yourself. Examples of packaged programs include video games on a disk and work-related programs, such as word processing for typing documents and electronic spreadsheets for analysis.

■ By "needs," we mean various organizing, managing, or business needs. That is, they are *information-related* or *decision-making* needs. Becoming **computer competent**—learning how to use the computer to meet your information needs—will improve your productivity. It will also make you a more valuable employee.

How much do you have to know to be computer competent? Clearly, in today's fast-changing technological world, you cannot learn everything—but very few people need to. You don't have to be a computer scientist to make good use of a microcomputer. Indeed, that is precisely the point of this book. Our goal is not to teach you everything there is to know, but only what you *need* to know to get started. Thus, we present only what we think you will find most useful—both now and in the future.

FIGURE 1-1

End users: People are using microcomputers to meet their information needs.

Four Kinds of Computers

Computers are of four types: microcomputers, minicomputers, mainframes, and supercomputers.

This book focuses principally on microcomputers. However, it is almost certain that you will come in contact, at least indirectly, with other kinds of computers. Thus, we describe many features that are common to these larger machines.

Computers are electronic devices that can follow instructions to accept input, process that input, and produce information. There are four types of computers: *microcomputers, minicomputers, mainframe computers,* and *supercomputers.*

Microcomputers

The most widely used and the fastest-growing type of computer is the **microcomputer.** (See Figure 1-2.) There are two categories of microcomputers—*desktop* and *portable*.

- **Desktop computers** are small enough to fit on top or along the side of a desk and yet are too big to carry around. (See Figure 1-3.) **Personal computers** are one type of desktop. These machines run comparatively easy-to-use application software. They are used by a wide range of individuals, from clerical people to managers. **Workstations** are another type of desktop computer. Generally, these machines are more powerful. They are designed to run more advanced application software. Workstations are used by engineers, scientists, and others who process lots of data. The distinction between personal computers and workstations is now blurring. The principal reason is that personal computers are now nearly as powerful as workstations and are able to run many of the same programs.

FIGURE 1-2

Microcomputers in use—
past, present, and future.

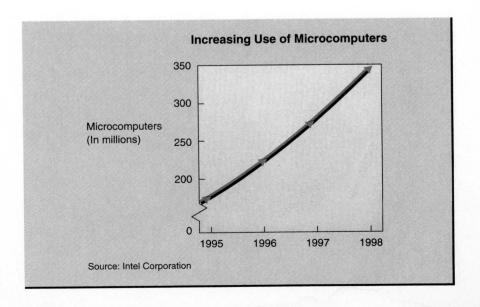

Increasing Use of Microcomputers

Microcomputers
(In millions)

350

300

250

200

0

1995   1996   1997   1998

Source: Intel Corporation

FIGURE 1-3
Desktop computer (Gateway 2000).

■ **Portable computers** are microcomputers that are small enough and light enough to move easily from one place to another. There are four categories of portable computers—*laptops, notebooks, subnotebooks,* and *personal digital assistants.*

    Laptops, which weigh between 10 and 16 pounds, may be either AC-powered, battery-powered, or both. The AC-powered laptop weighs 12 to 16 pounds. The battery-powered laptop weighs 10 to 15 pounds, batteries included, and can be carried on a shoulder strap. The user of a laptop might be an accountant or financial person who needs to work on a computer away from the desk.

    Notebooks are a smaller version of the laptop. (See Figure 1-4.) They weigh between 5 and 10 pounds and can fit into most briefcases. The user of a

FIGURE 1-4
Notebook computer (IBM ThinkPad 750).

FIGURE 1-5
Personal digital assistant
(Motorola Envoy Personal
Communicator).

notebook PC might be a student, salesperson, or journalist, who uses the computer for note-taking. It is especially valuable in locations where electrical connections are not available. Notebook computers are the most popular portable computer today.

Subnotebooks are for frequent flyers and life-on-the-road types. Subnotebook users give up a full-size display screen and keyboard in exchange for less weight. Weighing between 2 and 6 pounds, these computers fit easily into a briefcase.

Personal Digital Assistants (PDA) are much smaller than even the subnotebooks. The typical PDA combines pen input, writing recognition, personal organizational tools, and communications capabilities in a very small package. A PDA user might be a worker at a warehouse who records changes in inventory or a busy executive handling daily communications. (See Figure 1-5.)

Minicomputers

Also known as **midrange computers, minicomputers** are desk-sized machines. They fall between microcomputers and mainframes in their processing speeds and data-storing capacities. Medium-size companies or departments of large companies typically use them for specific purposes. For example, they might use them to do research or to monitor a particular manufacturing process. Smaller-size companies typically use minicomputers for their general data processing needs, such as accounting.

Mainframe Computers

Mainframes are large computers occupying specially wired, air-conditioned rooms. They are capable of great processing speeds and data storage. (See Figure 1-6.) They are used by large organizations—businesses, banks, universities, and government agencies—to handle millions of transactions. For example, insurance companies use mainframes to process information about millions of policyholders.

FIGURE 1-6
Mainframe computer (IBM
ES/9000).

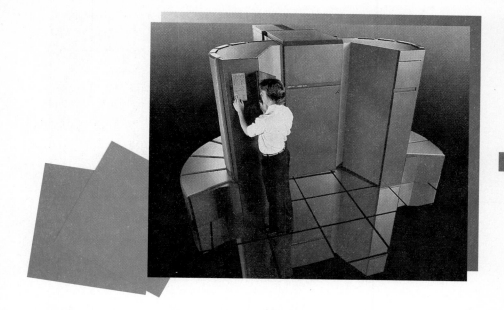

FIGURE 1-7
Supercomputer (Cray Y-MP
Computer System).

Supercomputers

The most powerful type of computer is the **supercomputer.** These machines are special, high-capacity computers used by very large organizations. For example, NASA uses supercomputers to track and control space explorations. Supercomputers are also used for oil exploration, simulations, and worldwide weather forecasting. (See Figure 1-7.)

Let us now get started on the road to computer competency. We begin by describing the role of the microcomputer in an information system.

The Five Parts of an Information System

An information system has five parts: people, procedures, software, hardware, and data.

When you think of a microcomputer, perhaps you think of just the equipment itself. That is, you think of the monitor or the keyboard. There is more to it than that. The way to think about a microcomputer is as part of an information system. An **information system** has five parts: *people, procedures, software, hardware,* and *data.* (See Figure 1-8.)

- **People:** It is easy to overlook people as one of the five parts of a microcomputer system. Yet that is what microcomputers are all about—making people, end user like yourself, more productive.

- **Procedures: Procedures** are rules or guidelines for people to follow when using software, hardware, and data. Typically, these procedures are documented in manuals written by computer specialists for particular organizations. Software and hardware manufacturers also provide manuals with their products. An example is the *Lotus 1-2-3 Reference Manual.*

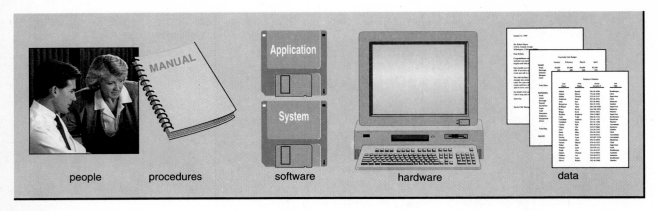

people   procedures   software   hardware   data

FIGURE 1-8
The five parts of an information system.

FIGURE 1-9
Two well-known microcomputer hardware systems: the IBM Performance Series multimedia and the Apple Macintosh Performa 5200 CD.

- **Software: Software** is another name for a program or programs. A **program** is the step-by-step instructions that tell the computer how to do its work. The purpose of software is to convert *data* (unprocessed facts) into *information* (processed facts).

- **Hardware:** The **hardware** consists of the equipment: keyboard, mouse, monitor, system unit, and other devices. Hardware is controlled by software. It actually processes the data to create information. (See Figure 1-9.)

- **Data: Data** consists of the raw, unprocessed facts. Examples of raw facts are hours you worked and your pay rate. After data is processed through the computer, it is usually called **information.** An example of such information is the total wages owed you for a week's work.

In large computer systems, there are specialists who deal with writing procedures, developing software, and capturing data. In microcomputer systems, however, end users often perform these operations. To be a competent end user, you must understand the essentials of software, hardware, and data.

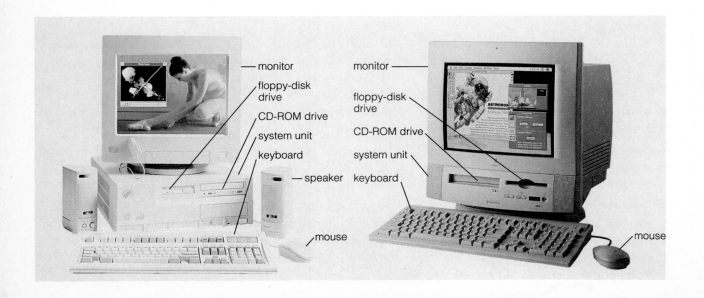

monitor
floppy-disk drive
CD-ROM drive
system unit
keyboard
speaker
mouse

monitor
floppy-disk drive
CD-ROM drive
system unit
keyboard
mouse

Software

Software is of two kinds: application software and system software.

Software, as we mentioned, is another name for programs. Programs are the instructions that tell the computer how to process data into the form you want. In most cases, the words *software* and *programs* are interchangeable.

There are two major kinds of software—*application software* and *system software*. You can think of application software as the kind you use. Think of system software as the kind the computer uses. (See Figure 1-10.)

Application Software

Application software might be described as "end-user" software. Application software performs useful work on general-purpose tasks such as word processing and cost estimating.

Application software may be *packaged* or *custom-made*.

- **Packaged software** are programs prewritten by professional programmers that are typically offered for sale. There are thousands of different types of application packages available for microcomputers alone.

- **Custom-made software,** or **custom programs,** are programs written for a specific purpose and for a specific organization. Using computer languages, programmers create this software to instruct the company computer to perform whatever tasks the organization wants. A program might compute payroll checks, keep track of goods in the warehouse, calculate sales commissions, or perform similar business functions.

There are certain general-purpose programs that we call "basic tools" in this book. These programs are widely used in nearly all career areas. They are the kind of programs you *have* to know to be considered computer competent. The most popular basic tools are:

- *Word processing programs,* used to prepare written documents
- *Spreadsheet programs,* used to analyze and summarize numerical data
- *Database managers,* used to organize and manage data and information

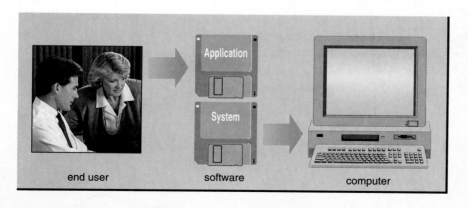

end user   software   computer

FIGURE 1-10
End users interact with application software. System software interacts with the computer.

■ *Graphics programs,* used to visually analyze and present data and information

■ *Communications programs,* used to transmit and receive data and information

■ *Integrated programs,* which combine some or all of these applications in one program. Also, *software suites,* in which separate applications are sold as a group.

There are certain programs that we call "power tools" in this book. These programs are more specialized than the basic tools. Power tools are widely used within certain career areas. They are the kind of programs you *should* know to be truly computer competent in the future. The most popular power tools are:

■ *Personal information managers,* used to increase productivity through organization

■ *Groupware,* designed to coordinate group activities and increase team productivity

■ *Project management,* used to plan projects, schedule people, and control resources

■ *Desktop publishing,* which combines text and graphics to create professional-quality documents

■ *Multimedia,* which integrates all kinds of information into a single presentation

■ *Artificial intelligence,* which simulates human thought processes and actions.

System Software

The user interacts with application software. **System software** enables the application software to interact with the computer. (Refer to Figure 1-10.) System software is "background" software. It includes programs that help the computer manage its own internal resources.

The most important system software program is the **operating system,** which interacts between the application software and the computer. The operating system handles such details as running ("executing") programs, storing data and programs, and processing data. System software frees users to concentrate on solving problems rather than on the complexities of operating the computer.

Microcomputer operating systems change as the machines themselves become more powerful and outgrow the older operating systems. Today's computer competency, then, requires that you have some knowledge of the following most popular microcomputer operating systems:

■ *DOS,* the standard operating system for International Business Machines (IBM) and IBM-compatible microcomputers.

■ *Windows,* not an operating system but an environment that extends the capability of DOS.

■ *Windows 95,* a new operating system that does not require DOS.

■ *Windows NT,* a powerful operating system designed for powerful microcomputers.

- *OS/2 Warp,* the operating system developed by IBM for powerful microcomputers.
- *Macintosh operating system,* the standard operating system for Apple Corporation's Macintosh computers.
- *Unix,* an operating system originally developed for minicomputers that can run on many of the more powerful microcomputers.

Hardware

Microcomputer hardware consists of devices for input, processing, storage, output, and communications.

Microcomputer hardware—the physical equipment—falls into five categories. They are *input devices, the system unit, secondary storage, output devices,* and *communications devices.* Because we discuss hardware in detail later in the book, we will present just a quick overview here.

Input Devices

Input devices translate data and programs that humans can understand into a form that the computer can process. The most common input devices for microcomputers are the keyboard and the mouse. (See Figure 1-11.) The **keyboard** on a computer looks like a typewriter keyboard, but it has additional specialized keys. A **mouse** is a device that typically rolls on the desktop. It directs the **insertion point,** or cursor, on the display screen. A mouse has one or more buttons for selecting commands. It is also used to draw figures.

FIGURE 1-11
Microcomputer keyboard and mouse.

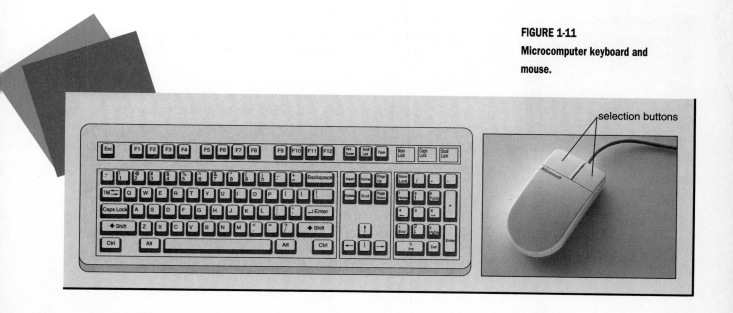

FIGURE 1-12
The system unit.

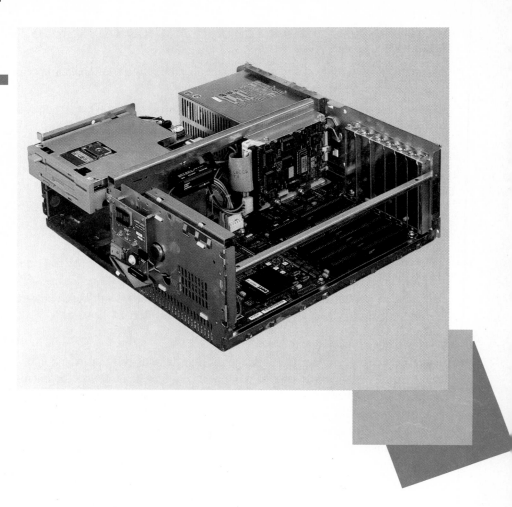

FIGURE 1-13
The Intel Pentium micro-
processor chip.

The System Unit

The **system unit** is electronic circuitry housed within the computer cabinet. (See Figure 1-12.) The two main parts of the system unit are:

■ The **central processing unit (CPU)** controls and manipulates data to produce information. A microcomputer's CPU is contained on a single integrated circuit or microprocessor chip. These chips are called **microprocessors.** (See Figure 1-13.)

■ **Memory,** also known as **primary storage** or **random access memory (RAM),** holds data and program instructions for processing the data. It also holds the processed information before it is output. Memory is sometimes referred to as *temporary* storage because it will be lost if the electrical power to the computer is disrupted or cut off. Data and instructions are held in memory only as long as the electrical power to the computer is on. Memory is located in the system unit on tiny memory chips.

Secondary Storage

Secondary storage also holds data and programs. However, it stores *permanently*. That is, the data and programs remain even after the electrical power is turned off. Secondary storage devices are located outside of the central processing unit, and are typically built into the system unit cabinet.

For microcomputers, the most important kinds of secondary storage "media" are as follows:

- **Floppy disks** (also called simply "diskettes") hold data or programs in the form of magnetized spots on plastic platters. The two sizes most commonly used are 3½-inch and 5½-inch diskettes. (See Figure 1-14.) The smaller size is more durable, can hold more, and is more widely used.

    A floppy disk is inserted into a **disk drive.** (See Figure 1-15.) This mechanism **reads** data from the disk. That is, the magnetized spots on the disk are converted to electronic signals and transmitted to primary storage inside the computer. A disk drive can also **write** data. That is, it can take the electronic information processed by the computer and record it magnetically onto the disk.

- A **hard disk** contains one or more metallic disks encased within a disk drive. Like floppy disks, hard disks hold data or programs in the form of magnetized spots. They also *read* and *write* data in much the same way as do floppy disks. However, the storage capacity of a hard-disk unit is many times that of a floppy disk and much faster.

- Unlike floppy and hard disks, **optical discs** hold data and programs by changing the reflecting surface of the disc. Some types of optical discs can read and write data. Some types can be written to only one time. The best-known type of optical disc, however, can only be read from. These are called **CD-ROM** for compact disc–read only memory.

Floppy and optical disks are inserted into and removed from their disk drives and are stored separately. The hard disk, by contrast, typically is not removable. (Refer to Figure 1-15.).

FIGURE 1-14
Two kinds of floppy disks:
3½-inch and 5¼-inch.

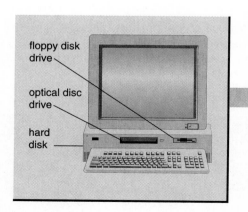

FIGURE 1-15
Three kinds of disk drives:
floppy, optical, and hard.

floppy disk drive

optical disc drive

hard disk

FIGURE 1-16
Newer monitors show sharp
images and vibrant colors.

FIGURE 1-17
Some printers can print color
images on paper.

Output Devices

Output devices are pieces of equipment that translate the processed information from the CPU into a form that humans can understand. One of the most important output devices is the **monitor,** or **video display screen,** which resembles a television screen. The quality of monitors has improved dramatically. Many monitors now offer crisp images and vivid colors. (See Figure 1-16.) Another important output device is the **printer,** a device that produces printed paper output. Some printers can also print in color. (See Figure 1-17.)

Communications Devices

Communications hardware sends and receives data and programs from one computer or secondary storage device to another. Many microcomputers use a **modem** (pronounced *"moh*-dem"). This device converts the electronic signals from the computer into electronic signals that can travel over a telephone line. A modem at the other end of the line then translates the signals for the receiving computer. A modem may be internal, or located inside a microcomputer's system cabinet. It may also be a separate unit, or external. (See Figure 1-18.)

FIGURE 1-18
An external modem connects
a microcomputer and a telephone.

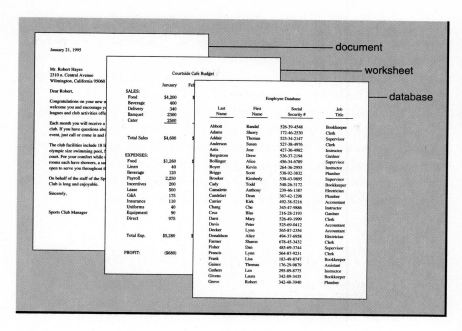

FIGURE 1-19
Three types of files: document, worksheet, and database.

Data

Data is contained in files for documents, worksheets, and databases.

Data is used to describe facts about something. If data is stored electronically in files, it can be used directly as input for the information system.

Three common types of files (see Figure 1-19) are:

- **Document files,** created by word processors to save documents such as memos, term papers, and letters.

- **Worksheet files,** created by electronic spreadsheets like Excel to analyze things like budgets and to predict sales.

- **Database files,** typically created by database management programs, contain highly structured and organized data. For example, an employee database file might contain all the workers' names, social security numbers, job titles, and other related pieces of information.

Connectivity

Connectivity is the microcomputer's ability to communicate with other computers and information sources.

Connectivity is the capability of the microcomputer to use information from the world beyond your desk. Data and information can be sent over telephone lines or cable and through the air. Thus, your microcomputer can be *connected* to other computers. It can also be connected to many computerized data banks and other sources of information that lie well beyond your desk.

Connectivity is a very significant development, for it expands the uses of the microcomputer severalfold. Central to the concept of connectivity is the **computer network.** A network is a communications system connecting two or more computers. Networks connect people as close as the next office and as far away as halfway around the world.

The **National Information Highway (NIH)** is a term used to describe the future of communication networks and computers. The basis of today's NIH, also known as the **National Information Infrastructure (NII)** or the **information superhighway,** is the **Internet.** Internet is a huge computer network available to nearly everyone with a microcomputer and a means to connect to it. It is a resource for information about an infinite number of topics.

A Look at the Future: You and Computer Competency

Computer competency is understanding the rules and the power of microcomputers. Competency lets you take advantage of increasingly productive software, hardware, and the connectivity revolution that are expanding the microcomputer's capabilities.

The purpose of this book is to help you be computer competent not only in the present but also in the future. Having competency requires your having the knowledge and understanding of the rules and the power of the microcomputer. This will enable you to benefit from three important developments: more powerful software, more powerful hardware, and connectivity to outside information resources. It will also help you to remain computer competent and to continue to learn in the future.

Powerful Software

The software now available can do an extraordinary number of tasks and help you in an endless number of ways. More and more employers are expecting the people they hire to be able to use it. Thus, we spend the next three chapters describing basic tools, power tools, and system software.

Powerful Hardware

Microcomputers are now much more powerful than they used to be. Indeed, the newer models have the speed and power of room-size computers of only a few years ago. However, despite the rapid change of specific equipment, their essential features remain unchanged. Thus, the competent end user should focus on these features. Chapters 5 through 7 explain what you need to know about hardware: the central processing unit, input/output devices, and secondary storage. A Buyer's Guide is presented at the end of this book for those considering the purchase of a microcomputer system.

Connectivity

The principle of *connectivity* is a rapidly evolving development. No longer are microcomputers and competent end users bound by the surface of the desk. Now they can reach past the desk and link up with other computers to share data, programs, and information. Accordingly, we devote Chapters 8 and 9 to discussing connectivity: communications, files, databases, and the Internet. An Internet Guide describing how to access and use the Internet is presented at the back of this book.

Changing Times

Are the times changing any faster now than they ever have? It's hard to say. People who were alive when radios, cars, and airplanes were being introduced certainly lived through some dramatic changes. Has technology made our own times even more dynamic? Whatever the answer, it is clear we live in a fast-paced age.

Most businesses have become aware that they must adapt to changing technology or be left behind. Many organizations are now making formal plans to keep track of technology and implement it in their competitive strategies. For example, banks have found that automated teller machines (ATMs) are vital to retail banking. (See Figure 1-20.) Not only do they require fewer human tellers, but they can also be made available 24 hours a day. ATM cards can be used in many places to buy anything from gas to groceries to movie tickets. Many banks are also trying to popularize home banking, so that customers can use microcomputers for certain financial tasks. In addition, banks are exploring the use of some very sophisticated application programs. These programs will accept and analyze cursive writing (the handwriting on checks) directly as input.

FIGURE 1-20
Automated teller machines are examples of technology used in business strategy.

Clearly, such changes do away with some jobs—those of many bank tellers and cashiers, for example. However, they create opportunities for other people. New technology requires people who are truly capable of working with it. These are not the people who think every piece of equipment is so simple they can just turn it on and use it. Nor are they those who think each new machine is a potential disaster. In other words, new technology needs people who are not afraid to learn it and are able to manage it. The real issue, then, is not how to make technology better. Rather, it is how to integrate the technology with people.

After reading this book, you will be in a very favorable position compared with many other people in industry today. You will learn not only the basics of hardware, software, and connectivity. You will also learn the most *current* technology. You will therefore be able to use these tools to your advantage—to be a winner.

KEY TERMS

application software (9)

CD-ROM (14)

central processing unit (CPU) (12)

communications hardware (14)

computer (4)

computer competent (3)

computer network (16)

connectivity (15)

custom program (9)

custom-made software (9)

data (8)

database file (15)

desktop computer (4)

disk drive (13)

document file (15)

end user (3)

floppy disk (13)

hard disk (14)

hardware (8)

information (8)

information superhighway (16)

information system (7)

input device (11)

insertion point (11)

Internet (16)

keyboard (11)

laptop (5)

mainframes (6)

memory (12)

microcomputer (4)

microprocessor (12)

midrange computer (6)

minicomputer (6)

modem (14)

monitor (14)

mouse (11)

National Information Highway (NIH) (16)

National Information Infrastructure (NII) (16)

notebook (5)

operating system (10)

optical disc (14)

output device (14)

packaged software (9)

personal computer (4)

personal digital assistant (PDA) (6)

portable computer (5)

primary storage (12)

printer (14)

procedure (7)

program (8)

random access memory (RAM) (12)

read (13)

secondary storage (12)

software (8)

subnotebook (6)

supercomputer (7)

system software (10)

system unit (12)

video display screen (14)

worksheet file (15)

workstation (4)

write (13)

REVIEW QUESTIONS

True/False

1. Microcomputers are common tools in all areas of life.

2. Hardware consists of a monitor, a keyboard, and software.

3. DOS is the standard operating system for Apple Corporation's Macintosh computers.

4. Memory is also known as primary storage.

5. A modem is used to send electronic signals over telephone lines.

Multiple Choice

1. Computers are electronic devices that accept instructions, process input, and produce:
   a. information
   b. prewritten programs
   c. data
   d. end users
   e. system software

2. High-capacity computers used primarily for research purposes are:
   a. microcomputers
   b. minicomputers
   c. mainframes
   d. supercomputers
   e. personal computers

3. The central processing unit (CPU) is located in the:
   a. hard disk
   b. system unit
   c. memory
   d. monitor
   e. keyboard

4. When electrical power is disrupted or cut off, data and programs are lost in:
   a. secondary storage
   b. basic tools
   c. memory
   d. operating system
   e. hard disk

5. Files containing highly structured and organized data are:
   a. documents
   b. worksheets
   c. databases
   d. graphics
   e. communications

Fill in the Blank

1. _____ _____ are people who use microcomputers or have access to larger computers.

2. Also known as midrange computers, _____ are frequently used by departments within larger organizations.

3. Written _____ are guidelines or rules to follow when using software, hardware, and data.

4. Secondary _____ is used to store data and programs permanently.

5. _____ files are created by electronic spreadsheet programs.

Open Ended

1. What is computer competency?
2. Describe the five parts of an information system.
3. Name the five categories of microcomputer hardware.
4. What is the difference between memory and secondary storage?
5. What are connectivity and the Internet?

DISCUSSION QUESTIONS AND PROJECTS

1. *Your reasons for learning computing:* How are you already using computer technology? What's happened in the computer-related world in the last six months that you might have read about or seen on television? How are companies using computers to stay on the cutting edge? These are some questions you might discuss with classmates to see why computers are an exciting part of life.

   You might also consider the reasons why you want to gain computer competency. Imagine your dream career. How do you think microcomputers, from what you already know, can help you do the work you want to do? What kind of after-hours interests do you have? Assuming you could afford it, how could a microcomputer bring new skills or value to those interests?

2. *Dealing with computer anxiety:* Some newcomers to computers experience *computer anxiety,* or *technophobia*—great discomfort, even fear, about dealing with these machines. They may be afraid, for example, that they "aren't smart enough" to work with computers or that they will "mess up." Or they may worry that they will accidentally break something, or that they will embarrass themselves in front of others. There are a number of ways of dealing with such anxieties and fears. If computers make you uncomfortable, discuss which of the following solutions might help.

   a. Work with a partner. Ask another newcomer if you can sit together (whether in lecture or laboratory) and try working things through together.

   b. Talk back to an imaginary critic. Write out a script in which you talk to an imaginary hostile stranger who puts you down about your computer abilities. By talking back, you demolish what are really self-criticisms.

   c. Familiarize yourself with computers gradually. Go into a computer lab by yourself and simply "play around" with a microcomputer. Back off whenever the discomfort becomes too great. After a while, you'll find yourself less bothered by these machines.

   d. Confront all your computer anxieties at once. Try the technique psychologists call "flooding." Allow yourself to experience all your fears and anxieties at once, no matter how bad they make you feel. By hanging in there, you tolerate the discomfort until the fears run their course.

3. *http://www.msu.edu//staff/rww/netgrow.html*   Today, the most dramatic event related to information technology is the widespread use of the Internet. It is used by individuals, businesses, and learning institutions throughout the world. Its projected growth and potential capabilities promise to influence all of our daily lives in the not-too-distant future. To learn more about it, visit the Internet site located at the address given at the beginning of this question. Then expand your search for information on the Internet by using other Internet resources. (Hint: Use the Every Student's Internet Resource Guide: Computer Science and Computer Technology—Entry Number: 01 and/or Entry Number: 02.)

You and Computer Competency

PEOPLE AND PROCEDURES   **SOFTWARE**

People

People are competent end users working to increase their productivity. **End users** use microcomputers and prewritten programs (such as word processing and spreadsheet programs) to solve information-related or decision-making problems.

Procedures

Procedures are manuals and guidelines that instruct end users on how to use the software and hardware.

Software is another name for **programs**—instructions that tell the computer how to process data. Two kinds are application and system software.

Application Software

Application software performs useful functions.

APPLICATION SOFTWARE	
BASIC TOOLS	**POWER TOOLS**
Word processors	Personal information managers
Spreadsheet programs	Groupware
Database managers	Project managers
Graphics programs	Desktop publishing
Communications programs	Multimedia
Integrated programs	Artificial intelligence

System Software

System software is "background" software that helps a computer manage its internal resources. An example is the **operating system.** Popular microcomputer operating systems:

SYSTEM SOFTWARE	
OPERATING SYSTEM	**DESCRIPTION**
DOS	Today's standard operating system for IBM and IBM-compatible microcomputers
Windows	Environment that extends capability of DOS
Windows 95	New operating system that does not require DOS
Windows NT	Operating system for very powerful microcomputers
OS/2 Warp	Developed for very powerful microcomputers
Macintosh operating system	Standard operating system for Apple's Macintosh computers
Unix	Runs on many powerful microcomputers

TYPE	DESCRIPTION
Microcomputers	Desktop and portable computers, widely used and number increasing fast
Minicomputers	Medium-sized, also known as midrange, used by medium-sized organizations and departments within larger organizations
Mainframes	Large computers for large organizations
Supercomputers	High-capacity machines for specialized uses like research

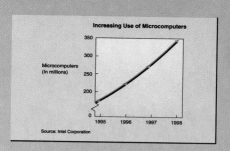

Increasing Use of Microcomputers

Microcomputers (In millions)

Source: Intel Corporation

HARDWARE

Input Devices

Input devices take data and put it into a form the computer can process. Especially important is the **keyboard,** a typewriter-like keyboard with specialized keys.

The System Unit

The **system unit** consists of electronic circuitry with two parts:

- **The central processing unit (CPU)**—controls and manipulates data to produce information
- **Memory (primary storage)**—temporarily holds data, program instructions, and processed data

Secondary Storage

Secondary storage stores data and programs. Three storage "media":

- **Floppy disk**—removable flexible 3½-inch or 5¼-inch plastic disks
- **Hard disk**—nonremovable, enclosed disk drive
- **Optical disk**—removable, **CD-ROM** best known

Output Devices

Output devices output processed information from CPU. Two important output devices:

- **Monitor**—TV screen-like device to display results
- **Printer**—device that prints out images on paper

Communications Devices

These send and receive data and programs from one computer to another. A device that connects a microcomputer to a telephone is a **modem.**

DATA AND CONNECTIVITY

Data

Data describes something and is typically stored electronically in a file. A **file** is a collection of characters organized as a single unit. Common types of files:

- **Document:** letters, research papers, memos
- **Worksheet:** budget analyses, sales projections
- **Database:** structured and organized data

Connectivity

Connectivity is a concept describing the ability of end users to tap into resources well beyond their desktops. Two important aspects of connectivity are:

- **Computer networks**—microcomputers can be linked to other microcomputers, minicomputers, or mainframes to share data and resources.
- **National Information Highway (NIH)**—also known as the **National Information Infrastructure (NII)** or **information superhighway**—is a term used to describe the future of communication networks and computers. **Internet** is the foundation for the NIH.

Application Software:

Basic Tools

Think of the microcomputer as an *electronic tool.* People may not consider themselves as being very good at typing, calculating, drawing, or looking up information. A microcomputer, however, can help you to do all these things—and much more. All it takes is the right kind of software—the programs that go into the computer. We describe some of the most important ones in this chapter.

COMPETENCIES

After you have read this chapter, you should be able to:

1. Explain the features common to all kinds of application software.
2. Describe application software for word processing, spreadsheets, database managers, graphics, and communications.
3. Describe integrated software that combines all these tasks.
4. Describe software suites that combine separate Windows applications.

Not long ago, trained specialists were required to perform many of the operations you can now perform with a microcomputer. Secretaries used typewriters to create professional-looking business correspondence. Market analysts used calculators to project sales. Graphic artists drew by hand. Data processing clerks created and stored files of records on large computers. Now you can do all these tasks—and much more—with a microcomputer. And many of these tasks can be done with just *one* application program.

General-Purpose Application Packages

Some features are common to all kinds of application packages.

Word processing, electronic spreadsheets, database managers, graphics programs, communications programs, and software that combines all five tasks are *general-purpose* application packages. That is, they may be used by many people for many different kinds of tasks. This is why we call them "basic tools." Some well-known software publishers are Microsoft, Lotus, and Novell.

Some features are common to most packaged programs. The following are the most important.

Version and Release

Software packages are continually being improved and revised. When a package first appears, it is assigned the number 1.0. As the package changes, the number changes. The number before the period refers to the **version,** and the number after the period refers to the **release.** Changes in a version number indicate major changes; changes in releases refer to minor changes.

Insertion Point

The **insertion point** or **cursor** shows you where you can enter data next. Typically, it is a blinking vertical bar on the screen. It can have other shapes depending on the software you are using. You can move the insertion point around using a mouse or the directional arrow keys.

Menus

Almost all software packages have **menus.** Typically, the menus are displayed in a menu bar at the top of the screen. When one of the menu items is selected, a pull-down menu appears. This is a list of commands associated with the selected menu. (See Figure 2-1.)

Shortcut Keys

Instead of using menus, many applications use **shortcut keys** for frequently used commands. They make it easier and faster to select certain commands. Many of these shortcuts use the **function keys**, F1, F2, and so on. Other shortcuts use key combinations typically consisting of the Alt, Ctrl, or Shift key used in combination with a letter, number, or function key. For example, in WordPerfect 6.1, the shortcut key F3 saves a file and the key combination Ctrl and O opens a file.

FIGURE 2-1

A menu bar and pull-down menu (WordPerfect for Windows, version 6.1).

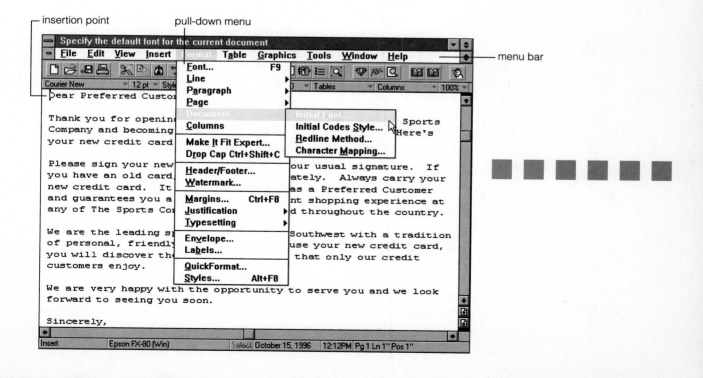

FIGURE 2-2

A Help screen (Excel for Windows 95, version 7.0).

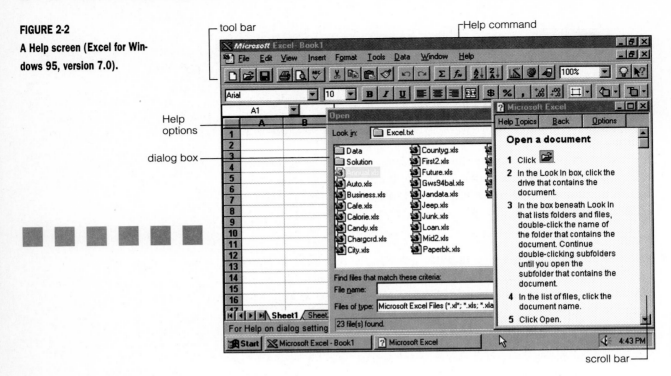

Help

For most application packages, one of the menus on the menu bar is **Help.** When selected, the help options appear. These options typically include a table of contents, a search feature to locate reference information about specific commands, and access to special learning features such as tutorials and step-by-step instructions. Additionally, most applications even provide what is called **context-sensitive help.** These help systems locate and display reference information directly related to the task you are performing. (See Figure 2-2.)

Tool Bars

Tool bars, also known as **button bars,** typically are below the menu bar. They contain **icons** or graphic representations for commonly used commands. This offers the user a graphic approach to selecting commands. It is an example of a **graphical user interface (GUI)** in which graphic objects rather than menus can be used to select commands. (See Figure 2-2.)

Dialog Box

Dialog boxes frequently appear after selecting a command from a pull-down menu. These boxes are used to specify additional command options. (See Figure 2-2.)

Scroll bars

Scroll bars are usually located on the right and/or the bottom of the screen. They enable you to display additional information not currently visible on the screen. (See Figure 2-2.)

WYSIWYG

Pronounced "wizzy-wig," **WYSIWYG** stands for "What You See Is What You Get." This means that the image on the monitor looks the same as the final printed document. Application programs without WYSIWYG cannot always display an exact representation of the final printed document. For instance, some word processors without WYSIWYG will not display footnotes and page numbers on the screen. However, they do appear on the printed copy. The WYSIWYG feature allows the user to preview the document's appearance before it is printed out.

Edit

Everybody makes mistakes entering data and information. The ability to change or to edit entries is a feature common to almost all applications. The **edit** feature makes revising and updating easy and is one of the most valuable features.

Cut, Copy, and Paste

Perhaps you have entered information that is wrong, or you decide you do not want to include the information at all. Or, perhaps you may want the same information to appear in multiple locations. You can easily make these changes using **cut, copy,** and **paste.** First, you select the information to be removed or copied by highlighting it. Then you choose the command to cut or to copy. If you select cut, the information simply disappears from your screen. If you select copy, the information remains but a copy is made. Then, by moving the insertion point to another location and selecting the paste command, the selected information appears at the new location. (See Figure 2-3.)

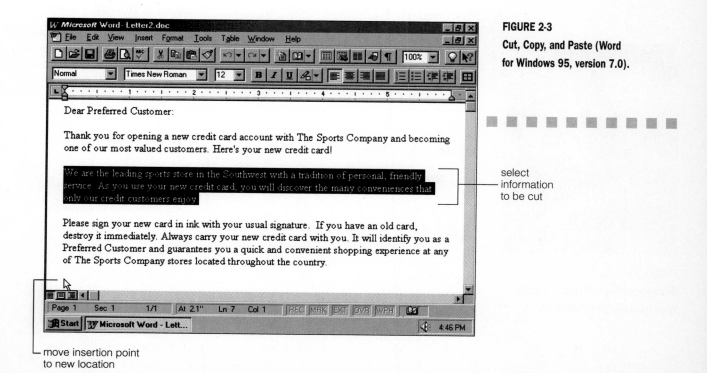

FIGURE 2-3

Cut, Copy, and Paste (Word for Windows 95, version 7.0).

select information to be cut

move insertion point to new location

FIGURE 2-4

Common application soft-
ware features.

■ ■ ■ ■ ■ ■ ■ ■ ■

COMMON FEATURES

FEATURE	DESCRIPTION
Version and Release	Indicates major and minor changes in software
Insertion Point	Shows where data can be entered
Menu	Presents commands available for selection
Shortcut Keys	Special-purpose keys for frequently used commands
Help	Presents explanations of various commands
Tool Bar	Presents graphic objects for commands
Dialog Box	Used to specify additional command options
Scroll Bars	Used to display additional information
WYSIWYG	"What You See Is What You Get"
Edit	Changes entered information
Cut, Copy and Paste	Deletes, moves, or copies information
Undo	Restores work prior to last command

Undo

It is easy to incorrectly select a command. Frequently, these accidently selected commands do things that makes changes that are not intended—for example, deleting a paragraph or a formula. No need to panic . . . use **undo.** This feature restores your work to how it was before the last command was selected.

See Figure 2-4 for a summary of the most important common features of general-purpose application packages.

Let us now describe the categories of application software that we are calling basic software tools.

FIGURE 2-5

Word processing software: Microsoft
Word Designed for Windows 95.

Word Processors

Word processing is used to create, edit, save, and print documents.

Word processing software is used to create, edit, save, and print documents. (See Figure 2-5.) **Documents** can be any kind of *text* material. Some examples of documents are letters, memos, term papers, reports, and contracts. Once it was thought that only secretaries would use word processors. Now they are used extensively in managerial and professional life. Indeed, it has been found that, among the basic software tools, word processors produce the highest gains in productivity.

If you have used a typewriter, then you know what word processing *begins* to feel like. You type in text on the keyboard. However, with word processing, you view the words you type on a computer monitor instead of on a piece of paper. After you are finished, you "save" (store) your words in a file on a floppy or hard disk. Then you turn on the printer and print out the results on paper.

The beauty of this method is that you can make changes or corrections—before printing out the document. Even after your document is printed, you can easily go back and make changes. You can then print it again. Want to change a report from double spacing to single spacing? Alter the width of the margins on the left and right? Delete some paragraphs and add some others from yet another document? A word processor allows you to do all these with ease. Indeed, *deleting, inserting, and replacing*—the principal editing activities—can be done just by pressing keys on the keyboard.

Popular word processing packages include Ami Pro, Word, and WordPerfect. Some important features shared by most word processors are described in the following sections.

Word Wrap and the Enter Key

One basic word processing feature is **word wrap.** On a typewriter, you must decide when to finish typing a line. You indicate the end of a line by pressing a carriage return key. A word processor automatically moves the insertion point to the next line once the current line is full. As you type, the words "wrap around" to the next line. To begin a new paragraph or leave a blank line, you press the **Enter** key.

Search and Replace

A **search** or **find** command allows you to locate any character, word, or phrase in your document. When you search, the insertion point moves to the first place the item appears. If you want, the program will continue to search for all other locations where the item appears.

The **replace** command automatically replaces the word you search for with another word. For example, you could search for the word *Chicago* and replace it with the word *Denver.* You can do this at every place *Chicago* appears. Or you can do this only where you choose to. The search and replace commands are useful for finding and fixing errors. For example, suppose you misspell a client's name. You could search for the incorrect spelling and replace it with the correct spelling.

Other Features

- Text can be aligned within the margins in various ways. The most common is left alignment. This means the text is displayed with an even left margin and a ragged right margin. Another common alignment is full justification. This means that the text on both the left and right margins is even.

- Text can be displayed in a variety of ways including boldfaced, underlined, and italicized.

- Tables of contents, footnotes, end notes, page numbers, tables, bulleted lists, and other features found in research papers can be easily created.

- Spelling can be checked automatically, by running your text through a **spelling checker** program. These programs identify incorrectly spelled words and suggest correct spellings. Many also include a feature to automatically correct spelling and expand abbreviations as you type.

FIGURE 2-6
Clip art (PowerPoint for
Windows 95, version 7.0).

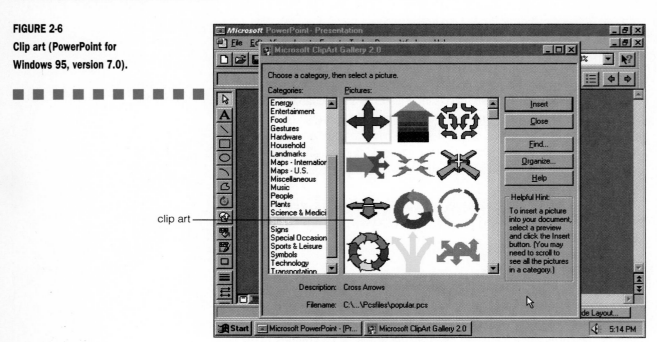

clip art

- In a similar manner, **grammar checkers** identify poorly worded sentences, excessively long sentences, and incorrect grammar.
- **Thesaurus** programs enable you to quickly find the right word or an alternative word with a similar meaning.
- A **mail merge** or **form letter** feature allows you to merge different names and addresses. You can mail out the same form letter to different people.
- Graphics enhancements can improve the look of documents. For example, **drawing programs** let you create line art. **Clip art** allows you to include available graphic images. (See Figure 2-6.) And **word art** allows you to manipulate text into various shapes.

Spreadsheets

A spreadsheet is an electronic worksheet used to organize and manipulate numbers and display options for "what-if" analysis.

The **spreadsheet** is based on the traditional accounting worksheet. Paper worksheets have long been used by accountants and managers to work up balance sheets, sales projections, and expense budgets. Spreadsheets are used by financial analysts, accountants, contractors, and others concerned with manipulating numeric data.

Spreadsheets allow you to try out various "what-if" possibilities. This is a powerful feature. You can manipulate numbers by using stored formulas and calculate different outcomes. For example, a retail store manager can estimate quarterly prof-

row headings

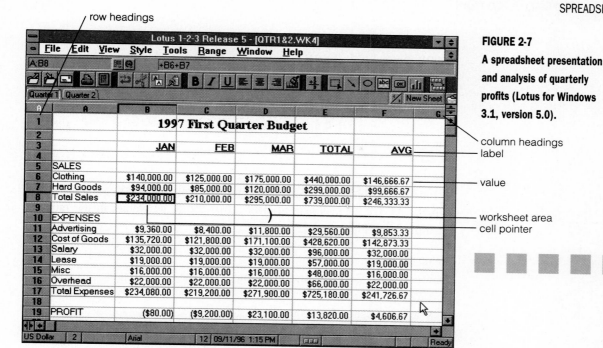

its by projecting sales over a three-month period. (See Figure 2-7.) The manager can then subtract expenses from sales. Expenses might include such things as advertising, cost of goods sold, and salaries. If expenses are too high to produce a profit, the manager can experiment on the screen with reducing some expenses and see the results almost instantly. For example, the number of employees, and hence salaries, might be reduced.

A spreadsheet has several parts. (See Figure 2-7.) The **worksheet area** of the spreadsheet has letters for **column headings** across the top. It also has numbers for **row headings** down the left side. The intersection of a column and row is called a **cell.** The cell holds a single unit of information. The position of a cell is called the **cell address.** For example, "B8" is the address for the cell located in column B and row 8. A **cell pointer**—also known as the **cell selector**—indicates where data is to be entered or changed in the spreadsheet. The cell pointer can be moved around in much the same way that you move the insertion point in a word processing program. In our illustration, the cell pointer is located in position B8.

Popular spreadsheet packages include Excel, Lotus 1-2-3, and Quattro Pro. Some common features of spreadsheet programs include the following:

Format

Labels are often used to identify information in a worksheet. (See Figure 2-7.) Usually a label is a word or symbol, such as a pound sign (#). A number in a cell is called a **value.** Labels and values can be displayed or formatted in different ways. A label can be centered in the cell or positioned to the left or right. A value can be displayed to show decimal places, dollars, or percent (%). The number of decimal positions (if any) can be altered, and the width of columns can be changed.

Formulas

Formulas are instructions for calculations. They calculate results using the number or numbers in referenced cells. For example, in our illustration, the spreadsheet is concerned with computing total sales. The formula to calculate January's total sales is shown near the top of the screen: +B6+B7. (See Figure 2-7). This means add the value in B6 (clothing sales) to the value of B7 (hard good sales). The total is displayed in cell B8.

Functions

Functions are built-in formulas that perform calculations automatically. For example, the Lotus function @SUM(B6..E6) adds all the values in the range of cells from B6 to E6.

Recalculation

Recalculation is one of the most important features of spreadsheets. If you change one or more numbers in your spreadsheet, all related formulas will recalculate automatically. Thus, you can substitute one value for another in a cell and observe the effect on other related cells in the spreadsheet.

By manipulating the values, you can use spreadsheet formulas to explore your options. For example, consider our illustration. If the January-to-March sales are *estimates,* you can change any or all of the values in cells B6 through D7. All of the associated cells including the total in cell E8 and the average in cell F8 will change automatically. (See Figure 2-7.) This is called **what-if analysis.**

Analysis Tools

Many programs include built-in **analysis tools** that help perform complicated what-if analysis. You can use **goal seeking tools** and **solver tools** to find the values needed to achieve a particular end result. **Scenario tools** allow you to test the effect of different combinations of data. For example, a contractor might need to keep the cost of building a house within a budget. The contractor can run cost calculations on various grades of materials and on the going pay rates for labor.

Other Features

Most spreadsheets also include additional capabilities for visually displaying and rearranging data. Among them are the following features:

■ **Data displayed in graphic form:** Most spreadsheets allow users to present their data in graphic form. That is, you can display numerical information as pie charts, bar graphs, and line graphs. Some spreadsheet programs even display data in graphs and charts that have a three-dimensional look.

■ **Graphics on worksheets:** This feature gives users the ability to place graphical elements such as lines, arrows, and boxes directly onto the worksheet. In addition, you can display charts and graphs directly on the worksheet. These charts and graphs automatically update when the numbers in the spreadsheet change.

■ **3-D spreadsheets:** If a file contains only one spreadsheet, it has two dimensions, namely, rows and columns. If a file contains more than one spreadsheet, it has three dimensions, namely, rows, columns, and spreadsheets. For instance, an account representative may keep quarterly sales data in separate spreadsheets all stored in one file named "SALES."

■ **Dynamic file links:** Some software offers **dynamic file links,** which allow you to link cells in one worksheet file to cells in other worksheet files. Whenever a change occurs in one file, the linked cells in the other files are automatically updated.

Database Managers

A database manager organizes a large collection of data so that related information can be retrieved easily.

A *database* is a collection of related data that has been entered into a computer system and stored for future use. Information in the database is organized so that selected items can be retrieved easily. Database management programs are used by salespeople to keep track of clients. They are also used by purchasing agents to keep track of orders and by inventory managers to monitor products in their warehouses. Database managers are used by many people inside and outside of business, from teachers to police officers. We describe databases in detail in Chapter 9.

A **database manager** or **database management system (DBMS)** is a software package used to set up, or *structure,* a database. It is also used to retrieve information from a database. An example of one database manager is Access. (See Figure 2-8.) This database contains address information about employees. The list

FIGURE 2-8

A database containing employee records (Access for Windows 3.1, version 2.0).

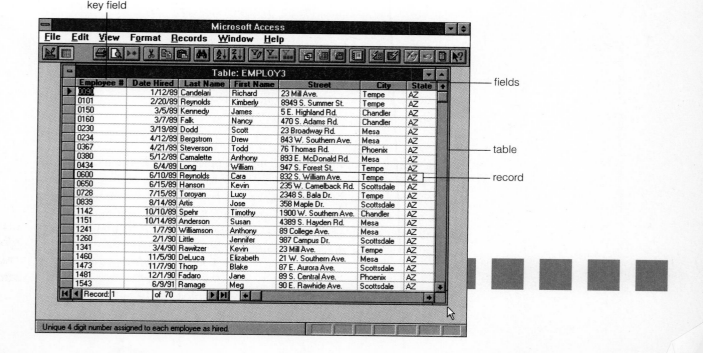

of employee numbers, names, and addresses is a **table.** Each line of information about one employee is called a **record.** Each column of information within a record is called a **field**—for example, last name.

Another table might contain benefit information. For example, it might include information about each employee's retirement, dental, and medical plans. These two tables are linked or related by a common field called a **key field.** The information in a key field must be unique for each record in a table. In this case the key field is the employee number. This is a **relational database.** That is, the address table and the benefits table are related by a key field containing common employee numbers.

To see the value of a relational database, imagine that you are a benefits administrator. You have been asked by your boss to notify all employees using a particular dental plan that rates have changed. If the employee records were stored only on sheets of paper, it might take days or weeks to locate the appropriate names and addresses.

With a database, the names and addresses of all affected employees can be located within moments. The database software first goes to the benefits table to locate all employees who use the dental plan. Then the database software goes to the address table. There, the appropriate employee numbers are used to locate the names and addresses of all employees using that dental plan.

Popular database management programs include Access, Approach, dBASE, and Paradox. Database managers have different features, depending on their sophistication. A description of the principal features of database manager software for microcomputers follows.

Locate and Display

A basic feature of all database programs is the capability to locate records in the file quickly. In our example, the program searches each record for a match in a particular field to whatever data you specify. This is called *querying* a database. The records can then be displayed on the screen for viewing, updating, or editing. For example, if an employee moves, the address field needs to be changed. The record is quickly located by searching the database to find the employee record that matches the name field you specify. Once the record is displayed, the address field can be changed.

Sort

Database managers make it easy to change the order of records in a file. Normally, records are entered into the database in the order they occur, such as the date a person is hired. This may not be the best way, however. There are a number of ways you can quickly rearrange the records in the file. For example, you might want to print out an entire alphabetical list of employees by last name. For tax purposes, you might want to list employees by social security number.

Calculate and Format

Many database programs contain built-in math formulas. In the office, for example, you can use this feature to find the highest or lowest commissions earned. You can calculate the average of the commissions earned by the sales force in one part of the country. This information can be organized as a table and printed out in a report format.

Other Features

Among other capabilities offered by some database management programs are the following:

■ **Customized data-entry forms:** A person new to the database program may find some of the descriptions for fields confusing. For example, a field name may appear as "CUSTNUM" for "customer number." However, the form on the screen may be customized so that the expression "Enter the customer number" appears in place of "CUSTNUM." Fields may also be rearranged on the screen, and boxes and lines may be added.

■ **Professional-looking reports:** A custom-report option enables you to design the elements you want in a report. Examples are the descriptions appearing above columns and the fields you wish to include. You can even add graphic elements, such as boxes or lines, so that the printed report has a professional appearance. Although the database itself may have, say, 10 fields, the report can be customized to display only the five or so important fields.

■ **Program control languages:** Most people using a database management program can accomplish everything they need to do by making choices from the menus. Many database management programs include a programming control language so that advanced users can create sophisticated applications. In addition, most allow direct communication to specialized mainframe databases through languages like SQL (Structured Query Language).

Graphics

There are three types of graphics programs: analytical for analysis, presentation for communication, and drawing for illustration.

Research shows that people learn better when information is presented visually. A picture is indeed worth a thousand words—or numbers. The popularity of graphics programs is expected to continue.

There are three types of graphics programs. *Analytical* graphics programs are used to analyze data. *Presentation* graphics programs are used to create attractive finished graphs for presentations and reports. *Drawing* programs are used to create illustrations.

FIGURE 2-9

Various types of analytical graphs (Excel for Windows 3.1, version 5.0).

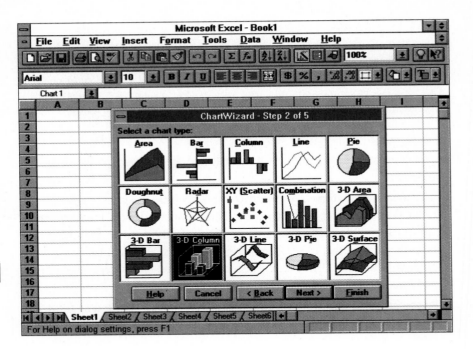

Analytical Graphics

Analytical graphics make numerical data much easier to grasp than when it is in the form of rows and columns of numbers. Most analytical graphics programs come as part of spreadsheet programs, such as Excel. (See Figure 2-9.) Thus, they are used by the same people who use spreadsheets. They are helpful in displaying economic trends, sales figures, and the like for easy analysis. Analytical graphics may be viewed on a monitor or printed out.

Presentation Graphics

You can use **presentation graphics** to communicate a message or to persuade other people, such as supervisors or clients. Thus, presentation graphics are often used by marketing or sales people, as well as many others.

Presentation graphics look more sophisticated than analytical graphics, using color, titles, and other features a graphic artist might use. (See Figure 2-10.) Using special equipment, you can convert graphics displays into slides, transparencies, or electronic presentations. The more powerful presentation graphics packages even include animation capabilities.

Popular presentation packages are Freelance, Harvard Graphics, Persuasion, and PowerPoint.

Drawing Programs

There is yet another kind of graphics program, one used by professional illustrators, such as people doing commercial art or drafting. These **drawing programs** are used to help create artwork for publications work. (See Figure 2-11.) They allow

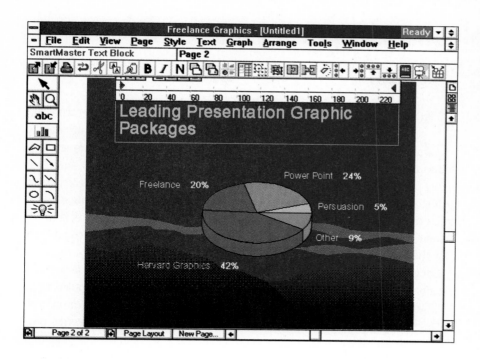

FIGURE 2-10
Example of presentation
graphics (Freelance for
Windows, version 2.0).

you to create attractive, sophisticated line art by combining lines, arcs, circles, and other shapes. Popular drawing packages are Adobe Illustrator, Aldus Freehand, and Micrografx Designer.

FIGURE 2-11
Example of a drawing pro-
gram (Aldus Freehand, ver-
sion 5.0).

Communications

Communications software lets you send data to and receive data from another computer.

Communications software enables microcomputer users to connect with and share resources. (See Figure 2-12.) Communications programs are used by all kinds of people inside and outside of business. Examples are students doing papers, consumers buying products, and lawyers researching the law. (See Figure 2-12.) Other examples are investors getting stock quotations and economists getting government statistical data. A sales representative might use this software and a modem to retrieve an electronic file from a distant, telephone-linked information source. The file might be a list of clients. The representative could then copy the file to his or her own diskette or hard disk.

Communications programs give microcomputers a powerful feature, as we have mentioned—namely, that of *connectivity.* Connections with microcomputers open up a world of services previously available only to users of mainframe computers. Recent developments in the National Information Highway and the Internet provide new and exciting opportunities for computer users. We devote all of Chapter 8 and a special Internet Guide to these topics. Some popular communications software includes Crosstalk, ProComm, and Smartcom. Some common features of most communications programs include:

FIGURE 2-12
Legal research (WinCin, Legal Forum).

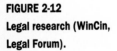

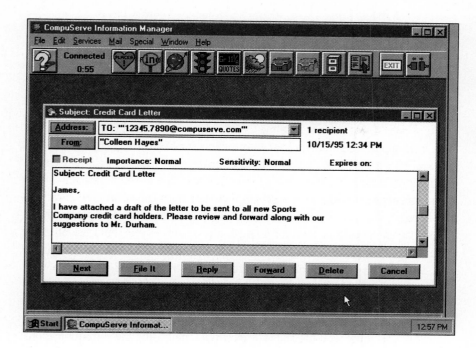

FIGURE 2-13
Example of an electronic mail screen (CompuServ, Information Manager).

Data Banks

With a communications program, you can access enormous computerized databases: data banks of information. Some of these, such as Dialog, resemble huge electronic encyclopedias.

Message Exchanges

Communications programs enable you to leave and receive messages on *electronic bulletin boards* or to use *electronic mail services.* (See Figure 2-13.) Electronic bulletin boards exist for people interested in swapping all kinds of software or information. Such people might be job seekers, lawyers, activists, rock music fans, or students—the possibilities are almost endless. Many organizations have "electronic mailboxes." For instance, you can transmit a report you have created on your word processor to a faraway company executive or to a college instructor.

Financial Services

With communications programs, you can look up airline reservations and stock quotations. You can order discount merchandise and even do home banking and bill paying.

Share Resources

Many business people use communications software with networks to allow sharing of expensive equipment like laser printers and hard-disk drives. Users are able to share data and programs.

Integrated Packages and Software Suites

Integrated software is an all-in-one application package. Software suites are individual windows applications that are sold together.

We have described five important kinds of application software. What happens if you want to take the data in one program and use it in another? Suppose you want to take information stored in the database manager and use it in a spreadsheet. This can be difficult to do with separate application packages. With an integrated package, however, it is easy to share data.

An **integrated package** is a program containing a collection of applications that work together and share information with each other. For example, to create a report on the growth of sales for a sporting goods store, you could use all parts of an integrated package. You could use the database to search and retrieve yearly sales data. The spreadsheet would be used to analyze the data and graphics to visually present the data. You could use the word processor to write the report that includes tables from the spreadsheet and visuals from the graphics program. (See Figure 2-14.)

Finally, you could send the report by electronic mail using the communications capability. Two well-known integrated packages are Lotus Works and Microsoft Works. Packages of this sort are easy to use. They are especially useful for microcomputers that do not have a lot of storage capacity.

An integrated package has a common structure allowing data to be exchanged easily between the applications within the package. Nevertheless, each application is generally less powerful than separate "stand-alone" application software. The next chapter explains how programs such as Windows allow users to share data

FIGURE 2-14

Example of an integrated package's spreadsheet and word processor (Microsoft Works for Windows 95, version 4.0).

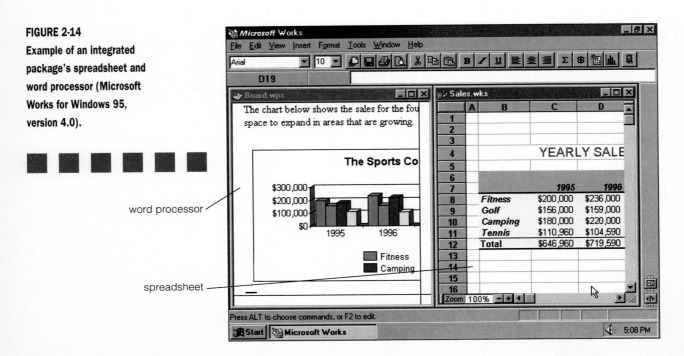

word processor

spreadsheet

between *completely different* stand-alone programs—not just between the applications available within one integrated package.

Some software companies are selling their separate windows application programs as a group—called **software suites.** The most popular software suite is Microsoft Office, which comes in different versions. One—Microsoft Office for Windows 3.1, Professional version—includes five individual Windows application packages. (See Figure 2-15.) The word processor is Word, the spreadsheet is Excel, the database is Access, the presentation graphics program is PowerPoint, and the communications program is Mail. Although more expensive than most integrated packages, software suites are much less expensive than purchasing each of the applications separately. Another popular software suite is Lotus SmartSuites.

For a summary of the basic application software, see Figure 2-16.

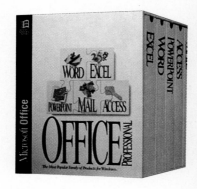

FIGURE 2-15
A software suite (Microsoft Office for Windows 3.1, Professional version).

BASIC TOOLS

APPLICATION	POPULAR PACKAGES
Word processors	Ami Pro, Word, WordPerfect
Spreadsheets	Excel, Lotus 1-2-3, Quattro Pro
Database managers	Access, Approach, dBASE, Paradox
Presentation graphics	Freelance, Harvard Graphics, Persuasion, PowerPoint
Drawing programs	Adobe Illustrator, Aldus Freehand, Micrografx Designer
Communications	Crosstalk, ProComm, Smartcom
Integrated packages	Microsoft Works, Lotus Works
Software suites	Lotus SmartSuite, Microsoft Office

FIGURE 2-16
Basic application software tools.

A Look at the Future

Tutorials, special software, and hardware add-ons help students learn complex software tasks.

Application software is one of those areas in which there are always new developments. How, then, can you keep up with newer versions?

Of course you can always take a class, which is often the easiest way. Many software manufacturers also produce *tutorials*—step-by-step directions and practice sessions. These may be available in books, on floppy disks, or on videotape cassettes. In the future, as software features multiply, the pressure will increase to make the learning process more efficient.

Already some *attempts at simplification* are being marketed. An add-on console (The Simplifier) can be plugged into a microcomputer keyboard. Its special cartridges contain instructions for students to help interpret complex commands in spreadsheet programs. Assistance is also available for learning other complex tasks. For instance, one word processing program (Wordbench) forces students to learn to write. It does this by limiting writing space, prohibiting users from going back to edit, and concealing words as they are typed.

Software manufacturers are providing more by including special capabilities right in the software. For example, Microsoft uses *wizards,* or a guided approach to performing selected tasks. PowerPoint, Microsoft's presentation software, has two such wizards. One is called the AutoContent wizard. After asking you a few questions about your presentation, the AutoContent wizard helps you to communicate and organize your ideas by suggesting an outline. The other wizard, Pick a Look, helps you create a look or style for your presentation. It provides over 100 professionally developed color and design combinations.

KEY TERMS

analysis tool (32)

analytical graphics (36)

button bar (26)

cell (31)

cell address (31)

cell pointer (31)

cell selector (31)

clip art (30)

column heading (31)

context-sensitive help (26)

copy (27)

cursor (25)

cut (27)

database management system (DBMS) (33)

database manager (33)

dialog box (26)

document (28)

drawing program (30 & 36)

dynamic file link (33)

edit (27)

Enter (29)

field (34)

find (29)

form letter (30)

formula (32)

function key (25)

function (32)

goal seeking tool (32)

grammar checker (30)

graphical user interface (GUI) (26)

Help (26)

icon (26)

insertion point (25)

integrated package (40)

key field (34)

label (31)

mail merge (30)

menu (25)

paste (27)

presentation graphics (36)

recalculation (32)

record (34)

relational database (34)

release (25)

replace (29)

row heading (31)

scenario tool (32)

scroll bar (26)

search (29)

shortcut key (25)

software suite (41)

solver tool (32)

spelling checker (29)

spreadsheet (30)

table (34)

thesaurus (30)

tool bar (26)

undo (28)

value (31)

version (25)

what-if analysis (32)

word art (30)

word processing (28)

word wrap (29)

worksheet area (31)

WYSIWYG (27)

REVIEW QUESTIONS

True/False

1. The insertion point or cursor indicates where you may enter data next.
2. Word wrap is a feature common to database managers.
3. Quattro Pro is a widely used word processor.
4. Spreadsheet programs are typically used to store and retrieve records quickly.
5. With communications programs, you can look up airline reservations and stock quotations.

Multiple Choice

1. The feature common to most application packages that allows you to see a printed document before it is printed:
   a. insertion point
   b. menu
   c. help
   d. WYSIWYG
   e. dialog box
2. When using a word processor, the command that is used to reinsert text into a document is:
   a. cut
   b. paste
   c. copy
   d. merge
   e. align
3. In spreadsheets, the common feature that specifies instructions for calculation is:
   a. formulas
   b. format
   c. recalculation
   d. consolidation
   e. value

4. A tool used frequently by marketing people to communicate a message or to persuade clients:
   a. word processors
   b. spreadsheets
   c. analytical graphics
   d. database managers
   e. presentation graphics

5. A collection of separate Windows applications sold as a group:
   a. combined
   b. suite
   c. communication
   d. integrated
   e. spreadsheet

Fill in the Blank

1. The _____ box is a feature common to many application programs that presents additional command options.

2. The _____ is based on the traditional accounting worksheet.

3. _____ _____ programs are used to keep track of details such as inventory records or client lists.

4. _____ software lets you send data to and receive data from another computer.

5. Microsoft Works and Lotus Works are _____ packages.

Open Ended

1. What is context-sensitive help?

2. How do formulas and recalculation work in a spreadsheet?

3. Explain the purpose of analytical graphics. Explain the purpose of presentation graphics. Explain the purpose of drawing programs.

4. Name three well-known spreadsheet packages.

5. What is the difference between an integrated package and a software suite?

DISCUSSION QUESTIONS AND PROJECTS

1. *Three ways to acquire application software:* The following exercise can be extremely useful. Concentrate on a category of software of personal interest to you—say, word processing or spreadsheets. Go to the library and find information on the following three methods of acquiring software. Which route seems to be the best for you? Why?

   a. *Public domain software* is software you can get for free. Someone writes a program and offers to share it with everyone without charge. Generally, you find these programs by belonging to a microcomputer users group. Or you find them by accessing an electronic bulletin board using your telephone-linked computer. Be aware that the quality of the software can vary widely. Some may be excellent and some may be poor.

b. *Shareware* is inexpensive. It is distributed free, in the same way as public domain software. After you have used it for a while and decide you like it, you're supposed to pay the author for it. Again, the quality varies. Some shareware is excellent.

c. *Commercial software* consists of brand-name packages, such as those we mentioned in this chapter. Prices and features vary. Fortunately, there are several periodicals that provide ratings and guides. *PC World* polls its readers to find out the best software brands in various categories. The magazine releases the results in its October issue. Other periodicals (for example, *PC* magazine, *MacWorld, Infoworld*) also have surveys, reviews, and ratings.

2. *New versions and releases:* Software companies seem to be offering new versions and releases of their application packages all the time. For example, in one twelve-month period, Lotus released four variations of its 1-2-3 spreadsheet program.

a. Take one application package (like Lotus 1-2-3, WordPerfect, or dBase) and find out how many variations have been released in the past two years.

b. If you own one variation of an application package and a new one is released, does yours become obsolete? Discuss and defend your position.

c. If you own one variation of a software package and a new version is released, should you upgrade to the newer version? What factors should be considered? If you decide to upgrade, how would you go about doing it?

d. Why do you suppose software manufacturers offer new variations of their software?

3. *http://www.halcyon.com/knopf/jim.html* Shareware began in 1982 with Jim Knoph. To learn more about the beginning of shareware and to obtain access to some available shareware, check out the Internet address given at the beginning of this question. Locate the VSL (Virtual Software Library) site on the Internet to learn about even more shareware and free software. (Hint: Use the Every Student's Internet Resource Guide: Computer Science and Computer Technology—Entry Number: 02.)

Applications Software: Power Tools

Applications software does "useful work." The five basic tools or types of general-purpose applications programs are used by many people for different kinds of tasks.

WORD PROCESSING	SPREADSHEETS	DATABASE MANAGERS

 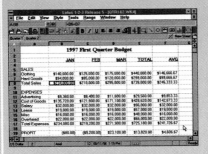 

A **word processor** creates, edits, saves, and prints **documents**. Especially useful for deleting, inserting, and replacing. Principal features:

Word Wrap and Enter Key

Word wrap automatically moves insertion point to new line. **Enter key** enters new paragraph or blank line.

Search and Replace

Search command allows users to quickly find a character, word, or phrase in a document. **Replace** command allows users to automatically replace with other text.

Other Features

- Aligning, bolding, underlining, and italicizing.
- Inserting table of contents, footnotes, end notes, page numbers, and bulleted lists.
- **Spelling** and **grammar checking.**
- Providing **thesaurus, mail-merge** capabilities, **drawing programs, clip-art,** and **word-art.**

Examples of Packages

Ami Pro, Word, and WordPerfect

A **spreadsheet** presents and analyzes data. A **worksheet area** is bounded by **column** and **row headings.** A **cell** is the intersection of column and row. The position of a cell is called **cell address.** The **cell pointer (cell selector)** indicates where data is to be entered. Principal features:

Format

Labels (column and row headings) and **values** (numbers in cells) can be displayed in different ways.

Formulas and Functions

Formulas are instructions for calculations. **Functions** are built-in formulas.

Recalculation

Recalculation is automatic recomputation.

Analysis Tools

Built-in tools for **what-if, goal-seeking, solving,** and **scenario** analyses.

Other Features

- Graphing data on spreadsheet.
- 3-D spreadsheets.
- Linking worksheet files.

Examples of Packages

Excel, Lotus 1-2-3, Quattro Pro

A **database manager** (or **database management system, DBMS**) is used to structure a database. A database is a collection of related data. **Relational databases** are organized as fields, records, and tables for easy retrieval of selected items. Principal features:

Locate and Display

A database query used to locate information that can be displayed on the screen for viewing or updating.

Sort

Users can sort through records and rearrange them in different ways.

Calculate and Format

Math formulas may be used to manipulate data. Data may be printed out in different report formats.

Other Features

- Customized data-entry forms.
- Professional-looking reports.
- Program control languages, like SQL (Structured Query Language).

Examples of Packages

Access, Approach, dBASE, Paradox

COMMON FEATURES

FEATURE	DESCRIPTION	FEATURE	DESCRIPTION
Version and Release	Indicates major and minor changes in software	Dialog Box	Used to specify additional command options
Insertion Point	Shows where data can be entered	Scroll Bars	Used to display additional information
Menu	Presents commands availabe for selection	WYSIWYG	"What You See Is What You Get"
Shortcut Keys	Special-purpose keys for frequently used commands	Edit	Changes entered information
Help	Presents explanations of various commands	Cut, Copy and Paste	Deletes, moves, or copies information
Tool Bar	Presents graphic objects for commands	Undo	Restores work prior to last command

GRAPHICS

Graphics programs display results of data manipulation for easier analysis, presentation, and illustration. Three types of graphics programs are analytical, presentation, and drawing programs.

Analytical Graphics

Analytical graphics programs put data in a form easier to analyze (e.g., bar charts, line graphs).

Presentation Graphics

Presentation graphics help communicate results or persuade, using color and titles.

Drawing Programs

Drawing programs help professional illustrators create attractive, sophisticated artwork for publications.

Examples of Packages

Most analytical graphics come as part of spreadsheet programs. Examples of presentation graphics: Freelance, Harvard Graphics, Persuasion, PowerPoint. Examples of drawing programs: Adobe Illustrator, Aldus Freehand, Micrografx Designer.

COMMUNICATIONS

Communications software enables users to connect with and share resources with others. Communications programs permit *connectivity*—they allow microcomputers to connect with other information resources.

Data Banks

Large computerized databases (e.g., electronic encyclopedias) are available.

Message Exchanges

Electronic bulletin boards and **electronic mail services** are available.

Financial Services

Users may look up stock quotations and airline reservations, order discount merchandise, and do home banking.

Share Resources

Laser printers, hard disks, and other expensive hardware can be shared on networks.

Examples of Packages

Crosstalk, ProComm, Smartcom

PACKAGES AND SUITES

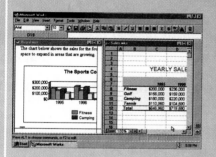

Integrated Packages

An **integrated package** is an all-in-one software program. It includes word processor, spreadsheets, database manager, graphics, and communications. Some features:

- Common structure for easy data exchange between applications.
- Less expensive than software suite.
- Each application not as powerful as "stand-alone" application.

Examples of Packages

Lotus Works and Microsoft Works

Software Suites

A **software suite** is a collection of individual windows applications packages sold together. Some features:

- Windows (discussed in detail in next chapter) allows sharing of data between completely different applications programs.
- Less expensive than buying each individual software package.

Examples of Packages

Lotus SmartSuite and Microsoft Office

Application Software:

Power Tools

Expect surprises—exciting ones, positive ones. This is the view to take in achieving computer competency. If at first the surprises worry you, that's normal. Most people wonder how well they can handle something new. But the latest technological developments also offer you new opportunities to vastly extend your range. As we show in this chapter, software that for years was available only for mainframes has recently become available for microcomputers. Here's a chance to join the computer-competent of tomorrow.

P*ower tools:* This is the characterization we have given to a whole new generation of software and hardware only recently available for microcomputers. Power tools include personal information managers, groupware, project management software, desktop publishing, multimedia, and artificial intelligence, including robotics, knowledge-based and expert systems, and virtual reality. Is there really a need to know anything about these new developments? There is if you want to be like those professionals in every area who are at the forefront of their disciplines. They are there because they have found more efficient ways to use their time and talents. You owe it to yourself, therefore, to at least be aware of what this software and hardware can do.

Personal Information Managers

A personal information manager is a program that helps you get organized and keeps you organized.

Stop and think for a minute about what you do in a typical day, week, month, and year. Professionals in all kinds of jobs do similar things. They schedule meetings, make to-do lists, and record important names, addresses, and telephone numbers. They jot down notes, make future plans, and record important dates like anniversaries and birthdays.

You may use some of the same tools that many professionals use to keep track of all these things. Such tools include calendars, Rolodex files, address books, index cards, wall charts, notepads, binders, and Post-it notes. That's what **personal information managers (PIMs)** do and more. (See Figure 3-1.)

PIMs are designed to get you organized and keep you organized. Most important, they are designed to help maximize your personal productivity. Typically, they include electronic calendars, to-do lists, address books, and notepads. Some have automatic reminders that produce a sound when important meetings are to begin. Others alert users whenever electronic mail has been received. Examples of PIM software are Computer Associates International Inc.'s UpToDate, Franklin Quest Co.'s Ascend, and Lotus Organizer.

PIMs are quite handy. You could join the thousands of managers who review their electronic calendars each morning to see what appointments they have. Later, while you're working on a spreadsheet, say, someone calls to schedule an important business meeting. You just type a command that "pops up" the PIM on the screen and type in the meeting time on your calendar. You then save the information. With another command, you make the PIM disappear from the screen and return to your spreadsheet.

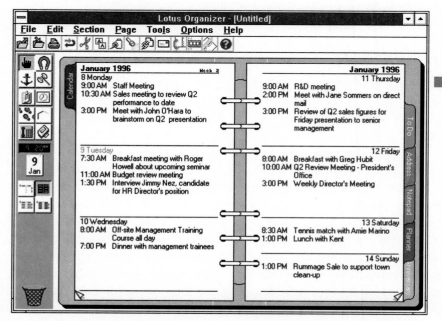

FIGURE 3-1

Personal information manager (Lotus Organizer).

FIGURE 3-2
Group scheduling (Lotus
Organizer for Windows).

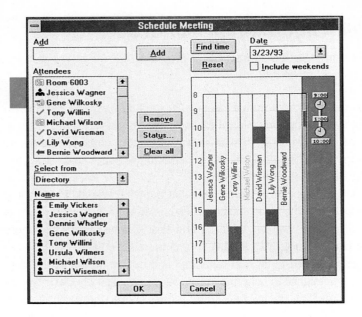

PIMs are called **memory-resident programs.** Also known as **TSR**s (for terminate and stay resident), these programs stay in the computer's memory (primary storage) all the time, until the computer is turned off. The value of a PIM is that it enables you to keep your desk free of notepads, phone directories, and calculators.

PIMs are good for scheduling your own time. However, one of the most difficult tasks is to schedule group meetings with busy people. A recent version of Organizer can help people who are connected by a network. It graphically shows the time slots when each person is available and can identify a time when everyone is free. (See Figure 3-2.) Applications that extend beyond personal productivity to group productivity are called *groupware*—the topic of our next section.

Groupware

Groupware supports group activities over networks to increase team productivity.

Most application software is designed for individuals working alone. These programs focus on personal or individual productivity. However, in most organizations today, the focus is on teams and team productivity.

As more and more networks become established, a new kind of software is becoming popular. Known as **groupware** or *collaborative technology,* this software provides services to support group activities. These include scheduling and holding meetings, communicating, collaborating on ideas, and sharing documents, knowledge, and information. With groupware, two or more people can work on the same information at the same time. This type of software is one of the fastest growing and most widely used network applications. Businesses are investing heavily in groupware to improve group productivity. (See Figure 3-3.)

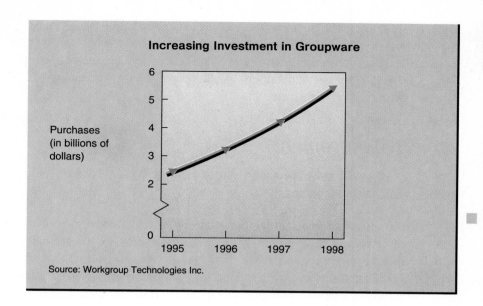

FIGURE 3-3
Investment in groupware—
past, present, and future.

The most widely used groupware software is Lotus Notes with nearly a million users. Basically, Lotus Notes is a way to share a database over a network so that many users can create and share information. The database is made up of *documents* containing many different kinds of information. They include text, graphics, sounds, images, and even videos. Users can create these documents using so-called *forms*. Users can *view* summaries of the database, share information, collaborate with others, and do many other group activities. (See Figure 3-4.)

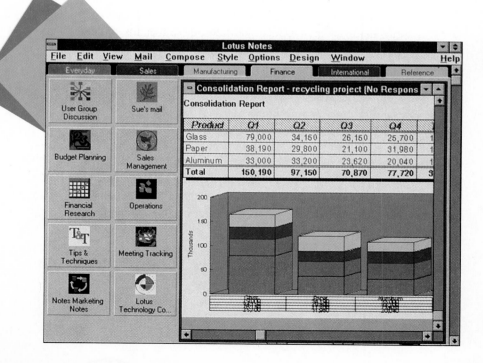

FIGURE 3-4
Groupware (Lotus Notes).

There are hundreds of commercially available Lotus Notes applications, ranging from work flow management to sales order processing. Additionally, Lotus Notes can link or connect users with many kinds of application software such as Lotus 1-2-3, Freelance, Organizer, and Ami Pro. Another popular groupware program is Microsoft's Windows for Workgroups.

Project Management

Project management software allows you to plan projects, schedule people, and control resources.

There are many occasions in business where projects need to be watched to avoid delays and cost overruns. A **project** may be defined as a one-time operation composed of several tasks that must be completed during a stated period of time. Examples of large projects are found in construction, aerospace, and political campaigns. Examples of smaller jobs might occur in advertising agencies, corporate marketing departments, and management information systems departments. You may have projects like term papers and lab experiments.

Project management software enables users to plan, schedule, and control the people, resources, and costs needed to complete a project on time. For instance, a contractor building a housing development might use it to keep track of the materials, dollars, and people required for success. Examples of project management software are Harvard Project Manager, Microsoft Project for Windows, Project Scheduler, SuperProject, and Time Line.

A typical use of project management software is to show the scheduled beginning and ending dates for each task in order to complete a particular project on time. It then shows the dates when each task was actually completed. Two important tools found in project management software are Gantt charts and PERT charts.

Gantt Charts

A **Gantt chart** uses bars and lines to indicate the time scale of a series of tasks. (See Figure 3-5.) You can see whether the tasks are being completed on schedule. The time scale may range from minutes to years.

PERT Charts

A **PERT (Program Evaluation Review Technique) chart** shows not only the timing of a project but also the relationships among its tasks. (See Figure 3-6.) The chart identifies which tasks must be completed before others can begin. The relationships are represented by lines that connect boxes stating the tasks, completion times, and dates. The critical path, the sequence of tasks that takes the longest to complete, is also identified. With project management software, tasks and their completion times can be easily changed to see the effect on the overall schedule.

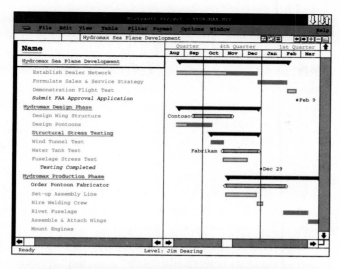

FIGURE 3-5
Gantt chart (Microsoft Project).

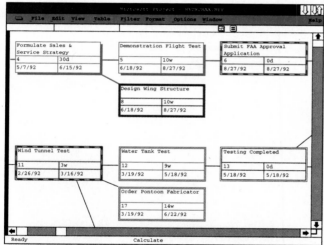

FIGURE 3-6
PERT chart (Microsoft Project).

Desktop Publishing

A desktop publishing program allows you to mix text and graphics to create publications of professional quality.

How would you like to generate a report that combined text and graphics and *really* impressed people with its looks? Suppose you wanted to create a report that looked like an article in a newsmagazine? When you present a report prepared on a word processing program, you are basically concerned with content; the appearance is secondary. When you do that same report with a desktop publishing program, the looks can be outstanding. An example of a page spread prepared by desktop publishing is shown in Figure 3-7.

Many publications—most books and magazines, for instance—are created by professionals trained in graphic arts and typesetting. They use equipment that often costs several thousand dollars. However, there are many publications where such experience and expenses are not necessary. Examples are newsletters, forms, catalogs, brochures, posters, menus, and advertisements. These are all candidates for desktop publishing. Real estate agents may use desktop publishing for sales sheets. Travel agents may use it for advertisements, architects for proposals, and government officials for presentations.

Desktop publishing is the process of using a microcomputer, a laser printer, and the necessary software to mix text and graphics. Some word processing programs are being developed with this capability. However, here we are concerned with specialized software that allows you to create publications that are of professional quality. The software enables you to select a variety of typestyles, just like those that commercial printers use. It also allows you to create and select graphic images. The laser printer produces a higher-quality printed result than is possible with other

FIGURE 3-7
Page produced by desktop publishing software.

TRAVEL

Edited by Karen Bantam

Sensible Souvenirs
Egyptian design motifs and the mystical Scarab

Lorem ipsum dlor sit amet, consectetuer adipiscing elit, sed diam nonummy nibh euismod tincidunt ut laoreet dolore magna aliquam erat volutpat. Ut wisi enim ad minim veniam, quis nostrud exerci tation ullamcorper suscipit lobortis nisl ut aliup ex ea commodo consequat. Duis autem vel eum iriure dolor in hendrerit in vulputate velit esse molestie consequat, vel illum dolore eu feugiat nulla facilisis at vero eros et accumsan et iusto odio dignissim qui blandit praesent ltatum zzril delenit augue duis dolore te feugait nulla facilisi. Lorem ipsum dolor sit amet, consectetuer adipiscing elit, sed diam nonummy nibh euismod tincidunt ut laoreet dolore magna aliquam erat volutpat. Ut wisi enim ad minim veniam, quis nostrud eu feugiat nulla.

The Single Traveler
Shipboard romance... Is the Love Boat for real?

Eros et accumsan et iusto odio dignissim qui blandit praesent luptatum zzril delenit augue duis dolore te feugait nulla facilisi. Nam liber tempor cum soluta nobis eleifend option congue nihil imperdiet doming id quod mazim placerat facer possim assum. Lorem ipsum dolor sit amet, consectetuer adipiscing elit. Ut wisi enim ad minim veniam, quis nostrud exerci tation ullamcorper suscipit lobortis nisl ut aliquip ex ea commodo consequat. Duis autem vel eum iriure dolor in hendrerit in vulputate velit esse molestie consequat, vel illum dolore eu feugiat nulla facilisis at vero eros et accumsan et iusto odio dignissim qui blandit praesent luptatum zzril delenit augue duis dolore te feugait nulla facilisi. Lorem ipsum dolor sit amet, consectetuer adipiscing elit, sed diam nonummy nibh euismod tincidunt ut laoreet dolore magna aliquam erat volutpat. Ut wisi enim ad minim veniam, quis nostrud exerci tation ullamcorper suscipit lobortis nisl ut aliquip ex ea commodo consequat. Duis autem vel eum iriure dolor in hendrerit in vulputate velit esse molestie consequat, vel illum dolore eu feugiat nulla facilisis at vero eros et accumsan et iusto odio dignissim qui blandit praesent luptatum zzril delenit augue duis dolore te.

Places with a Past
Sun worshippers abound where Greek tragedies once unfolded

Euismod tincidunt ut laoreet dolore magna aliquam erat volutpat. Ut wisi enim ad minim veniam, quis nostrud exercitation lamcorper suscipit lobortis nisl ut aliquip ex ea commodo consequat. Autem vel eum iriure dolor in

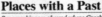

FIGURE 3-8
Desktop publishing (Quark Express).

microcomputer printers. A typical display screen from a desktop publishing program is shown in Figure 3-8. Popular programs are First Publisher, PageMaker, Quark Express, and Ventura Publisher.

Desktop publishing lets you place various kinds of text and graphics together in a publication designed almost any way you want. For instance, imagine you are helping a marketing manager for an airplane manufacturer to prepare a presentation on a new aircraft. You could use a word processing program to type the text. You could then use other software to create graphics. Or you might use graphics that have already been created from a graphics program. You can even use images that have been scanned from photographs. The desktop publishing program lets you integrate all these and look at your work on the monitor as one page. You can also look at two facing pages in reduced size or an enlarged view of a partial page. You can rearrange text and columns. You can enlarge or reduce any element and choose from all kinds of typestyles and sizes.

Desktop publishing programs let you decide how many columns of text will be placed on a page. **Style sheets** automate the selection of size and style of text for headings, captions, and so on. Their use promotes consistency throughout a document. You can select with a single mouse click the size, width, and shading of the lines and boxes that separate and emphasize text. You can place a graphic image anywhere on a page. Text will automatically realign around an image or overwrite the image.

If you are not trained as a graphic designer, desktop publishing programs will not make you into one. However, they can help. Ventura, for example, offers 25 sample style sheets. These can be used for brochures, newsletters, books, and so on. As you become more experienced, you can modify these style sheets or even create your own.

FIGURE 3-9

Multimedia systems in use—
past, present, and future.

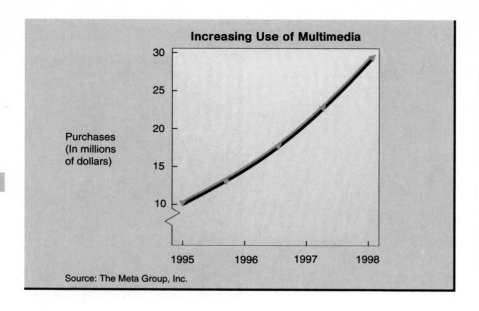

Increasing Use of Multimedia

Purchases
(In millions
of dollars)

Source: The Meta Group, Inc.

Once a document is composed on the screen, it must be transmitted to an output device that can print it out. This task is accomplished by what are known as **page description languages.** A page description language describes the shape and position of letters and graphics to the printer. An example is Adobe's PostScript, which is used in the PageMaker product. Other examples are Interpress from Xerox and Document Description Language (DDL) from Imagen.

Multimedia

Multimedia integrates all kinds of information. Multimedia PCs are specially equipped microcomputers. Hypermedia databases store multimedia data.

FIGURE 3-10

Multimedia presentation: the leopard.

Multimedia is one of the fastest-growing computer applications. More than 1 in 3 microcomputer systems sold today are equipped for multimedia. The trend is expected to continue. (See Figure 3-9.)

Multimedia, also called **hypermedia,** is the integration of all sorts of media into one form of presentation. These media may include text, graphics, animation, video, music, and voice.

Consider how a zoology professor might use multimedia for a lecture on felines. For hardware, he attaches a microcomputer and a CD-ROM drive to a speaker system and a large monitor. For software, he uses a readily available application, *The San Diego Zoo Presents . . . The Animals!,* written by The Software Toolworks. After a brief introduction, the professor begins the multimedia lesson by showing photos of leopards in their natural surroundings. (See Figure 3-10.) Then he shows a video clip of leopards hunting on an African plain. He then presents a narrated story explaining the animal and its environment, followed by a few pages of detailed

FIGURE 3-11
Multimedia PC (IBM Aptiva).

information. All of this is stored on the CD-ROM. Even better, if students want more information about leopards or other animals, the instructor can quickly present information on 225 animals. The CD-ROM also contains 1,500 photos, 150 video clips, 12 narrated stories, and 100 pages of information.

Multimedia PC

The typical **multimedia PC** is similar to many other powerful microcomputer systems. It has a fast microprocessor and a large hard-disk drive. Additionally, multimedia systems have a soundboard, speakers, and CD-ROM drive. (See Figure 3-11.) The soundboard and speakers capture and play back sound. The CD-ROM drive is needed to store the massive data requirements for multimedia. For instance, just 1 minute of video with stereo sound requires 25 MB of disk space. The most common use for multimedia systems is to run previously created applications stored on CD-ROM. There are thousands of commercially available multimedia applications. (See Figure 3-12.)

TOP-SELLING CD-ROMS

RANK	TITLE	PUBLISHER
1	Myst	Broderbund
2	Dark Forces	Lucas Arts
3	Doom II: Hell on Earth	ID/GT
4	NASCAR Racing	Virgin
5	NBA Live '95	Electronic Arts

Source: G. Meir Inc., May 1995

FIGURE 3-12
The five top-selling CD-ROMs.

FIGURE 3-13
Authoring software (Icon-Author).

Most multimedia PCs are used to run multimedia applications. Of course, someone must create these applications. Creating multimedia applications requires additional hardware and software. Microphones, video cameras, and scanners may be used to capture inputs. Additional hardware is required to save these inputs. While CD-ROMs are excellent for running multimedia applications, they are "read-only" and cannot be used to save data. Special optical discs with large storage capacities are typically used to save and create multimedia applications. Special software called *authoring software* is used to create presentations by linking various types of input. (See Figure 3-13.)

Hypermedia Databases

Typical database management systems are not able to handle multimedia data. They are designed to store numeric-only data. **Hypermedia databases** store and link a wide range of data including graphics, animation, video, music, and voice. They are based on the concept of card files, just like note cards, only these are electronic. Information is recorded on basic filing units called *cards*. A card is a computer screen filled with data comprising a single record. Cards in turn are organized into related files (bodies of information) called *stacks*. Cards and stacks are easily created and edited by the user through the use of typing and drawing tools.

You can create various connections between cards and stacks, and by fields of information on the cards, by means of *buttons*. A button is an area of the screen that is sensitive to the "click" of a mouse. Using your mouse to guide the cursor, you move to one of these buttons on the screen. You then click the mouse, and you are connected to another card or stack.

By clicking buttons, you can "navigate" through the cards and stacks to locate information or to discover connections between ideas contained in the stacks. For example, suppose an electronic "encyclopedia" or "textbook" has been developed containing information about Native Americans. Figure 3-14 shows how you might do research on this subject. Each stack contains pertinent data: numbers, maps, text, charts, sounds, or pictures. You can define buttons to link the information. The links may be sequential, going from one card to the next in a stack. Or the links may be nonsequential so that you can jump from one topic to another. Once the links have been created you can sort through and access related information in a way that's convenient to you.

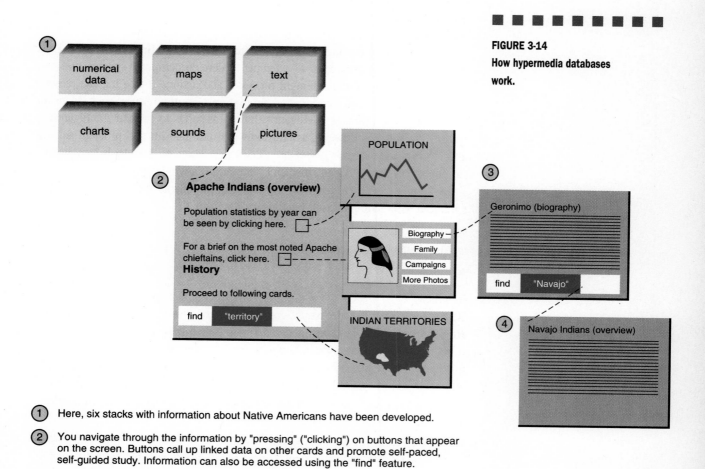

FIGURE 3-14
How hypermedia databases work.

① Here, six stacks with information about Native Americans have been developed.

② You navigate through the information by "pressing" ("clicking") on buttons that appear on the screen. Buttons call up linked data on other cards and promote self-paced, self-guided study. Information can also be accessed using the "find" feature.

③ Linking data is not a one-way street. From any card, you can access other cards to probe deeper into a line of thought.

④ Or you can embark on an entirely new course of investigation.

Artificial Intelligence

AI attempts to simulate human thought processes and actions. Three areas are robotics, knowledge-based and expert systems, and virtual reality.

Does human intelligence really need the presence of "artificial intelligence," whatever that is? Indeed, you might worry, do we need the competition? Actually, the goal of artificial intelligence is not to replace human intelligence, which is probably not replaceable. Rather, it is to help people be more productive. Let us describe how this might work.

In the past, computers used calculating power to solve *structured* problems, the kinds of tasks described throughout this book. People—using intuition, reasoning, and memory—were better at solving *unstructured* problems, whether building a product or approving a loan. Most organizations have been able to computerize the tasks once performed by clerks. However, knowledge-intensive work, such as that performed by many managers, is only beginning to be automated.

Now the field of computer science known as **artificial intelligence (AI)** is moving into the mainstream. AI attempts to develop computer systems that can mimic or simulate human thought processes and actions. These include reasoning, learning from past actions, and simulation of human senses such as vision and touch. True artificial intelligence that corresponds to human intelligence is still a long way off. However, several tools that emulate human problem solving and information processing have been developed. Many of these tools have practical applications for business, medicine, law, and many other fields.

Let us now consider three areas in which human talents and abilities have been enhanced with "computerized intelligence":

- Robotics
- Knowledge-based systems
- Virtual reality

Robotics

Robotics is the field of study concerned with developing and using robots. **Robots** are computer-controlled machines that mimic the motor activities of humans. Some toylike household robots (such as the Androbots) have been made for entertainment purposes. Most, however, are used in factories and elsewhere. They differ from other assembly-line machines in that they can be reprogrammed to do more than one task. Robots are often used to handle dangerous, repetitive tasks. There are three types of robots:

- **Industrial robots:** Industrial robots are used in factories to perform certain assembly-line tasks. Examples are machines used in automobile plants to do welding, painting, and loading. (See Figure 3-15.) In the garment industry, robot pattern cutters create pieces of fabric for clothing. Some types of robots have claws for picking up objects.

FIGURE 3-15
Industrial robot: spraying
and polishing on car plant
production line.

■ **Perception systems:** Some robots imitate some of the human senses. For example, robots with television-camera vision systems are particularly useful. They can be used for guiding machine tools, for inspecting products, for identifying and sorting parts, and for welding. (See Figure 3-16.) Other kinds of perception systems rely on a sense of touch, such as those used on microcomputer assembly lines to put parts into place.

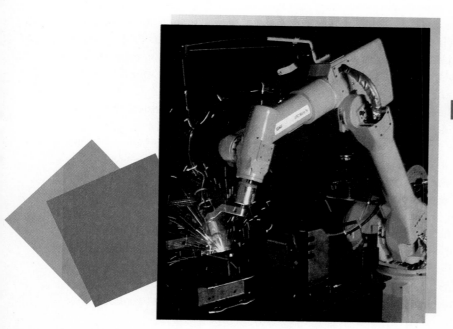

FIGURE 3-16
Perception system: vision-
system robot, used for
welding.

■ **Mobile robots:** Some robots act as transporters, such as "mailmobiles." They carry mail through an office, following a preprogrammed route. Others act as computerized carts to deliver supplies and equipment at medical centers.

Knowledge-Based (Expert) Systems

People who are expert in a particular area—certain kinds of law, medicine, accounting, engineering, and so on—are generally well paid for their specialized knowledge. Unfortunately for their clients and customers, they are expensive, not always available, and hard to replace when they move on.

What if you were to somehow *capture* the knowledge of a human expert? What if you then made it accessible to everyone through a computer program? This knowledge could be reasonably priced and always available. Indeed, if you were an expert yourself, you could use such a program to double-check your own judgments. Moreover, as an expert, you could create your own computer program containing much of what you know. All this is exactly what is being done with so-called *knowledge-based* or *expert systems*. **Expert systems** are computer programs that provide advice to decision makers who would otherwise rely on human experts. These programs are unlike conventional programs in several ways.

■ Conventional programs typically are used to perform routine tasks on data and to process sequentially from top to bottom. These programs use very highly structured logic. For example, a payroll program performs routine calculations using an employee database following a standard and precise sequence of operations.

■ Expert system programs are used to provide advice on very specialized tasks that typically require a human expert.

Rather than use a database, expert systems use knowledge bases. These contain specific facts, rules to relate these facts, and user input to formulate recommendations and decisions. These rules are used only when needed. The sequence of processing is determined by the interaction of the user and the knowledge base. Many expert systems use so-called *fuzzy logic,* which allows users to respond to questions in a very humanlike way. For example, if an expert system asked how your classes were going, you could respond, "great," "OK," "terrible," and so on.

Over the past decade, expert systems have been developed in areas such as medicine, geology, chemistry, military science, and photography. (See Figure 3-17.) There are expert systems with such names as Oil Spill Advisor, Bird Species Identification, and even Midwives Assistant. A system called Grain Marketing Advisor helps farmers select the best way to market their grain. Another, called Senex, shows how to treat breast cancer based on advanced treatment techniques.

Expert systems are created using a programming language or a shell. Expert system **shells** are special kinds of software that allow a person to custom-build a particular kind of expert system. For instance, the shell called VP-Expert has a database and can work with Lotus 1-2-3 and dBASE. This shell can then be used to build different kinds of expert systems. For example, VP-Expert has helped gardeners to assemble information about the most effective natural pest controls to use

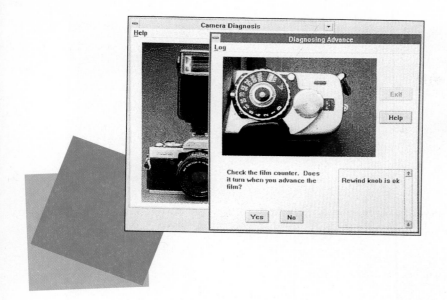

FIGURE 3-17
Expert system: diagnosing problems with cameras.

for specific purposes. Texas Instruments has developed an entire line of micro-computer-based shells called the Personal Consultant Series. These shells have been used to build Senex and Grain Marketing Advisor, among others we mentioned.

Virtual Reality

Suppose you could create and virtually experience any new form of reality you wish. You could see the world through the eyes of a child, a robot—or even a lobster. You could explore faraway resorts, the moon, or inside a nuclear waste dump, without leaving your chair. This simulated experience is rapidly becoming possible with a form of AI known as *virtual reality*.

Virtual reality is also known as **artificial reality** or **virtual environments.** Virtual reality hardware includes headgear and gloves. The headgear (one type is called Eyephones) has earphones and three-dimensional stereoscopic screens. The gloves (DataGlove) have sensors that collect data about your hand movements. Coupled with software (such as a program called Body Electric), this interactive sensory equipment lets you immerse yourself into a computer-generated world.

An example of virtual reality is shown in Figure 3-18. In the photo is a person wearing an interactive sensory headset and glove. The rest of the photo shows what the person is actually seeing—in this instance a molecular view of a human cell. When the person moves their head, the stereoscopic views change.

There are any number of possible applications for virtual reality. The ultimate recreational use might be something resembling a giant virtual amusement park. More seriously, we can simulate important experiences or training environments such as flying, surgical operations, spaceship repair, or nuclear disaster cleanup.

FIGURE 3-18
Virtual reality: looking inside a molecule.

A Look at the Future

The downsizing of computer applications will continue. So will the broadening of the scope of applications, as in current research into artificial life.

We can expect the trend of *downsizing of applications* to continue. That is, tasks that could once be performed only by mainframes will increasingly be done with microcomputers. Computer networks will link mainframes, microcomputers, workstations, and servers of all kinds—file servers, database servers, and communications servers. These developments will have an effect on the kinds of resources available to you in your career.

Just as important, we will probably also see a *broadening of the scope of applications.* Already well along in development, for instance, are *pen-based computers.* These are portable computers with handwriting-recognition capabilities that can identify printed letters, digits, and punctuation. They can even be modified to accept particular handwriting styles. Also presently being marketed are compact disc players that display audio and video programs on a TV set. These enable viewers to navigate by sight and sound through encyclopedias and atlases. These and similar devices may be forerunners to so-called *information appliances.* Such appliances would bundle a computer, telephone, fax machine, photocopier, color printer, and laser discs or CDs into one intelligent machine.

In the 21st century, the concepts applied in artificial intelligence, such as robotics, will be applied to all sorts of things. Even now, for instance, an experimental house in Japan, the "TRON House," has microprocessors and sensors built into everything. Windows open and close to maintain optimum ventilation. Background music reduces in volume when the telephone rings. Kitchen computers take the guesswork out of cooking. Bathroom computers monitor one's health. No doubt we will see a similar extension of computer technology to the workplace.

Most spectacularly, there are already attempts to go beyond artificial intelligence to something called *artificial life*. In this field, researchers are trying to develop programs that learn and develop on their own. Computers are used to simulate living systems and make computerized environments in which simulations of organisms eat, reproduce, and die. The outcome of these investigations may produce defenses against the computer viruses that have damaged networks and databases. They may also further our understanding of how human urban communities work.

KEY TERMS

artificial intelligence (AI) (60)

artificial reality (63)

expert system (62)

Gantt chart (52)

groupware (50)

hypermedia (56)

hypermedia database (58)

memory-resident program (50)

multimedia (56)

multimedia PC (57)

page description language (56)

personal information manager (PIM) (49)

PERT (Program Evaluation Review Technique) chart (52)

project (52)

project management software (52)

robot (60)

robotics (60)

shells (62)

style sheet (55)

TSR (50)

virtual environment (63)

virtual reality (63)

REVIEW QUESTIONS

True/False

1. PIMs typically include electronic calendars, to-do lists, address books, and notepads.

2. Groupware is also known as collaborative technology.

3. Desktop publishing software helps you to plan, schedule, and control the people, resources, and costs of a project.

4. Multimedia sales are expected to remain constant for the next few years.

5. Expert systems are programs that give advice to individuals who would otherwise rely on human experts.

Multiple Choice

1. A one-time operation composed of several tasks that must be completed during a stated period:
   a. plan
   b. organizer
   c. manager
   d. schedule
   e. project

2. The application software that allows you to mix text and graphics to create documents of professional quality:
   a. AI
   b. PIM
   c. groupware
   d. desktop publishing
   e. project management

3. The application that can link all sorts of media into one form of presentation:
   a. organizer
   b. word processor
   c. multimedia
   d. spreadsheet
   e. PIM

4. _____ supports group activities over networks.
   a. Hypermedia
   b. Groupware
   c. AI
   d. PIM
   e. A knowledge-based system

5. An area of artificial intelligence that simulates certain experiences using special headgear, gloves, and software that translates data into images:
   a. virtual reality
   b. expert system
   c. collaborative technology
   d. hypermedia
   e. shell

Fill in the Blank

1. Lotus Organizer is an example of a _____.

2. In desktop publishing, a _____ _____ helps you to create the basic appearance of single or multiple pages.

3. Linking text, graphics, animation, video, music, and voice into one presentation can be done using _____.

4. Unlike most assembly-line machines, _____ can be reprogrammed to do more than one task.

5. Expert system _____ are special programs that allow a person to custom-build an expert system.

Open Ended

1. What are personal information managers? What are they used for?

2. Explain what project management software does. Give an example of how one might be used.

3. What does a desktop publishing program let you do? What does a page description language do?

4. Explain how multimedia works.

5. What are the three areas of artificial intelligence?

DISCUSSION QUESTIONS AND PROJECTS

1. *New areas for expert systems:* There are numerous expert systems designed to pick winning stocks in the stock market. However, not everyone using these systems has become rich. Why? List and discuss three other areas in which you think it would be difficult to devise an expert system.

2. *A picture of things to come:* Over the next 10 to 15 years, say some experts, electronic miniaturization will produce small, portable devices that you can wear like clothing. These devices will do all kinds of wonderful things. For example, they will incorporate display screens, keyboards, CD memories, faxes, telephones, scanners, cameras, and satellite transmitters and will recognize handwriting and voice. What kind of wearable, lightweight "information and entertainment machine" would you design for yourself? What would it do?

3. *http://fas.sfu.ca/1/cs/research/groups/Vision*   One of the most exciting areas of robotics is visual perceptions systems. Computational vision is a process whereby computers are taught to use visual information. To learn more about this exciting area, connect to the Computational Vision Lab at Simon Fraser University using the Internet address given at the beginning of this question. Then expand your research on computer vision using other Internet resources. (Hint: Use the Every Student's Internet Resource Guide: Computer Science and Computer Technology—Entry Number: 01 and/or Entry Number: 02.)

Applications Software: Power Tools

Applications

Some recent important microcomputer applications are personal information managers, groupware, project management software, desktop publishing, multimedia and artificial intelligence—robotics, knowledge-based and expert systems, and artificial reality.

PERSONAL INFORMATION MANAGERS

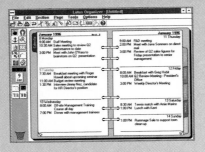

Personal information managers (PIMs) help keep you organized and maximize your personal productivity. They generally include electronic calendars, to-do lists, address books, and notepads.

Some PIMs are able to schedule group meetings with busy people.

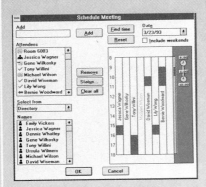

Examples of Packages

Computer Associates International Inc.'s UpToDate, Franklin Quest Co.'s Ascend, Lotus Organizer

GROUPWARE

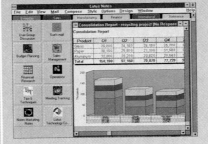

Groupware, also known as collaborative technology, allows groups of workers to schedule and hold meetings, communicate, collaborate on ideas, and share documents, knowledge, and information.

Lotus Notes, the most widely used groupware software, shares a database consisting of documents. The documents can contain text, graphics, images, and videos. Users create documents using forms and view summaries of the database.

Examples of Packages

Lotus Notes, Microsoft's Workgroup for Windows

PROJECT MANAGEMENT

Project management software allows you to plan, schedule, and control the people, resources, and costs of a project.

Two important tools found in project management software are:

Gantt Charts

A **Gantt chart** uses bars and lines to indicate the time scale of a series of tasks so you can see whether the tasks are being completed on schedule.

PERT Charts

A **PERT chart** shows not only the timing of a project but also the relationships among its tasks.

Examples of Packages

Harvard Project Manager, Microsoft Project for Windows, Project Scheduler, SuperProject, Time Line

TOP-SELLING CD-ROMS

RANK	TITLE	PUBLISHER
1	Myst	Broderbund
2	Dark Forces	Lucas Arts
3	Doom II: Hell on Earth	ID/GT
4	NASCAR Racing	Virgin
5	NBA Live '95	Electronic Arts

Source: G. Meir Inc., May 1995

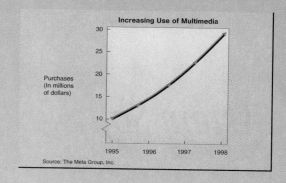

Increasing Use of Multimedia

Purchases (In millions of dollars)

Source: The Meta Group, Inc.

DESKTOP PUBLISHING

Desktop publishing is the process of using a microcomputer, laser printer, and necessary software to mix text and graphics and create publications of almost professional quality. Once a document is composed on the monitor screen, it is transmitted by a **page description language,** which describes the shape and position of letters and graphics, to a printer for printing out.

Examples of Packages

First Publisher, PageMaker, Quark Express, Ventura Publisher.

MULTIMEDIA

Multimedia or **hypermedia** combines and controls information in a variety of forms including: text, graphics, animation, video, music, and voice. Two key components of multimedia applications are multimedia PCs and hypermedia databases:

Multimedia PCs

Multimedia PCs are powerful microcomputers with large disk drives, sound boards, speakers, and CD-ROM drives. Multimedia PCs used for creating presentations require additional hardware such as: microphones, video cameras, scanners, and floptical disks. **Authoring software** is also required to create and link the different types of inputs.

Hypermedia Databases

Hypermedia databases store and link all kinds of data. The data is stored in **cards** and **stacks** and allows users to navigate this information in creative and useful ways through buttons.

ARTIFICIAL INTELLIGENCE

Artificial intelligence is a research field to develop computer systems simulating human thought processes and actions. Three areas include:

Robotics

Robotics is a research field to develop machines that can be reprogrammed to do more than one task. Some types are industrial robots, perception systems, and mobile robots.

Knowledge-Based (Expert) Systems

These are computer programs that duplicate the knowledge humans have for performing specialized tasks. They are unlike conventional programs in that they provide advice, use a knowledge base, fire rules, and process according to user interaction. **Fuzzy logic** is used to allow human-like input.

Virtual Reality

Also known as **artificial reality** or **virtual environments,** this consists of interactive sensory equipment to simulate alternative realities to the physical world.

System Software

Becoming a microcomputer end user is like becoming the driver of a car. You can learn just enough to start up the car, take it out on the street, and pass a driver's license test. Or you can learn more about how cars work. That way you can drive any number of vehicles, know their limitations, and compare performance. Indeed, you could go so far as to learn to be a mechanic. Similarly, by expanding your knowledge about microcomputers, you extend what you can do with them. You don't have to be the equivalent of a mechanic—a computer technician. But the more you know, the more you expand your computer competency and productivity.

All cars do the same thing—take you somewhere. But there was a time when you could choose between different automotive power systems: steam, electricity, diesel, or gasoline. Some systems were better for some purposes than others. You could have a car that was quiet or cheap to run, for instance. However, that same car perhaps took too long to start, wouldn't take you very far, or didn't have enough power on the hills.

Microcomputers are in a comparable phase of evolution. Some computers do some things better than others—are easier to learn, for instance, or run more kinds of application software. Why is this? One important reason is the *system software,* the "background" software that acts as an interface between the microcomputer and the user. System software also acts as an interface between the application program and the input, output, and processing devices. (See Figure 4-1.) The most important types of microcomputer system software are *DOS, Microsoft Windows, OS/2 Warp, Macintosh,* and *Unix.* Which of these you can use depends in part on what kind of computer you have.

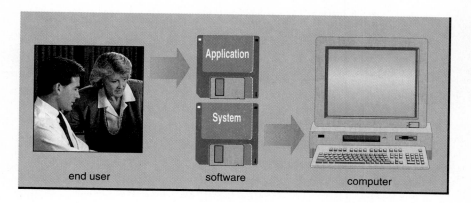

Why Learn About System Software?

Because standards are changing, users need to know more about system software than was previously required.

Are you buying a pricey racing machine that you don't really need? Or are you buying an inexpensive, practical vehicle that may nonetheless soon become obsolete? These are the kinds of things many people think about when buying cars. Similar considerations apply in buying microcomputers and software. It's important to know what each type of operating system can and can't do. (See Figure 4-2.) Moreover, you hope the buying decision you make will be good for the next several years.

FIGURE 4-2
The IBM ValuePoint (left) and Apple Macintosh Power PC (right) use different system software. Although similar in many ways, these systems also have significant differences.

If the study of system software seems to be remote from your concerns, it shouldn't be. Here's why:

- **Competing system software:** In earlier editions of this book there might not have been a need for this chapter. The kind of microcomputer system software that predominated was the one for IBM and IBM-compatibles known as DOS. These IBM and IBM-compatibles are often referred to as *DOS-based* microcomputers. The other popular system software was the one designed for the Apple Macintosh. Without specialized hardware and software, Macintosh programs wouldn't run on DOS-based microcomputers, and DOS programs wouldn't run on Macintosh computers. Today's very powerful microcomputers are demanding more and more from last year's system software. Now there are several competing forms of system software.

- **DOS limitations:** If DOS was so popular, why didn't the microcomputer industry just stay with it? The answer is that it has some practical limitations, as we shall discuss. Because it is so widespread, DOS will probably continue to be used for the next several years. Thus, it is well worth learning. However, as more powerful microcomputers become commonplace, other system software will replace DOS. In sum, DOS is popular today but will likely fade in the years to come.

- **One computer, many kinds of system software:** Now there are microcomputers that run more than one kind of system software. Employers may require that you know more than one kind. For instance, many office workers may need to know how to work with DOS, Microsoft Windows, and OS/2. These systems can run on the same computer.

- **More networking:** More and more computers are being connected together to share information and resources. Not all operating systems can efficiently support network operations. And some of the ones that do can support only certain types of networks.

- **More sophisticated users:** Previously, microcomputer users were satisfied with the performance offered by DOS. However, users are becoming more sophisticated. Now they want to be able to fully exploit the power of these newer microcomputers. They are beginning to demand that microcomputers run programs that previously could run only on minicomputers and mainframes. To do this, more sophisticated system software is required.

Even if you use only *one* type of system software, such as Windows, it's important to realize that such software is frequently revised. Revisions are made in order to handle new technology such as newly developed input and output devices. As system software changes, you need to know what the effects are on your old application software.

Four Kinds of Programs

System software consists of the bootstrap loader, diagnostic routines, basic input-output system, and operating system.

System software deals with the physical complexities of how the hardware works. System software consists of four kinds of programs: bootstrap loader, diagnostic routines, basic input-output system, and operating system. The last one, the operating system, is the one we are most concerned with in this chapter. However, we will briefly mention the others, which operate automatically.

- The **bootstrap loader** is a program that is stored permanently in the computer's electronic circuitry. When you turn on your computer, the bootstrap loader obtains the operating system from your hard disk (or floppy disk) and loads it into memory. This is commonly called **booting** the system.

- The **diagnostic routines** are also programs stored in the computer's electronic circuitry. They start up when you turn on the machine. They test the primary storage, the central processing unit (CPU), and other parts of the system. Their purpose is to make sure the computer is running properly. On some computers, the screen may say "Testing RAM" (a form of computer memory) while these routines are running.

- The **basic input-output system** consists of service programs stored in primary storage. These programs enable the computer to interpret keyboard characters and transmit characters to the monitor or to a floppy disk.

- The **operating system,** the collection of programs of greatest interest to us, helps the computer manage its resources. The operating system takes care of a lot of internal matters so that you, the user, don't have to. For instance, it interprets the commands you give to run programs. It also enables you to interact with the programs while they are running. It manages memory, data, and files.

One set of programs within the operating system is called **utility programs.** These programs perform common repetitive tasks or "housekeeping tasks." One important utility program is used for **formatting** (or **initializing**) blank floppy disks. This program is very important. Although you can purchase disks already formatted, many are not and must be formatted before you can use them. Formatting prepares the disk so that it will accept data or programs. With a formatted disk, you can use a utility program to **copy** or duplicate files and programs from another disk. You can **erase** or remove old files from a disk. You can make a **backup** or duplicate copy of a disk. You can **rename** the files on a disk—that is, give them new filenames.

Every computer has an operating system. Larger computer systems like mainframes and minicomputers have very sophisticated ones. A popular operating system for IBM's mainframes, for example, is MVS. Digital Equipment Corporation (DEC) uses VAX/VMS as the operating system for its minicomputers. These operating systems have very powerful capabilities, including virtual memory, multiprogramming, and multiprocessing.

An operating system with **virtual memory** increases the amount of memory available to run programs. Without virtual memory, an entire program must be read into the computer system's memory before it can run. Therefore, the size of memory determines the largest program that can be run. With virtual memory, the operating system divides large programs into parts and stores these parts on a secondary storage device, usually a disk. Each part is then read into the computer system's memory only when needed. This allows a computer system to run very large programs.

Multiprogramming and multiprocessing allow more than one person to use a computer system. For **multiprogramming,** the operating system interrupts and switches rapidly back and forth between several programs while they are running. This allows several different users to run different programs seemingly at the same time. For **multiprocessing,** the operating system controls two or more central-processing units. This allows several different users to independently run different programs at the same time.

There are several similarities between larger computer and microcomputer operating systems. One difference, however, is that the larger systems tend to focus on multiple users of a computer system. Microcomputer operating systems, on the other hand, tend to focus on single users.

For end users, the most important operating systems are those for microcomputers. To achieve computer competency, it is important for you to know something about the principal types of operating systems on the market for microcomputers today. These are *DOS, Microsoft Windows, OS/2 Warp, Macintosh,* and *Unix.*

For a summary of system software programs, see Figure 4-3.

DOS

DOS is the standard. It is widely used, runs thousands of applications, and requires inexpensive hardware.

DOS stands for *Disk Operating System.* Its original developer, Microsoft Corporation, sells it under the name *MS-DOS.* (The "MS," of course, stands for Microsoft.) It is the standard operating system for all microcomputers advertising themselves as "IBM-compatible" or "DOS-based," such as Compaq. Whatever machine it is used with, it is usually referred to simply as *DOS.*

There have been several upgrades since MS-DOS was introduced. The 1981 original was labeled version 1.0. (See Figure 4-4.) Since then there have been numerous new versions, including 6.0, 6.1, and 6.2. An important characteristic of the more recent or newer versions is that they are "backward compatible." That is, you can still run application programs with them that you could run on the older versions. The newest versions feature pull-down menus. (See Figure 4-5.) With pull-down menus, you use your mouse-directed insertion point or cursor to unfold ("pull down") a menu from the top of your display screen.

SYSTEM SOFTWARE PROGRAMS

PROGRAM	FUNCTION
Bootstrap loader	Reads operating system from disk and loads into memory.
Diagnostic routines	Tests parts of system to ensure computer is running properly.
Basic input-output	Transmits characters from the keyboard to a monitor or disk.
Operating system	Helps manage computer resources. Most important types are DOS, Microsoft Windows, OS/2, Macintosh, and Unix.

FIGURE 4-3
Types of system programs.

DIFFERENT VERSIONS OF MS-DOS

VERSION	FEATURES
1.0	Original operating system for IBM PC and compatibles. Supported only floppy-disk drives.
2.0	Developed for IBM XT microcomputer. First version to support hard-disk drives.
3.0	Appeared about the same time as IBM AT microcomputer. Starting with 3.2 release, supported networking and 3½-inch disk drives.
4.0	Included pull-down menus and other sophisticated modifications.
5.0	Allowed access to more memory and task switching.
6.0	Included disk compression, advanced memory and file management, and virus protection.

FIGURE 4-4
Different versions of MS-DOS.

Advantages

There is no question that DOS has many advantages. The reasons for learning it are very compelling.

- **Widely used:** DOS is the most popular microcomputer operating system ever sold. It is installed on 85 percent of all the microcomputers (personal computers) in the world.

- **Number of applications:** An enormous number of application programs have been written for DOS. Indeed, more specialized software is available for DOS than for any other operating system. This software includes not just the basic tools and power tools mentioned in Chapters 2 and 3 but many others as well.

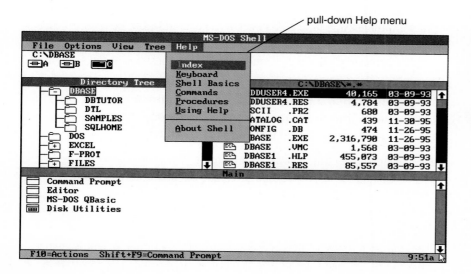

pull-down Help menu

FIGURE 4-5
Example of pull-down menu from MS-DOS 6.0.

■ **Runs on inexpensive hardware:** DOS runs on many computers—old and new—that are reasonably priced. In addition, DOS is available for all kinds of domestic- and foreign-made IBM-compatible machines. The IBM Personal Computer set the standard for the business market. However, the appearance of similarly designed competitors has driven prices down, making microcomputers available to more people.

Disadvantages

DOS is software, but software can perform only as well as the hardware for which it was designed. The first version of DOS was introduced in 1981 for microcomputers with floppy-disk drives. This first version did not support hard disk drives. Since that time, hardware has evolved significantly, and new versions have also evolved. Fortunately, these newer versions of DOS were written so that older application programs could still work with them. Unfortunately, DOS' ability to fully use all the power of today's microcomputers has been constrained. This is because DOS must support these older application packages.

■ **Limited primary storage:** Before an application program can be used, it must be stored in the computer's primary storage. An application program running with DOS has direct access to only 640 kilobytes (about 640,000 characters) of primary storage. With the newer versions of DOS, several additional kilobytes can be accessed. However, most of the new spreadsheet, database management, and graphics programs require more primary storage. New microcomputers have much more primary storage. Still, DOS by itself as the operating system cannot access all of this available primary storage. This restriction is an inherent limitation of DOS.

■ **"Single tasking" only: Multitasking** is the term given to operating systems that allow a single user to run several application programs at the same time. We discuss multitasking further in the next section. Unfortunately, MS-DOS by itself can only do *single tasking:* It can support only one user and one application program at the same time. The newer versions of MS-DOS, however, do support *task switching.* That is, they can switch or interrupt one application to do another application. But they cannot run both applications at the same time.

■ **Character-based interface:** In DOS, users issue commands by typing or by selecting items from a menu. This approach is called a **character-based interface** or **command line interface.** Many users find another arrangement for issuing commands, the graphical user interface, much easier.

The widespread use and success of Microsoft's MS-DOS has encouraged other software companies to introduce similar competing products. The two best known are PC-DOS by IBM and Novell DOS by Novell Incorporated. Although the most recent versions of MS-DOS, PC-DOS, and Novell DOS are very similar, Microsoft's MS-DOS is by far the most widely used.

The long-term future of DOS is clear. It will likely continue to be updated, with newer versions designed to minimize its current disadvantages. However, DOS will eventually be replaced by newer operating systems that take advantage of new technologies.

Microsoft Windows

Windows is an operating environment, while Windows 95 and Windows
NT are powerful new operating systems.

There are three basic variations of Microsoft Corporation's windowing programs. The first is simply called Windows. The other two are Windows 95
and Windows NT.

Windows

Unlike Windows 95 and Windows NT, **Windows** is not an operating system. It is
a program that runs with DOS. (See Figure 4-6.) Windows extends the capabilities
of DOS by creating an easy-to-use **operating environment.** Other companies
make similar programs: Desqview by Quarterdeck Office Systems and NewWave by
Hewlett-Packard Company.

Windows is designed to run on IBM and compatible microcomputers with particular kinds of microprocessors. They are the Intel 80486 ("486") chip and Pentium chip.

ADVANTAGES Windows extends the capabilities of DOS to include:

■ **Multitasking:** When DOS is combined with Windows, a number of applications
("multiple tasks") can share the same microprocessor. With multitasking you
could be running a word processing program and a database management program at the same time. While printing a report using the word processing program, the other program could search a database for more information. Windows does this by switching back and forth between the two applications.

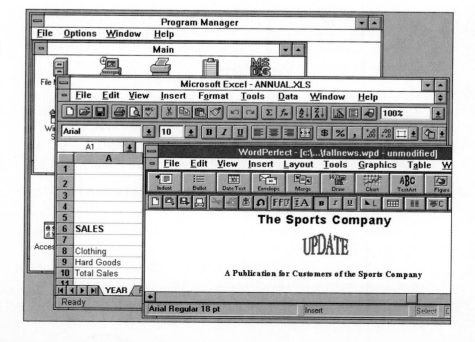

FIGURE 4-6
Windows 3.1 running
with DOS.

■ **Graphical user interface:** Windows (and other windowing programs available for DOS) offers a graphical user interface (GUI). A graphical user interface allows the user to move a mouse (or use keyboard commands) to move a pointer or cursor on the screen. The user positions the pointer on graphic symbols called **icons** or on pull-down menus and then clicks (presses a button on) the mouse. For example, to specify printer commands using Windows, the user can simply click on the printer icon.

■ **Number of applications:** Although more programs have been written for DOS, there are thousands of programs written for Windows.

■ **More memory:** As mentioned before, DOS by itself has limited access to memory, thereby severely limiting software and hardware capabilities. Windows, however, has a **memory manager** that allows access well beyond 640 kilobytes. Windows can access billions of characters of memory.

■ **Sharing data between applications:** Windows can share data from one application with other applications. For example, you may have created a cost report using a word processing program. The report contains a table based on a spreadsheet analysis of various items. If the two applications were linked, a change in the spreadsheet's values would automatically be reflected in the word processing document.

DISADVANTAGES Windows has dramatically improved upon DOS. Of course, Windows has some limitations.

■ **Minimum system configuration:** Windows requires a more powerful microcomputer to run. To effectively use Windows, the system should have at least a 486 microcomputer. It also requires at least four times as much memory as DOS and a hard disk.

■ **Unrecoverable errors:** When running the earlier versions of Windows, users sometimes encountered the message "Unrecoverable application error" on their screen. This means that the application program cannot proceed and the user must restart the program to begin again. Fortunately, these unrecoverable errors are rare with the newer versions of Windows.

Windows 95

Unlike Windows, **Windows 95** does not require DOS to run. (See Figure 4-7.) It is a new, powerful operating system. Introduced by Microsoft in 1995, Windows 95 is considered by many to be the future replacement for Windows and for DOS. It is an advanced operating system designed for today's very powerful microcomputers.

ADVANTAGES Windows 95 has some major advantages compared to Windows. These include:

■ **Multiprocessing:** Multiprocessing is similar to multitasking except that the applications are run independently and at the same time. For instance, you could be printing a word processing document and using a database management program at the same time. With multitasking, the speed at which the document is

FIGURE 4-7
Windows 95.

printed is affected by the demands of the database management program. With multiprocessing, the demands of the database management program do not affect the printing of the document.

- **Flexibility:** Windows 95 does not require DOS and is able to run with a much wider variety of powerful computers and microprocessors.

- **Internet access:** As we will discuss in the Internet Guide, to connect to the Internet through an online service, your microcomputer must have TCP/IP and Internet utilities. Both are built into Windows 95. To gain access using Windows 95, all you have to do is click the appropriate icon. (See Figure 4-7.)

- **Easy upgrades:** Installation of new hardware such as a modem can be very complex and difficult. A new standard called Plug and Play (to be discussed in detail in Chapter 5) promises to greatly simplify the installation process. Windows 95 is the first operating system for DOS-based computers to fully support Plug and Play.

DISADVANTAGES Compared to Windows, Windows 95 has two major disadvantages.

- **Minimum system configuration:** Like Windows, Windows 95 requires at least a 486 microprocessor and a hard disk drive to operate effectively. Windows 95, however, requires more hard disk space—nearly 5 times as much. Additionally, Windows 95 requires much more memory—3 to 4 times as much.

- **Fewer applications:** Compared to DOS and Windows, fewer applications have been written specifically for Windows 95. It can, however, run most DOS and Windows applications.

Windows NT

Windows NT is a very sophisticated and powerful operating system. (See Figure 4-8.) It is not considered a replacement for either Windows or Windows 95. Rather, it is an advanced alternative designed for very powerful microcomputers and networks.

ADVANTAGES Windows NT has some major advantages when compared to Windows 95. These advantages include:

■ **Multiuser:** Windows NT allows more than one person, or **multiusers,** to use the same computer at the same time. At one time, multiuser systems were considered to have a very significant cost advantage. Now, as hardware costs have come down, this advantage for microcomputers is not nearly as significant.

■ **Networking:** In many business environments, workers often use computers to communicate with one another and to share software using a network. This is made possible and controlled by special system software. Windows NT has network capabilities and security checks built into the operating system. This makes network installation and use relatively easy.

DISADVANTAGES Windows NT has some disadvantages when compared to Windows 95.

■ **Minimum system configuration:** Like Windows 95, the system should have at least the power of a 486 microprocessor. However, Windows NT requires more memory and more than twice the hard disk space as Windows 95.

■ **Upgrade support:** Windows NT does not provide the same level of support for Plug and Play as Windows 95. Therefore, upgrading or installation of new hardware under Windows NT can be much more difficult.

FIGURE 4-8

Windows NT.

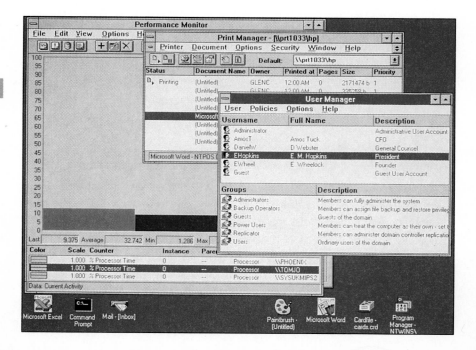

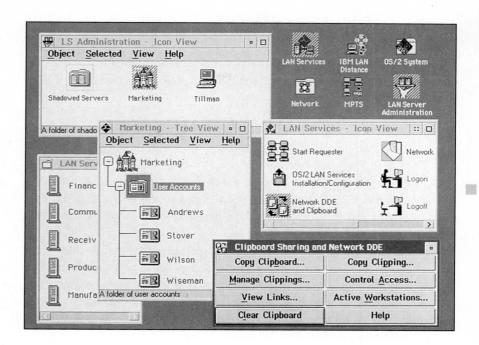

FIGURE 4-9
OS/2 Warp.

OS/2

OS/2 was originally developed jointly by IBM and Microsoft.

OS/2 stands for Operating System/2. (See Figure 4-9.) It was originally developed jointly by IBM and Microsoft (who have since gone their separate ways). The most recent version is OS/2 Warp.

Advantages

Like Windows 95 and Windows NT, OS/2 Warp is designed for very powerful microcomputers and has several advanced features. Some of its advantages include:

- **Minimum system configuration:** OS/2 Warp requires nearly the same system configuration as Windows 95. Compared to Windows NT, however, OS/2 requires only one third the memory and less than half the hard disk space.

- **Multiprocessing:** Like Windows NT, OS/2 Warp supports multiprocessing. Windows 95 does not support multiprocessing.

Disadvantages

OS/2 Warp has some disadvantages compared to Windows 95 and Windows NT:

- **Networking:** Compared to Windows NT, neither OS/2 Warp nor Windows 95 have the same level of network and security capabilities.

- **Upgrade support:** Like Windows NT, OS/2 Warp does not provide the same level of support for Plug and Play as does Windows 95. Therefore, upgrading or installation of new hardware can be much more difficult.

Macintosh Operating System

The Macintosh operating system, which runs only on Macintosh computers, offers a high-quality graphical user interface and is very easy to use.

What can you do with OS/2 Warp or Microsoft Windows that you can't do with an Apple Macintosh computer? That's what many people are asking. If it's a graphical user interface or Plug and Play capabilities you want, that's been available for some time with the Mac. In the opinion of many industry observers, OS/2 Warp and Microsoft Windows look very similar to the Macintosh operating system. To appreciate the differences, let us look at how the Macintosh works.

The **Macintosh operating system** is contained in two primary files—the System file and the Finder. These two files work together to perform the standard operating system procedures. These procedures include tasks such as formatting disks, copying files, erasing files, and running application programs. These files also manage the user interface, displaying menus and activating tasks that are chosen from the menus by the user.

Remember that the advantages and disadvantages of microcomputer operating systems are associated with the microprocessors for which they were originally designed. DOS, Microsoft Windows, and OS/2 were designed for microprocessor chips built by Intel, most recently the 486 and Pentium chips. Macintoshes, on the other hand, are built around Motorola's 68040 and PowerPC microprocessors. These Motorola chips cannot run DOS application programs, and the Intel chips cannot run Macintosh application programs. In the beginning, Apple found its Macintoshes hard to sell to corporations because nearly all business application programs—such as Lotus 1-2-3—were written to run on DOS-based machines.

Apple has introduced numerous versions of its operating system. A recent version is the Macintosh **System 7.5** designed for Apple computers using Motorola's PowerPC microprocessor. This operating system is a significant milestone for Apple. It is a very powerful operating system like Windows NT and OS/2. System 7.5 has network capabilities and can read DOS, Windows, and OS/2 files.

Advantages

The Apple Macintosh popularized the graphical user interface, including the use of windows, pull-down menus, and the mouse. (See Figure 4-10.) The graphical user interface has several advantages:

- **Ease of use:** The graphical user interface has made the Macintosh popular with many newcomers to computing. This is because it is easy to learn. In fact, studies show that user training costs are *half* as much for Macintoshes as for DOS-based computers.

- **Quality graphics:** Macintosh has established a high standard for graphics processing. This is a principal reason why the Macintosh is popular for desktop publishing. Users are easily able to merge pictorial and text materials to produce professional-looking newsletters, advertisements, and the like.

FIGURE 4-10
**The Macintosh graphical
user interface.**

- **Multitasking:** Like the Microsoft Windows programs and OS/2, the Macintosh System 7 enables you to do multitasking. That is, several programs can run at the same time.

- **Easy upgrades:** Like Windows 95, the Macintosh System 7 supports Plug and Play. As mentioned earlier, Macintosh was the first operating system to support this concept.

Disadvantages

Many characteristics that were previously considered disadvantages may no longer prove to be so. Nevertheless, let us consider what these disadvantages are.

- **A "business" machine?** Apple has had to struggle against the corporate perception that its products are not for "serious business users." Corporate buyers have had a history of purchasing from IBM and other vendors of large computers. Many have viewed Apple from the beginning as a producer of microcomputers for students, game players, and hobbyists. This is changing fast.

- **Multiprocessing:** Unlike Windows NT and OS/2 Warp, Macintosh System 7.5 does not support multiprocessing.

- **Compatibility difficulties:** The incompatibility of DOS with Macintosh microprocessors made Macintoshes less attractive to corporate users interested in compatibility and connectivity. However, hardware and software are now available for the Mac to allow it to run DOS, Windows, and OS/2 applications. In addition, communications networks connect Macintoshes to other computers that use DOS. Apple has cooperated with Digital Equipment Corporation (DEC) and others to produce communications links between Macintoshes, IBM PCs, and mainframe computers.

Unix

Unix can run on many different computers (is "portable"), can perform multitasking, can be shared by several users at once, and can network reliably.

U**nix** has been around for some time. It was originally developed by AT&T for minicomputers and is very good for multitasking. It is also good for networking between computers. It has been, and continues to be, popular on very powerful microcomputers called workstations. (See Figure 4-11.)

Unix initially became popular in industry because for many years AT&T licensed the system to universities for a nominal fee. This led to Unix being carried by recent computer science and engineering graduates to their new places of employment.

One important consequence of its scientific and technical orientation is that Unix has remained popular with engineers and technical people. It is less well known among businesspeople. All that, however, is changing. The reason: With the arrival of very powerful microcomputers, Unix is becoming a larger player in the microcomputer world.

Let us consider the advantages and disadvantages of Unix.

FIGURE 4-11
Unix workstation: Sun IPX

Advantages

Unix has the advantage of being a portable operating system. That means that it is used with ("is portable to") different types of computer systems. It is used with microcomputers, minicomputers, mainframes, and supercomputers. The other operating systems are designed for microcomputers and are not nearly as portable. Having said this, however, we must hastily state that there are *different versions* of Unix, as we will describe. Let us first consider the advantages.

- **Multitasking:** Unix enables you to do multitasking. It allows you to run several programs at the same time, each one sharing the CPU.

- **Multiprocessing:** Unix, like Windows NT and OS/2 Warp, is able to run several programs independently and at the same time.

- **Networking:** Unix is able to share files over electronic networks with several different kinds of equipment. Although the other operating systems can also do this, Unix systems have been successfully and reliably sharing across networks for years.

Disadvantages

Unix was a minicomputer operating system used by programmers and computer science professionals some time before the rise of the microcomputer. This means it has certain qualities that make it useful to programmers—lots of supporting utility programs and documentation, for instance. However, some of its features make it difficult for end users. Let us consider the disadvantages.

- **Limited business application software:** This is a great barrier at the moment. There are many engineering application programs. Unfortunately, there are fewer business application programs. Businesses that are dependent on off-the-shelf programs for microcomputers will find offerings very limited.

- **No Unix standard:** This may be *the* biggest stumbling block. There is no Unix standard. This means that an application written for one version of Unix may not run on other versions. The principal microcomputer versions are AT&T's Unix System V, IBM's AIX, Novell's UnixWare 2, and the University of California/Berkeley's 4.2 Unix. An organization called the X/Open Co. is trying to create a standard. This organization is a consortium of major computer suppliers led by DEC, Hewlett-Packard, Novell, and SunSoft.

- **More difficult to learn:** Unix is a very powerful and complex operating system. Its commands are frequently long and complex. Because of this, many microcomputer users find Unix difficult to learn and use.

Unix is a popular operating system for researchers and educators. Some observers think it could yet become a leader among microcomputer operating systems.

The principal advantages and disadvantages of the present microcomputer operating systems are summarized in Figure 4-12.

FIGURE 4-12

Advantages and disadvantages of present microcomputer operating systems.

■ ■ ■ ■ ■ ■ ■ ■ ■

COMPARISONS OF OPERATING SYSTEMS

OPERATING SYSTEM	ADVANTAGES	DISADVANTAGES
DOS	Many existing users and applications; system requirements	Limited primary storage; single tasking only; character-based interface
Windows	Multitasking; graphical user interface; many applications; more memory; share data between applications	System requirements; occasional unrecoverable errors
Windows 95	Multitasking; graphical user interface; more memory; share data between applications; multiprocessing; flexibility; Internet access; easy upgrades	System requirements; few applications
Windows NT	Multitasking; graphical user interface; more memory; share data between applications; multiprocessing; multiuser; flexibility; networking capabilities	System requirements; few applications; upgrade support
OS/2 Warp	Multitasking; graphical user interface; more memory; share data between applications; system requirements; multiprocessing; flexibility	Few applications; networking capabilities; upgrade support
Macintosh	Ease of use; quality graphics; graphical user interface; multitasking; upgrade support	Market perception; no multiprocessing compatibility
Unix	Multitasking; multiprocessing; multiuser; networking capabilities	Limited business applications; no standard version; difficult to learn

A Look at the Future

The popularity of DOS is declining while Windows is increasing in popularity. Many new operating systems will use object-oriented programming.

We continually read that this or that operating system is going to overturn DOS as the most widely used microcomputer operating system. However, DOS remains strong and, when coupled with Windows, it will likely remain strong through the next few years. Although opinions vary, most expect DOS used alone to decline in the next few years and Windows to increase. Following that, most expect DOS and Windows to give way to other operating systems.

In the near future, DOS, Windows, and Macintosh will probably continue to serve many people. These include students, people with microcomputers at home, and owners of small businesses. Windows, Windows 95, and OS/2 Warp will first be used in larger businesses, higher education, and local government. Eventually, they will replace DOS.

One thing is certain for the future of operating systems. Newer, more powerful, and easier-to-use versions will keep evolving. These new systems will be created with *object-oriented programming.* It involves creating the operating system with a series of interchangeable software objects or modules. This differs from the way DOS and other popular operating systems are constructed. They use layer after layer of lines of computer code instead. Using object-oriented programming, new operating systems can be developed faster and more efficiently.

Microsoft Corporation is developing a major new version of Windows. This operating system is expected to have a user interface to match Windows 95, an advanced Internet connection, and powerful network security capabilities. Apple, IBM, and Hewlett-Packard are working on a joint project called Taligent. This project is expected to provide the foundation for IBM's next major revision of OS/2, called Workplace. Taligent is also the foundation for Apple's next generation of operating systems, code-named "Copland" (likely to be called System 8) and "Gershwin." These operating systems may already have been released by the time you read this. Another Microsoft Corporation project, code-named "Cairo," is under development to upgrade the high-end Windows NT operating system.

KEY TERMS

backup (73)

basic input-output system (73)

booting (73)

bootstrap loader (73)

character-based interface (76)

command line interface (76)

copy (73)

diagnostic routine (73)

DOS (74)

erase (73)

formatting (73)

icon (78)

initializing (73)

Macintosh operating system (82)

memory manager (78)

multiprocessing (74)

multiprogramming (74)

multitasking (76)

multiuser (80)

operating environment (77)

operating system (73)

OS/2 (81)

rename (73)

System 7.5 (82)

Unix (84)

utility program (73)

virtual memory (74)

Windows (77)

Windows 95 (78)

Windows NT (80)

REVIEW QUESTIONS

True/False

1. One computer can only run one kind of system software.
2. Virtual memory increases the amount of memory available to run application programs.
3. Mainframe and minicomputer systems tend to focus on multiple users of a single computer system.
4. Macintosh computers are designed to use the 486 microprocessor.
5. One of Unix's primary strengths is the large number of applications written for it.

Multiple Choice

1. The collection of programs that helps the computer manage its resources:
   a. bootstrap loader
   b. applications
   c. operating system
   d. diagnostic routines
   e. backup
2. An operating environment:
   a. Windows
   b. Windows 95
   c. Windows NT
   d. OS/2
   e. Macintosh
3. The ability to have a number of applications running at the same time:
   a. GUI
   b. integrated
   c. windowing software
   d. multitasking
   e. networking
4. An operating system developed jointly by IBM and Microsoft Corporation:
   a. Unix
   b. OS/2
   c. Windows NT
   d. Desqview
   e. Macintosh
5. Designed to run the System 7.5 operating system:
   a. Unix
   b. OS/2
   c. Windows
   d. Desqview
   e. Macintosh

Fill in the Blank

1. _____ the system means that the computer has been turned on and the operating system has been loaded into memory.

2. Of all the microcomputer operating systems, _____ is able to run on the least expensive hardware.

3. Windows 95 is an operating _____ .

4. The System file and the Finder are the two primary files in the _____ operating system.

5. The lack of a standard version for _____ is likely its most significant disadvantage.

Open Ended

1. What, in a phrase, is the difference between application software and system software?

2. What are utility programs?

3. What is meant by multitasking?

4. What is a graphical user interface?

5. What is meant by the term *multiuser*?

DISCUSSION QUESTIONS

1. *Apple or IBM?* Suppose you're working for a small company that needs 10 new microcomputers. The computers must all be the same and will be networked to share data and programs. It's your decision—you can buy either Apple Macintoshes or IBM-compatibles. Which microcomputer and what operating system would you choose, and why?

2. *An operating system for everybody?* Readers always have the advantage over writers because the words they read exist in the present, not in the uncertain future. As we write this, we don't know how Microsoft's "Cairo," the IBM—Apple Corporation Taligent experiment, Apple's "Copland" (likely to be called System 8), or "Gershwin" will turn out. To find out more about them, go to the library or use the Internet to research these topics.

3. *http://www.microsoft.com*   A good place to learn about anything is to go to the source. To learn more about Windows 95, go to the Microsoft home page at the address given at the beginning of this question. Then locate Apple and IBM's home page to learn more about their operating systems. (Hint: Use the Every Student's Internet Resource Guide: Computer Science and Computer Technology—Entry Number: 02.)

Systems Software

Applications

Systems software does "background work" (like helping the computer do internal tasks). Five different kinds of operating systems are: DOS, Microsoft Windows, OS/2, Macintosh, and Unix. Three basic variations of Microsoft Windows: Windows, Windows 95, and Windows NT.

SYSTEM SOFTWARE PROGRAMS

PROGRAM	FUNCTION
Bookstrap loader	Reads operating system from disk and loads into memory.
Diagnostic routines	Tests parts of system to ensure computer is running properly.
Basic input-output	Transmits characters from the keyboard to a monitor or disk.
Operating system	Helps manage computer resources. Most important types are DOS, Microsoft Windows, OS/2, Macintosh, and Unix.

WINDOWS	WINDOWS 95	WINDOWS NT

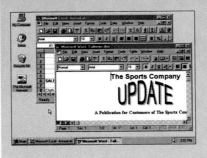

Windows is not an operating system. It is a program that runs with DOS as the operating system. Windows extends the capability of DOS. Compared to DOS:	**Windows 95** is an operating system. It does not require DOS. Windows 95 is an advanced operating system for powerful microcomputers. Compared to Windows:	**Windows NT** is an operating system that offers an advanced alternative to Windows and Windows 95. It is designed for very powerful microcomputers and networks. Compared to Windows 95:

Advantages

- **Multitasking** is possible (several applications sharing multiprocessor that switches between applications).
- **Graphical user interface (GUI)** is provided. Commands can be executed by manipulating graphic symbols called **icons.**
- More memory can be accessed.
- Share data between applications.

Disadvantages

- System requirements are much greater than DOS.
- Unrecoverable errors were a problem with earlier versions of Windows.

Advantages

Like Windows, it supports multitasking, graphical user interface, more memory access, and data sharing. Additionally:

- **Microprocessing** capability allows multiple applications to run independently and at the same time.
- Flexibility to run with wider variety of powerful computers and microprocessors.
- Internet utilities to connect to an online service.
- Plug and Play support to simplify new hardware installation.

Disadvantages

- System requirements are much greater than Windows.
- Few applications written specifically for Windows 95.

Advantages

Like Windows 95, it supports multitasking, graphical user interface, more memory access, data sharing, multiprocessing, and flexibility. Additionally:

- **Multiuser** capability allows more than one user to operate at the same time.
- Easy to install and use networking capabilities.

Disadvantages

- System requirements much greater than for Windows 95.
- Plug and Play is not supported.

DOS is the most widely used operating system for IBM and IBM-compatible computers. There are six versions of MS-DOS. All are "backward compatible"—applications programs can run on newer versions of DOS.

DIFFERENT VERSIONS OF MS-DOS

VERSION	FEATURES
1.0	Original operating system for IBM PC and compatibles. Supported only floppy-disk drives.
2.0	Developed for IBM XT microcomputer. First version to support hard-disk drives.
3.0	Appeared about the same time as IBM AT microcomputer. Starting with 3.2 release, supported networking and 3½-inch disk drives.
4.0	Included pull-down menus and other sophisticated modifications.
5.0	Allowed access to more memory and task switching.
6.0	Include disk compression, advanced memory and file management and virus protection.

OS/2	MACINTOSH OPERATING SYSTEMS	UNIX

OS/2 is an operating system initially developed jointly by IBM and Microsoft. Compared to Windows NT:

Advantages

Like Windows NT, it supports multitasking, graphical user interface, more memory access, data sharing, flexibility, and multiprocessing.

- Systems requirements are slightly less.

Disadvantages

Like Windows NT, it does not support Plug and Play and system requirements much greater than Windows 95. Additionally:

- Networking capabilities are not as advanced.
- Multiuser capability not supported.

Several operating systems have been designed for Apple's **Macintosh**. New versions have been developed as new versions of the Macintosh have been developed.

Advantages

- Easy to learn and to use.
- Offers a high standard for graphics processing.
- Can do multitasking—running of multiple programs at the same time.
- Can share data with other applications programs.

Disadvantages

- Some corporate buyers do not view Macintosh as a serious business machine.
- Does not support multiprocessing
- Programs written for DOS will not run on a Macintosh unless specialty hardware and software have been installed.

Unix, originally developed for minicomputers, is able to run on more powerful models of microcomputers. Unix is available in a number of different versions, many of which are not compatible.

Advantages

- Allows multitasking—running of multiple programs.
- Allows multiprocessing—running multiple programs independently and at the same time.
- Allows multiple users to share computer simultaneously.
- History of sharing files over electronic networks with different equipment.

Disadvantages

- Few business applications programs are presently available.
- No one Unix standard exists; there are several versions (principal ones: Unix System V, Berkeley 4.2 Unix, SunOS).
- Commands are often long and complex, making it difficult for some users to learn and to use.

The Processing Unit

How is the data in "data processing" actually *processed?* That is the subject of this chapter. Why do you need to know anything about it? The answer lies in three words: *speed, capacity,* and *flexibility.* After reading this chapter, you will be able to judge how fast, powerful, and versatile a particular microcomputer is. As you might expect, this knowledge is valuable if you are planning to buy a new microcomputer system. (The Buyer's Guide at the end of this book provides additional buying information.) It will also help you to evaluate whether or not an existing microcomputer system is powerful enough for today's new and exciting applications.

COMPETENCIES

After you have read this chapter, you should be able to:

1. Explain the two main parts of the central processing unit—the control unit and the arithmetic-logic unit.
2. Understand the workings and the functions of memory.
3. Describe how a computer uses binary codes to represent data in electrical form.
4. Describe the components of the system unit in a microcomputer.

Some time you may get the chance to watch when a technician opens up a microcomputer to fix it. You will see that it is basically a collection of electronic circuitry. There is no need for you to understand how all these components work. However, it is important to understand the principles. Once you do, you will then be able to determine how powerful a particular microcomputer is. This will help you judge whether it can run particular kinds of programs and can meet your needs as a user.

The CPU

The central processing unit has two components—the control unit and the arithmetic-logic unit.

The part of the computer that runs the program (executes program instructions) is known as the **processor** or *central processing unit (CPU)*. In a microcomputer, the CPU is on a single electronic component, the **micro-**

processor chip, within the *system unit* or *system cabinet.* The system unit also includes circuit boards, memory chips, ports, and other components. A microcomputer's system cabinet may also house disk drives, but these are considered separate from the CPU. (See Figure 5-1.)

In Chapter 1 we said the system unit consists of electronic circuitry with two main parts, the processor (the CPU) and memory. Let us refine this further by stating that the CPU itself has two parts: the control unit and the arithmetic-logic unit. In a microcomputer, these are both on the microprocessor chip.

The Control Unit

The **control unit** tells the rest of the computer system how to carry out a program's instructions. It directs the movement of electronic signals between memory—which temporarily holds data, instructions, and processed information—and the arithmetic-logic unit. It also directs these control signals between the CPU and input and output devices.

The Arithmetic-Logic Unit

The **arithmetic-logic unit,** usually called the **ALU,** performs two types of operations—arithmetic and logical. *Arithmetic* operations are, as you might expect, the fundamental math operations: addition, subtraction, multiplication, and division. *Logical* operations consist of comparisons. That is, two pieces of data are compared to see whether one is equal to (=), less than (<), or greater than (>) the other.

FIGURE 5-1

Inside a microcomputer system unit.

Memory

Memory temporarily holds data, program instructions, and information.

Memory—also known as **RAM, primary storage, internal storage,** or **main memory**—is the part of the microcomputer that holds

- Data for processing
- Instructions for processing the data—that is, the *program*
- Information—that is, processed data—waiting to be output or sent to secondary storage such as a floppy disk in a disk drive

One of the most important facts to know about memory is that part of its content is held only temporarily. In other words, it is stored only as long as the microcomputer is turned on. When you turn the machine off, the contents immediately vanish. We have said this before, but it bears repeating: The stored contents in memory are *volatile* and can vanish very quickly, as during a power failure, for example. It is therefore a good practice to repeatedly save your work in progress to a secondary storage medium such as a floppy disk or hard disk. For instance, if you are writing a report on a word processor, every 5 to 10 minutes you should stop and save your work. Some word processors and other application software have the ability to automatically save every few minutes.

The next important fact to know about memory is that its capacity varies in different computers. The original IBM Personal Computer, for example, could hold up to approximately 640,000 characters of data or instructions. By contrast, the IBM ValuePoint can hold 128 *million* characters, or over 24 times as much. If you are using an older computer with small memory, it may not be able to run such powerful programs as Excel. Thus, you need to look at the software package before you buy and see how much memory it requires.

Registers

Computers also have several additional storage locations called **registers.** These appear in the control unit and ALU and make processing more efficient. Registers are special high-speed staging areas that hold data and instructions temporarily during processing. They are parts of the control unit and ALU rather than memory. Their contents can therefore be handled much faster than the contents of memory can.

The Processing Cycle

To locate the characters of data or instructions in main memory, the computer stores them at locations known as **addresses.** Each address is designated by a unique number. Addresses may be compared to post office mailboxes. Their numbers stay the same, but the contents continually change.

Our illustration gives an example of how memory and the CPU work to process information. (See Figure 5-2.) Note that the various components of the CPU are linked by special electrical connections. In this example, the program will multiply two numbers—20 × 30, yielding 600. Let us assume the program to multi-

FIGURE 5-2
How the CPU and memory
work.

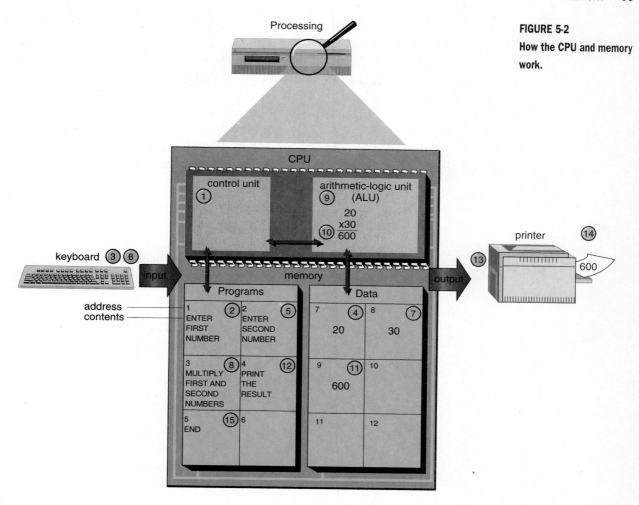

(1) The control unit recognizes that the entire program has been loaded into memory. It begins to execute the first step in the program.

(2) The program tells the user, ENTER FIRST NUMBER.

(3) The user types the number *20* on the keyboard. An electronic signal is sent to the CPU.

(4) The control unit recognizes this signal and routes the signal to an address in memory—address 7.

(5) After completing the above program instruction, the next program instruction tells the user, ENTER SECOND NUMBER.

(6) The user types the number *30* on the keyboard. An electronic signal is sent to the CPU.

(7) The control unit recognizes this signal and routes it to memory address 8.

(8) The next program instruction is executed: MULTIPLY FIRST AND SECOND NUMBERS.

(9) To execute this instruction, the control unit informs the arithmetic-logic unit (ALU) that two numbers are coming and that the ALU is to multiply them. The control unit next sends the ALU a copy of the contents of address 7 (*20*) and then sends a copy of the contents of address 8 (*30*).

(10) The ALU performs the multiplication: *20* x *30* = *600*.

(11) The control unit sends a copy of the multiplied results (*600*) back to memory, to address 9.

(12) The next program instruction is executed: PRINT THE RESULT.

(13) To execute this instruction, the control unit sends the contents of address 9 (*600*) to the printer.

(14) The printer prints the value *600*.

(15) The final instruction is executed: END. The program is complete.

ply these two numbers has been loaded into memory. The program asks the user to enter the two values (20 and 30). It then multiplies these two values together (20 × 30). Finally, it prints out the result (600) on a printer. Our illustration describes the process just after the program has been loaded into memory. Follow the steps in the figure to walk yourself through the diagram.

Note: This figure simplifies the actual processing activity in order to demonstrate the essential operations of the CPU. For instance, there are actually many more memory addresses—thousands or millions—than are shown here. Moreover, the addresses are in a form the computer can interpret—electronic signals rather than the numbers and letters shown here.

The Binary System

Data and instructions are represented electronically with a binary, or two-state, numbering system. The three principal binary coding schemes are ASCII, EBCDIC, and Unicode.

W e have described the storage and processing of data in terms of *characters*. How, in fact, are these characters represented inside the computer?

We said that when you open up the system cabinet of a microcomputer, you see mainly electronic circuitry. And what is the most fundamental statement you can make about electricity? It is simply this: It can be either *on* or *off*.

Indeed, there are many forms of technology that can make use of this two-state on/off, yes/no, present/absent arrangement. For instance, a light switch may be on or off, or an electric circuit open or closed. A magnetized spot on a tape or disk may have a positive charge or a negative charge. This is the reason, then, that the binary system is used to represent data and instructions.

The decimal system that we are all familiar with has 10 digits (0, 1, 2, 3, 4, 5, 6, 7, 8, 9). The **binary system,** however, consists of only two digits—0 and 1. In the computer, the 0 can be represented by electricity being off, and the 1 by electricity being on. Everything that goes into a computer is converted into these binary numbers. (See Figure 5-3.) For example, the letter *W* corresponds to the electronic signal 0 1 0 1 0 1 1 1.

Units of Measure for Capacity

Each 0 or 1 in the binary system is called a **bit**—short for *bi*nary digi*t*. In order to represent numbers, letters, and special characters, bits are combined into groups of eight bits called **bytes.** Each byte typically represents one character—in many computers, one addressable storage location. The capacity of main memory, then, is expressed in numbers of bytes. There are four commonly used units of measurement to describe memory capacity. (See Figure 5-4.)

- One **kilobyte**—abbreviated **K, KB,** or **K-byte**—is equivalent to approximately 1000 bytes. (More precisely, 1 kilobyte is equal to 1024 bytes. However, the figure is commonly rounded to 1000 bytes.) This is a common unit of mea-

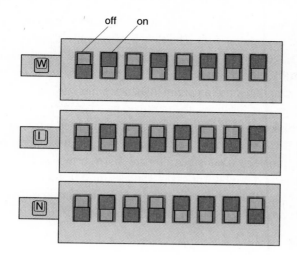

sure for memory or storage capacity of microcomputers. The older IBM PCs, for example, had a top capacity of 640K, or about 640,000 characters of data.

- One **megabyte**—**MB** or **M-byte**—represents 1 million bytes. Thus, a microcomputer system listed with a "16MB main memory" has primary storage capacity of about 16 million bytes.

- One **gigabyte**—**GB** or **G-byte**—represents about 1 billion bytes. This is a measure that until recently was used only with larger computers. Now it is also used to describe very powerful microcomputers.

- One **terabyte**—**TB** or **T-byte**—represents about 1 trillion bytes. This is a measure used with large computers.

Binary Coding Schemes

Now let us consider an important question. How are characters represented as 0s and 1s ("off" and "on" electrical states) in the computer? The answer is in the use of *binary coding schemes.*

Two of the most popular binary coding schemes use eight bits to form each byte. These two codes are *ASCII* and *EBCDIC.* (See Figure 5-5.) A recently developed code, *Unicode* uses sixteen bits.

- **ASCII,** pronounced "*as*-key," stands for *A*merican *S*tandard *C*ode for *I*nformation *I*nterchange. This is the most widely used binary code for microcomputers.

- **EBCDIC,** pronounced "*eb*-see-dick," stands for *E*xtended *B*inary *C*oded *D*ecimal *I*nterchange *C*ode. It was developed by IBM and is used on many IBM and other kinds of computers. As a result, EBCDIC is almost an industry standard for large computers.

- **Unicode** is a sixteen-bit code designed to support international languages like Chinese and Japanese. These languages have too many characters to be represented by the eight-bit ASCII and EBCDIC codes. It was developed by Unicode, Inc. with support from Apple, IBM, and Microsoft.

MEMORY CAPACITY

UNIT	CAPACITY
Kilobyte	one thousand bytes
Megabyte	one million bytes
Gigabyte	one billion bytes
Terabyte	one trillion bytes

FIGURE 5-4
Memory capacity.

BINARY CODES

CHARACTER	ASCII	EBCDIC
A	0100 0001	1100 0001
B	0100 0010	1100 0010
C	0100 0011	1100 0011
D	0100 0100	1100 0100
E	0100 0101	1100 0101
F	0100 0110	1100 0110
G	0100 0111	1100 0111
H	0100 1000	1100 1000
I	0100 1001	1100 1001
J	0100 1010	1101 0001
K	0100 1011	1101 0010
L	0100 1100	1101 0011
M	0100 1101	1101 0100
N	0100 1110	1101 0101
O	0100 1111	1101 0110
P	0101 0000	1101 0111
Q	0101 0001	1101 1000
R	0101 0010	1101 1001
S	0101 0011	1110 0010
T	0101 0100	1110 0011
U	0101 0101	1110 0100
V	0101 0110	1110 0101
W	0101 0111	1110 0110
X	0101 1000	1110 0111
Y	0101 1001	1110 1000
Z	0101 1010	1110 1001
0	0011 0000	1111 0000
1	0011 0001	1111 0001
2	0011 0010	1111 0010
3	0011 0011	1111 0011
4	0011 0100	1111 0100
5	0011 0101	1111 0101
6	0011 0110	1111 0110
7	0011 0111	1111 0111
8	0011 1000	1111 1000
9	0011 1001	1111 1001

FIGURE 5-5

ASCII and EBCDIC binary coding schemes for representing data.

When you press a key on the keyboard, a character is automatically converted into a series of electronic pulses. The CPU can recognize these pulses. For example, pressing the letter *W* on a keyboard causes an electronic signal to be sent to the CPU. The CPU then converts it to the ASCII value of 01010111.

Why are coding schemes important? Whenever files are used or shared by different computers or applications, the same coding scheme must be used. Generally, this is not a problem if both computers are microcomputers since both would most likely use ASCII code. And most microcomputer applications store files using this code. However, problems occur when files are shared between microcomputers and larger computers that use EBCDIC code. The files must be translated from one coding scheme to the other before processing can begin. Fortunately, special conversion programs are available to help with this translation.

The Parity Bit

As you know, there is often static on the radio. Similarly, there can be "static," or electronic interference, in a circuit or communications line transmitting a byte. When you are typing the letter *W*, for example, the *W* should be represented in the CPU (in ASCII) as

$$0\ 1\ 0\ 1\ 0\ 1\ 1\ 1$$

However, if the last 1 is garbled and becomes a 0, the byte will be read as 01010110—*V* instead of *W*. Is there a way, then, for the CPU to detect whether it is receiving erroneous data?

Indeed there is. Detection is accomplished by using a **parity bit**—an extra bit automatically added to a byte for purposes of testing accuracy. There are even-parity systems and odd-parity systems. In a computer using an even-parity system, the parity bit is set to either 0 or 1 so that the number of 1s is even. (See Figure 5-6.) For instance, when the letter *W* is pressed on the keyboard, the signal 01010111 is emitted. Before the signal is sent to the CPU, the number of 1s is counted—in this case, 5. A parity bit is added to the front and set to 1, thereby making the number of 1s even. The signal 101010111 is sent. When the signal is received by the CPU, the number of 1s is checked again. If it is odd, it means an error has occurred. This is called a *parity error.* When a parity error occurs, the CPU requests that the signal be sent again. If the parity error occurs again, the message "parity error" might appear on your display. (Odd-parity systems act just the reverse of even-parity systems.)

Of course, the system does not guarantee accuracy. For example, if *two* erroneous 0s were introduced in the byte for *W*, the computer would accept the byte as correct. This is because the two erroneous 0s would add up to an even 4 bits.

We have explained the principles by which a computer stores and processes data. We can now open up the system unit and take a look at some of the parts.

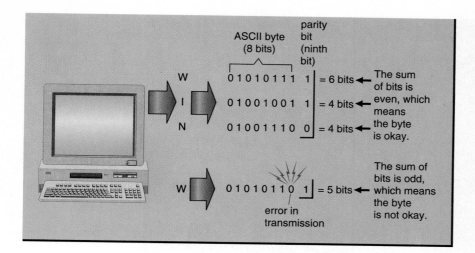

FIGURE 5-6
How parity bits check for
transmission errors.

The System Unit

It's important to understand what's inside the system unit, so that you can talk intelligently to computer specialists.

As mentioned, the part of the microcomputer that contains the CPU is called the *system unit.* The system unit is housed within the system cabinet. If you take off the cabinet, you will find that many parts can be easily removed for replacement. Almost all computers are modular. That is, entire sections can be replaced, as one would the parts of a car. In addition, microcomputers are *expandable.* That is, more memory may be added, as well as certain other devices.

Let us consider the following components of the system unit:

- System board
- Microprocessor chips
- Memory chips—RAM and ROM
- System clock
- Expansion slots and boards
- Bus lines
- Ports

System Board

The **system board** is also called the **motherboard.** (See Figure 5-7.) It consists of a flat board that usually contains the CPU and some memory *chips.* A **chip** consists of a tiny circuit board etched on a small square of sandlike material called silicon. A chip is also called a **silicon chip, semiconductor,** or **integrated circuit.** Chips are mounted on carrier packages, which then plug into sockets on the system board. In addition, system boards usually contain expansion slots, as we describe in another few paragraphs.

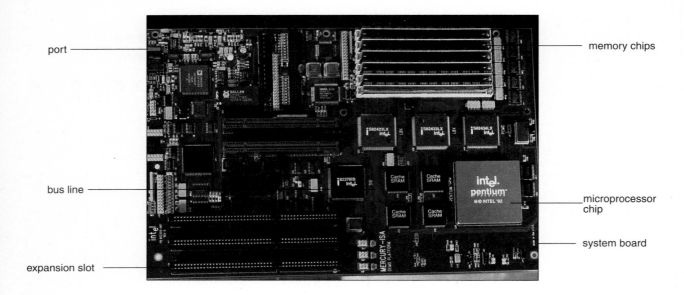

port —————— memory chips

bus line —————— microprocessor chip

—————— system board

expansion slot ——————

FIGURE 5-7
A microcomputer system board.

■ ■ ■ ■ ■ ■ ■ ■ ■

Microprocessor Chips

In a microcomputer, the CPU is contained on a single silicon chip called the *micro-processor*—"microscopic processor." Different microprocessors have different capabilities. (See Figure 5-8.)

Some chips or "families" of chips have become famous as the basis for several important lines of microcomputers. However, they are known by distinctly undramatic names: Their names are just their product numbers.

Chip capacities are often expressed in word sizes. A **word** is the number of bits (such as 16, 32, or 64) that can be accessed at one time by the CPU. The more bits in a word, the more powerful—and the faster—the computer. A 32-bit-word computer can access 4 bytes at a time. A 64-bit-word computer can access 8 bytes at a time. Therefore, the 64-bit computer is faster.

Microcomputers process data and instructions in millionths of a second, or **microseconds.** Supercomputers, by contrast, operate at speeds measured in nanoseconds and even picoseconds—1 thousand to 1 million times as fast as microcomputers. (See Figure 5-9.)

As we mentioned, the growing power of microprocessor chips is what is changing everything about microcomputers. Motorola's Power PC chip, for example, is the basis for Apple's Power PC Macintosh 710 (See Figure 5-10.) This machine can scroll through documents the length of *War and Peace* up to four times faster than Apple's previously most powerful machine, the Quadra 800. Intel's Pentium Pro chip is twice as powerful as its predecessor, the Pentium chip.

There are two types of microprocessors.

■ **CISC Chips:** The most common type of microprocessor is CISC ("complex instruction set computer"). This design was popularized by Intel and is the basis for their line of microprocessors. It is the most widely used chip design and has thousands of programs written specifically for it. Intel's Pentium is a recent CISC chip.

MICROPROCESSORS

MICROPROCESSOR		TYPICAL APPLICATIONS	USERS
Intel	80486	DOS, Windows, basic tools, personal information management	Single user, office staff, home user, home office user
	Pentium	Windows 95, OS/2 Warp, groupware, desktop publishing, project management	All of the above, networked users, workgroups
	Pentium Pro	Windows NT, Unix, multimedia, artificial intelligence, network communications, large database applications	All of the above, specialists
Motorola	68040	Macintosh operating system, basic tools, personal information management, desktop publishing	Single user, home user, home office user
	PowerPC	Unix, groupware, project management, artificial intelligence, network communications, large database applications	All of the above, networked users, workgroups, specialists

FIGURE 5-8
Typical microprocessor applications and users.

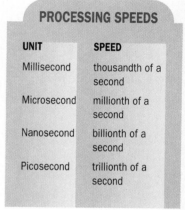

PROCESSING SPEEDS

UNIT	SPEED
Millisecond	thousandth of a second
Microsecond	millionth of a second
Nanosecond	billionth of a second
Picosecond	trillionth of a second

FIGURE 5-9
Processing speeds.

FIGURE 5-10
The Power Macintosh 710, which uses a Power PC microprocessor.

■ **RISC Chips:** RISC ("reduced instruction set computer") chips use fewer instructions. The design is becoming more widely used. This design is simpler, faster, and less costly than CISC chips. A recent Motorola chip developed with IBM and Apple is the Power PC chip. Two other recent RISC chips are Digital Equipment Corporation's (DEC) Alpha chip and MIPS' R4400 chip. These chips are used in many of today's most powerful microcomputers. (See Figure 5-11.)

The major advantage of the CISC chip is that it can run a large number of existing application programs. However, this advantage is offset somewhat by special programs called emulation programs. Emulation programs allow RISC chips to run CISC application programs. Unfortunately, the RISC advantage in speed is lost when the emulation programs are used. Another approach taken by two competitors to Intel's Pentium chip is to produce "RISC-like" chips. These chips are based on the CISC design but incorporate some of the techniques used in RISC chips. They can run applications designed for CISC chips with speeds comparable to RISC chips. Two such chips are AMD's K5 and Cyrix's M1 chips.

Some specialized processor chips are available. One example is the tiny built-in microprocessor used in **smart cards.** Smart cards are about the size of a credit card. They can be used to hold health insurance information, frequent flier records, or driver license information, to name a few. While this technology has been around for some time, it has received more attention lately. President Clinton has suggested a National Health Security smart card for all individuals. This card would be used for a number of applications, including monitoring federal financial assistance programs.

FIGURE 5-11
This IBM RISC System/6000 is one of several IBM workstations using the fast RISC chip.

Memory Chips

There are two well-known types of memory chips. One type is called *RAM*. The other type is *ROM*. **RAM (random-access memory)** chips hold the program and data that the CPU is presently processing. That is, it is *temporary* or volatile storage. (Secondary storage, which we shall describe in Chapter 7, is *permanent* storage, such as the data stored on diskettes. Data from this kind of storage must be loaded into RAM before it can be used.)

RAM is called temporary because as soon as the microcomputer is turned off, everything in RAM is lost. It is also lost if there is a power failure that disrupts the electric current going to the microcomputer. For this reason, as we mentioned earlier, it is a good idea to save your work in progress. That is, if you are working on a document or a spreadsheet, every few minutes you should save, or store, the material.

In addition, when programs or data are written, or encoded, to RAM, the previous contents of RAM are lost. This is called the *destructive write process*. However, when programs and data are read, or retrieved, from RAM, their contents are not destroyed. Rather, the read process simply makes a copy of those contents. Consequently, this activity is called the *nondestructive read process*.

RAM storage is frequently expressed in megabytes. Thus, a microcomputer with 16MB RAM has memory that will hold about 16 million characters of data and programs.

Knowing the amount of RAM is important! Some software programs may require more memory capacity than a particular microcomputer offers. For instance, Excel for Windows 95 requires 6MB of RAM. Additional RAM is needed to hold any data. However, many microcomputers—particularly older ones—may not have enough memory to hold the program, much less work with it.

Microcomputer memory in RAM is of four types. (See Figure 5-12.) These types are mentioned in the instruction manuals you use to install system software like DOS or application software like Excel.

- **Conventional memory: Conventional memory** consists of the first 640K of RAM. It is the area used by DOS and application programs.

- **Upper memory: Upper memory** is located between 640K and 1MB of RAM. DOS uses this area to store information about the microcomputer's hardware. However, it is frequently underused and can be used by application programs.

- **Extended memory: Extended memory** is available on most microprocessors. It includes directly accessible memory above 1MB. Some programs can use extended memory (for example, Windows), and some cannot.

- **Expanded memory: Expanded memory** is intended to help older microprocessors that cannot directly access memory over 1MB. Expanded memory is a special "island" of memory of up to 32MB that exists outside of the DOS 640K limit. That is, it temporarily uses a portion of the reserved memory area between 640K and 1MB and switches it with information from the island.

FIGURE 5-12

Types of RAM: conventional, upper, extended, expanded.

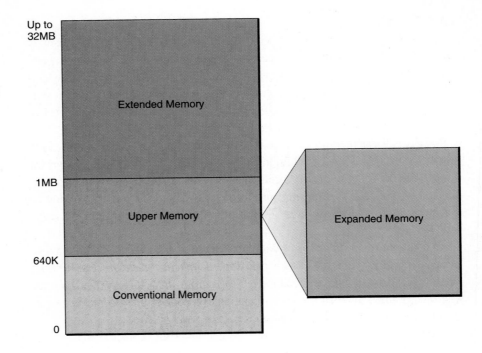

Another term you are apt to hear about in conjunction with RAM is **cache memory.** Cache (pronounced "cash") memory is an area of RAM set aside to store the most frequently accessed information stored in RAM. The cache acts as a temporary high-speed holding area between the memory and the CPU. In a computer with a cache (not all machines have one), the computer detects which information in RAM is most frequently used. It then copies that information into the cache, so that the CPU can access that information more quickly than usual.

ROM (read only memory) chips have programs built into them at the factory. Unlike RAM chips, the contents of ROM chips cannot be changed by the user. "Read only" means that the CPU can read, or retrieve, the programs written on the ROM chip. However, the computer cannot write—encode or change—the information or instructions in ROM.

ROM chips typically contain special instructions for detailed computer operations. For example, ROM instructions may start the computer, give keyboard keys their special control capabilities, and put characters on the screen. ROMs are also called **firmware.**

Two important variations on the ROM chip are the following:

■ **PROM (programmable read-only memory).** This means that a software manufacturer can write instructions onto the chip using special equipment. However, once it is written, it cannot be changed.

■ **EPROM (erasable programmable read-only memory).** This is a PROM chip that can be erased with a special ultraviolet light. New instructions can then be written on it. (There are also some electrically erasable chips—EEPROM.)

System Clock

The **system clock** controls the speed of operations within a computer. This speed is expressed in **megahertz** (abbreviated **MHz**). One megahertz equals 1 million cycles (beats) per second. The faster the clock speed, the faster the computer can process information. In computer ads, you may see that microcomputers built with Intel's Pentium chip typically have a 90 MHz or 100 MHz speed.

Expansion Slots and Boards

Computers are known for having different kinds of "architectures." Machines that have **closed architecture** are manufactured in such a way that users cannot easily add new devices. Most microcomputers have **open architecture.** They allow users to expand their systems by inserting optional devices known as **expansion boards.** Expansion boards are also called **plug-in boards, controller cards, adapter cards,** or **interface cards.**

The expansion boards plug into slots inside the system unit. Ports on the boards allow cables to be connected from the expansion boards to devices outside the system unit. Among the kinds of expansion boards available are the following:

- **Memory expansion boards:** These circuit boards consist of several additional RAM chips, which increase the capacity of the computer's memory. Early microcomputer users found that additional memory was their first requirement for handling newer, more sophisticated programs, such as integrated software. Memory can be added by using plug-in boards, which gives you expanded memory. Memory can also be added by inserting RAM chips directly onto the system board, which gives you extended memory. (See Figure 5-13.)

- **Network adapter cards:** These cards are used to connect a computer to one or more other computers. This forms a communication network whereby users can share data, programs, and hardware. The network adapter card plugs into a slot inside the system unit. The network adapter card typically connects the system unit to a cable that connects to the other devices on the network.

FIGURE 5-13
A microcomputer expansion board.

FIGURE 5-14
A PCMCIA card.

◼ ◼ ◼ ◼ ◼ ◼ ◼ ◼

◾ **Small computer system interface (SCSI—pronounced "scuzzy") card:** Most computers have only a limited number of expansion slots. A **SCSI card** uses only one slot and can connect as many as seven devices to the system unit. These cards are used to connect such devices as printers, hard disk drives, and CD-ROM drives to the system unit.

◾ **PC cards:** To meet the size and constraints of portable computers, credit card–sized expansion boards have been developed. These cards can be easily inserted and replaced from the outside of a portable computer. They are called **PC cards** or **PCMCIA (Personal Computer Memory Card International Association) cards.** (See Figure 5-14.) These cards can be used for a variety of purposes, including increasing memory and connecting to other computers.

A wide variety of other expansion boards exist. Some of the most widely used are the following. Video adapter cards are used to adapt a variety of color video display monitors to a computer. CD-ROM cards connect optical disc drives (which we discuss in Chapter 7), and sound boards can record and play back digital sound.

To access the capabilities of an expansion board, the board must be inserted into a slot in the system unit and the system reconfigured to recognize the new board. This reconfiguration can require setting special switches on the expansion board and creating special configuration files. This can be a complex and difficult task. A recent development known as **Plug and Play** promises to eliminate this task.

Plug and Play is a set of hardware and software standards recently developed by Intel, Microsoft, and others. It is an effort by hardware and software vendors to create operating systems, processing units, and expansion boards, as well as other devices, that are able to configure themselves. Ideally, to install a new expansion board all you have to do is insert the board and turn on the computer. As the computer starts up, it will search for these Plug and Play devices and automatically configure the devices and the computer system.

Plug and Play is an evolving capability. Only a few completely Plug and Play–ready systems exist today. However, observers predict that within the next few years this will become a widely adopted standard, and adding expansion boards will be a simple task.

Bus Lines

A **bus line**—or simply **bus**—connects the parts of the CPU to each other. It also links the CPU with other important hardware. Examples are RAM and ROM chips and ports connecting with outside devices. A bus is a data roadway along which bits travel. Such data pathways resemble a multilane highway. The more lanes there are, the faster traffic can go through. Similarly, the greater the capacity of a bus, the more powerful and faster the operation. A 64-bit bus has greater capacity than a 32-bit bus, for example.

Why should you even have to care about what a bus line is? The answer is that, as microprocessor chips have changed, so have bus lines. Many devices, such as expansion boards, will only work with one type of bus line.

The four principal bus lines (or "architectures") are the following:

- **Industry Standard Architecture (ISA):** This bus was developed for the IBM Personal Computer. First it was an 8-bit-wide data path, then (when the IBM AT was introduced) it was 16 bits wide. The older microprocessors and add-on expansion boards were able to satisfactorily move data along this 16-bit roadway. But then along came the 386 chip—which requires data paths that are 32 bits wide. And suddenly there was a competition between two 32-bit standards.

- **Micro Channel Architecture (MCA):** IBM decided to support the 386 chip with a 32-bit bus line that was entirely new. You cannot simply remove your expansion boards from an older computer and put them into a new IBM computer with Micro Channel. It simply won't work. If you are not concerned about transferring boards, IBM's new standard is not a problem. You can take full advantage of the faster processor. Recently, a 64-bit MCA bus was introduced.

- **Extended Industry Standard Architecture (EISA):** This 32-bit bus standard was proposed in September 1988 by nine manufacturers of IBM-compatibles, led by Compaq Computer Corporation. The purpose of EISA is to extend and amend the old ISA standard, so that all existing expansion boards can work with the new architecture. Like MCA, EISA has introduced a 64-bit bus.

- **Peripheral Component Interconnect (PCI):** The most recently developed category of buses is called **local buses.** These buses were originally developed to meet the tremendous video demands of today's graphical user interfaces. PCI is the most widely used local bus. (**VESA local bus [VL-bus]** is another widely used local bus.) PCI is a high-speed 64-bit bus that is nearly ten times faster than either MCA or EISA buses. Now, PCI buses are widely used to connect the CPU, memory, and expansion boards. Many observers predict that PCI will replace MCA and EISA buses in the future.

Ports

A **port** is a connecting socket on the outside of the system unit. This allows you to plug in a variety of devices, such as keyboards, mouse devices, video displays, modems, and printers. Ports may be parallel or serial. (See Figure 5-15.)

- Parallel ports are used to connect external devices that need to send or receive a lot of data over a short distance. These ports typically send eight bits of data simultaneously across eight parallel wires. Parallel ports are mostly used to connect printers to the system unit.

- Serial ports are used for a wide variety of purposes. They are used to connect a mouse, keyboard, modem, and many other devices to the system unit. Serial ports send data one bit at a time and are very good for sending information over a long distance.

Ports are used to connect input and output devices to the system unit. We usually refer to all hardware outside the system unit—but not necessarily outside the system *cabinet*—as **peripheral devices.** In many microcomputers, disk drives are built into the system cabinet. In some laptop computers, the keyboard and monitor are also an integral part of the system cabinet.

For a summary of system unit components, see Figure 5-16.

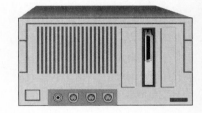

FIGURE 5-15
The ports in the back of a microcomputer.

SYSTEM UNIT

COMPONENT	FUNCTION
System board	Holds the various other system components
Microprocessor	Contains the CPU on a single chip
Memory	Holds programs and instructions
System clock	Controls the speed of computer operations
Expansion slots and boards	Increases memory and other system capabilities
Bus lines	Connects various internal system components
Ports	Connects outside devices to system unit

FIGURE 5-16
Components of the system unit.

A Look at the Future

Four new technologies could make computing faster: RISC, superconducting, optical computing, and neural networking. The result will be "downsizing applications."

We have already mentioned RISC (reduced instruction set computer) microprocessors. Some observers think the RISC chip will triple performance every one and a half to two years. Memory chips are also increasing in capacity. A new technology developed by Rambus Inc. promises RAM chips with ten times the speed of today's chips.

Another technological improvement may come in the form of the materials used for microprocessors. At the present time, microprocessor chips are made out of silicon. Such chips are called *semiconductors* because electricity flows through the material with some resistance. *Superconducting* material, in contrast, conducts electricity without resistance. Until recently, superconduction was considered impractical because the materials had to be continuously cooled to extremely low, subzero temperatures. However, research is now being done on "warm" superconductors. These offer the promise of faster on-and-off processing to give us lightning-quick computers.

A third area being explored is that known as *optical computing*. This technology features a machine consisting of lasers, lenses, and mirrors. An optical computing machine uses pulses of light rather than currents of electricity to represent the on-and-off codes of data. Light is much faster than electricity.

A fourth area, *neural networks,* is not a different kind of technology so much as a new arrangement using existing technology. Present computers—even supercomputers—are relatively slow because of a built-in structural limitation: The processor and the memory are physically separated. Although joined by a communications link, the processor spends a long time waiting for data coming from or going to memory. (The arrangement is known as the *von Neumann architecture,* after its originator, John von Neumann.) A neural network, however, consists of layers of processors interconnected somewhat like the neurons of biological nervous systems. One such computer developed by TRW has 250,000 processors and 5.5 million connections. As a result, data is transmitted to and from a processor at many times the speed of the old arrangements.

With these kinds of developments, it's clear that we are on the road to "downsizing applications." That is, computers will get not only smaller, as we are seeing with the newer portables, but also more powerful. Indeed, it's easy to believe—as some industry observers suggest—that by the year 2000 desktop computers will be as powerful as the first supercomputer.

KEY TERMS

adapter card (105)

address (94)

arithmetic-logic unit (ALU) (93)

ASCII (97)

binary system (96)

bit (96)

bus line, bus (106)

byte (96)

cache memory (104)

chip (99)

CISC chip (100)

closed architecture (105)

control unit (93)

controller card (105)

conventional memory (103)

EBCDIC (97)

EPROM (erasable programmable read-only memory) (104)

expanded memory (103)

expansion board (105)

Extended Industry Standard Architecture (EISA) (107)

extended memory (103)

firmware (104)

gigabyte, GB, G-byte (97)

Industry Standard Architecture (ISA) (107)

integrated circuit (99)

interface card (105)

internal storage (94)

kilobyte, K, KB, K-byte (96)

local bus (107)

main memory (94)

megabyte, MB, M-byte (97)

megahertz, MHz (105)

memory (94)

Micro Channel Architecture (MCA) (107)

microprocessor chip (92)

microseconds (100)

motherboard (99)

open architecture (105)

parity bit (98)

PC card (106)

PCMCIA (Personal Computer Memory Card International Association) card (106)

Peripheral Component Interconnect (PCI) (107)

peripheral device (107)

Plug and Play (106)

plug-in board (105)

port (107)

primary storage (94)

processor (92)

PROM (programmable read-only memory) (104)

RAM (random-access memory) (94, 103)

register (94)

RISC chip (102)

ROM (read-only memory) (104)

SCSI card (106)

semiconductor (99)

silicon chip (99)

smart card (102)

system board (99)

system clock (105)

terabyte, TB, T-byte (97)

Unicode (97)

upper memory (103)

VESA local bus (VL-bus) (107)

word (100)

REVIEW QUESTIONS

True/False

1. In a microcomputer, the CPU is located on a single chip called the microprocessor.
2. A grouping of eight bytes is called a bit.
3. Another name for the system board is the processor board.
4. CISC chips use fewer instructions than RISC chips.
5. A SCSI card can be used to connect several different devices to the system unit.

Multiple Choice

1. The ALU performs arithmetic operations and:
   a. stores data
   b. logical operations
   c. binary calculations
   d. reduced instruction calculations
   e. parity checks
2. The binary code that is widely used with microcomputers is:
   a. ASCII
   b. EBCDIC
   c. BCD
   d. DEC/MVS
   e. Unicode
3. The number of bits that can be processed at one time is a:
   a. register
   b. cycle
   c. byte
   d. word
   e. PROM
4. Two types of memory chips are RAM and:
   a. RISC
   b. main
   c. MCA
   d. CDROM
   e. ROM
5. The local bus that is predicted to replace the other types in the future is called:
   a. EISA
   b. ISA
   c. PCI
   d. MCA
   e. PCMCIA

Fill in the Blank

1. Data and instructions are stored in memory at locations known as _____.
2. A _____ bit is an extra bit that is added to a byte to help detect errors.
3. _____ memory is directly accessible above 1MB.
4. The system clock controls the _____ of operations within a computer.
5. _____ and _____ is a set of standards designed to assist in the reconfiguration of computer systems.

DISCUSSION QUESTIONS AND PROJECTS

1. *An inexpensive microcomputer system:* The prices of microcomputer systems have been decreasing for some time. You can buy them from computer stores, mail-order companies, and oftentimes from your college bookstore. Look through your local newspaper or through a computer magazine to locate three low-priced systems. Read each advertisement, make a list of all the computer terms used, and write down their definitions. Prepare a table comparing the three systems. Some factors to include in your table are: price, memory capacity, storage capacity, processor type, display type, expansion capability, and software included. If you were to purchase one of these systems, which one would you select, and why?

2. *The mobile office:* The mobile office does not have a fixed location, but like the traditional office has support facilities such as computers, printers, and fax and copy machines. The central piece of equipment is the notebook computer. Many jobs require being on the road away from home one week every month. For those road warriors, the mobile office is essential.

   Many hotels now offer specially equipped hotel rooms and business centers. For example, many Hyatt Hotels have the Hyatt Business Plan that provides guest rooms with microcomputers, modems, and fax machines. Additionally, a 24-hour business center provides printer, photocopy, and office-supply support.

   Suppose you have a job that requires a mobile office. Before making any hotel reservations, you should ensure that essential support facilities are available. Contact a major hotel chain to determine their support for mobile computing. Specifically, find out the following:

   a. Are in-room microcomputers and fax machines available? What are the charges?

   b. Is there a business center on site? What support is provided? What are the hours? What are the charges?

   c. If a business center is not available, will the front desk provide basic services such as faxing, copying, and printing? What are the charges?

3. *http://www.intel.com* The two largest manufacturers of microprocessor chips are Intel and Motorola. To learn more about recent microprocessor developments, connect to Intel's home page using the Internet address given at the beginning of this question. Then locate Motorola's home page to learn more about their microprocessors. (Hint: Use the Every Student's Internet Resource Guide: Computer Science and Computer Technology—Entry Number: 02.)

Input and Output

How do you get data to the CPU? How do you get information out? Here we describe the two most important places where the computer interfaces with people. The first half of the chapter covers input devices; the second half covers output devices.

People understand language, which is constructed of letters, numbers, and punctuation marks. However, computers can understand only the binary machine language of 0s and 1s. Input and output devices are essentially translators. Input devices translate symbols that people understand into symbols that computers can process. Output devices do the reverse: They translate machine output to output people can comprehend. Let us, then, look at the devices that perform these translations.

COMPETENCIES

After you have read this chapter, you should be able to:

1. Explain the difference between keyboard and direct-entry input devices and the POS terminal.

2. Describe the features of keyboards and the three types of terminals. These are dumb, smart, and intelligent terminals.

3. Describe direct-entry devices used with microcomputers. These include the mouse, touch screen, light pen, digitizer, pen-based computer, image scanner, fax, bar-code reader, MICR, OCR, OMR, and voice-input devices.

4. Describe monitors (desktop and portable) and monitor standards (CGA, EGA, VGA, Super VGA, and XGA).

5. Describe printers (dot-matrix, laser, ink-jet, thermal) and plotters (pen, ink-jet, electrostatic, and direct image).

6. Describe voice-output devices.

Input: Keyboard Versus Direct Entry

Input devices convert people-readable data into machine-readable form. Input may be keyboard or direct entry.

Input devices take data and programs people can read or understand and convert them to a form the computer can process. This is the machine-readable electronic signals of 0s and 1s that we described in the last chapter. Input devices are of two kinds: keyboard entry and direct entry.

- **Keyboard entry:** Data is input to the computer through a *keyboard* that looks like a typewriter keyboard but has additional keys. In this method, the user typically reads from an original document called the **source document.** The user enters that document by typing on the keyboard.

- **Direct entry:** Data is made into machine-readable form as it is entered into the computer; no keyboard is used.

FIGURE 6-1
A point-of-sale terminal.

An example of an input device that uses both is a **point-of-sale (POS) terminal.** This is the sort of "electronic cash register" you see in department stores. (See Figure 6-1.) When clerks sell a sweater, for example, they can record the sale by typing in the information (product code, purchase amount, tax) on the keyboard. Or they can use a hand-held **wand reader** or **platform scanner** to read special characters on price tags as direct entry. The wand reflects light on the characters. The reflection is then changed by photoelectric cells to machine-readable code. Whether by keyboard entry or direct entry, the results will appear on the POS terminal's digital display. (See Figure 6-1.)

Keyboard Entry

In keyboard entry, people type input. The input usually appears on a monitor.

Probably the most common way in which you will input data, at least at the beginning, is through a keyboard.

Keyboards

Keyboards have different kinds of keys. (See Figure 6-2.)

- **Typewriter keys:** The keys that resemble the regular letters, numbers, and punctuation marks on a typewriter keyboard are called **typewriter keys.** Note the position of the **Enter** key, which is used to enter commands into the computer.
- **Function keys:** The keys labeled *F1, F2,* and so on are the **function keys.** These keys are used for tasks that occur frequently (such as underlining in word processing). They save you keystrokes.

FIGURE 6-2
Traditional keyboard.

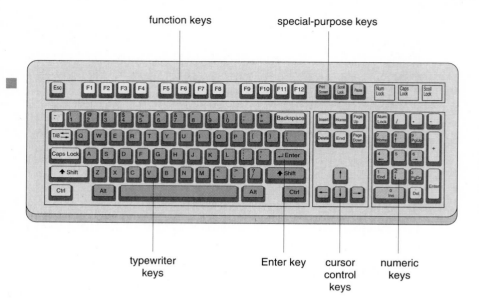

Numeric keys: The keys 0 to 9, called the **numeric keys** or **numeric keypad,** are used for tasks principally involving numbers. These may be useful when you are working with spreadsheets.

Special-purpose and cursor control keys: Examples of **special-purpose keys** are *Esc* (for "Escape"), *Ctrl* (for "Control"), *Del* (for "Delete"), and *Ins* (for "Insert"). These keys are used to help enter and edit data and execute commands. The **cursor control keys** or **directional arrow keys** are used to move the cursor.

As we mentioned in Chapter 5, these keys convert letters, numbers, and other characters into electrical signals that are machine readable. These signals are sent to the computer's CPU.

There are two basic keyboard designs. The traditional design or straight design is shown in Figure 6-2. The contour design splits and slopes the keyboard. (See Figure 6-3.) Many people prefer the contour design because it is more natural and comfortable.

FIGURE 6-3
Microsoft's Natural Keyboard.

Terminals

A **terminal** is a form of input (and output) device that consists of a keyboard, a monitor, and a communications link. There are three types of terminals:

A **dumb terminal** can be used to input and receive data, but it cannot process data independently. It is used only to gain access to information from a computer. Such a terminal may be used by an airline reservations clerk to access a mainframe computer for flight information.

A **smart terminal** has some memory. It allows users to perform some editing or verification of data before it is sent to a large computer. A bank loan officer might do some calculations associated with making a loan on the smart terminal. The loan officer would do this before the information is stored in the bank's mainframe.

- An **intelligent terminal** includes a processing unit, memory, and secondary storage such as a magnetic disk. Essentially, an intelligent terminal is a microcomputer with some communications software and a telephone hookup (modem) or other communications link. These connect the terminal to the larger computer.

Nearly all large organizations have terminals connected to their minicomputers and mainframe computers. At one time, all terminals were dedicated input devices. Now, microcomputers with the appropriate software and communications links can operate exactly like any of the dedicated terminals. With microcomputers dropping in price and increasing in power and flexibility, companies have tended to buy these instead of dedicated terminals.

Direct Entry

Direct entry creates machine-readable data that can go directly to the CPU. Direct entry includes pointing, scanning, and voice-input devices.

Direct entry is a form of input that does not require data to be keyed by someone sitting at a keyboard. Direct-entry devices create machine-readable data on paper or magnetic media, or feed it directly into the computer's CPU. This reduces the possibility of human error being introduced (as often happens when data is being entered through a keyboard). It is also an economical means of data entry. Direct-entry devices may be categorized into three areas: pointing devices, scanning devices, and voice-input devices.

Pointing Devices

Pointing, of course, is one of the most natural of all human gestures. There are a number of devices that use this method as a form of direct-entry input, as follows.

- **Mouse:** There are three basic **mouse** types. For one type the mouse has a ball on the bottom and is attached with a cord to the system unit. (See Figure 6-4.) When rolled on the tabletop, the mouse controls the cursor or pointer. The second type does not require a flat surface. The cursor is controlled by rotating a

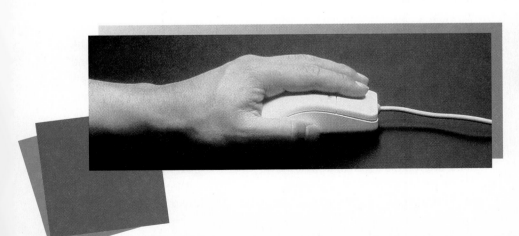

FIGURE 6-4
Microsoft mouse.

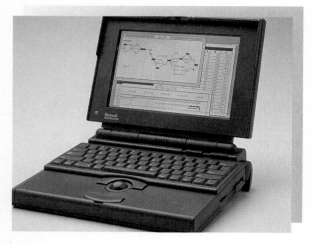

FIGURE 6-5 Trackball: Macintosh Notebook.

FIGURE 6-6 Touch–surface: Epson ActionNote 880.

FIGURE 6-7

A touch screen: An industrial application.

FIGURE 6-8

A light pen: A hospital application.

ball with your thumb. This type of mouse is often called a trackball or roller-ball. (See Figure 6-5.) The newest type is a touch-surface. The cursor is controlled by moving and tapping your finger on the surface of a pad. (See Figure 6-6.) The trackball and touch-surface are common on portable computers and are often built into keyboards.

At one time, the mouse was identified only with Apple microcomputers. However, it is now standard for almost all microcomputers. Many people like the mouse because it reduces the need to input commands through a keyboard.

■ **Touch screen:** A **touch screen** is a particular kind of monitor screen covered with a plastic layer. (See Figure 6-7.) Behind this layer are crisscrossed invisible beams of infrared light. This arrangement enables someone to select actions or commands by touching the screen with a finger. Touch screens are easy to use, especially when people need information quickly. You may see touch screens at bank automatic teller machines (ATMs) and at visitor information centers in airports and hotels. However, they also have military and industrial applications. More recently, they are being used with microcomputers in applications that formerly used a mouse.

■ **Light pen:** A **light pen** is a light-sensitive penlike device. (See Figure 6-8.) The light pen is placed against the monitor. This closes a photoelectric circuit and identifies the spot for entering or modifying data. Light pens are used by engineers, for example, in designing anything from microprocessor chips to airplane parts.

■ **Digitizer:** A **digitizer** is a device that can be used to trace or copy a drawing or photograph. The shape is converted to digital data. A computer can then represent the data on the screen or print it out on paper. A **digitizing tablet** enables you to create your own images using a special stylus. (See Figure 6-9.) The images are then converted to digital data that can be processed by the computer. Digitizers are often used by designers and architects.

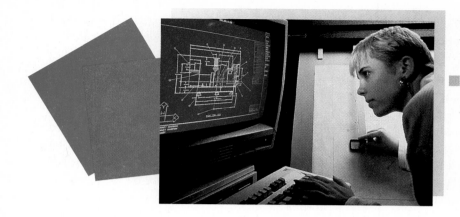

FIGURE 6-9
A digitizer: An industrial design application.

- **Pen-based computing:** A **pen-based computer** is a small (for example, 3.9 pounds) computer. It lets you write directly on the display screen with a stylus. (See Figure 6-10.) The system is less a triumph of hardware than of software. What is revolutionary is that these devices contain software that can recognize a person's handwriting. The handwriting can be stored as it was scrawled—not too difficult a task. More difficult is the task of converting a person's distinctive cursive writing—is that a "c" or an "e" or an "o"?—into typescript. Some pen-based computers do this.

Scanning Devices

Direct-entry scanning devices record images of text, drawings, or special symbols. The images are converted to digital data that can be processed by a computer or displayed on a monitor. Scanning devices include the following:

- **Image scanner:** An **image scanner** identifies images on a page. (See Figure 6-11.) It automatically converts them to electronic signals that can be stored in a computer. The process identifies pictures or different typefaces by scanning

FIGURE 6-10
A pen-based computer: Recording inventory.

FIGURE 6-11
An image scanner: Reproducing color images.

FIGURE 6-12
A fax machine: Sending documents electronically.

FIGURE 6-13
A bar-code reader: Recording product codes.

each image with light and breaking it into dots. The dots are then converted into digital code for storage. Image scanners are becoming widely used input devices. They are commonly used in desktop publishing to scan graphic images that can then be placed in a page of text.

- **Fax machines: Facsimile transmission machines,** commonly called **fax machines,** have become popular office machines because they can transfer documents at electronic speeds. (See Figure 6-12.) Fax machines scan the image of a document to be sent. The light and dark areas of the image are converted into a format that can be sent electronically over telephone lines. The receiving fax machine converts the signals back to an image and recreates it on paper. The machine uses a process much like those used by office photocopiers. Fax machines are useful to anyone who needs to send images rather than text. Examples are engineering drawings, legal documents with signatures, and sales promotional materials.

  Many people use **dedicated fax machines.** These are specialized devices that do nothing else except send and receive documents from one place to another. Indeed, these are found not only in offices and print shops but even alongside phone booths in hotel lobbies and airports.

  Many people use their microcomputers to send and receive fax. One way is to install a **fax board** into their system unit. Most users, however, install a **fax/modem board** that provides the independent capabilities of a fax and a modem.

- **Bar-code readers:** You are probably familiar with **bar-code readers** from grocery stores. (See Figure 6-13.) Bar-code readers are photoelectric scanners that read the **bar codes,** or vertical zebra-striped marks, printed on product containers. Supermarkets use a bar-code system called the Universal Product Code (UPC). The bar code identifies the product to the supermarket's computer, which has a description and the latest price for the product. The computer automatically tells the POS terminal what the price is. And it prints the price and the product name on the customer's receipt.

- **Character and mark recognition devices:** There are three kinds of scanning devices—formerly used only with mainframes—now found in connection with the more powerful microcomputers.

  Magnetic-ink character recognition (MICR) is a direct-entry method used in banks. This technology is used to automatically read those futuristic-looking numbers on the bottom of checks. A special-purpose machine known as a **reader/sorter** reads characters made of ink containing magnetized particles.

  Optical-character recognition (OCR) uses special preprinted characters, such as those printed on utility and telephone bills. They can be read by a light source and changed into machine-readable code. A common OCR device is the hand-held *wand reader.* (See Figure 6-14.) These are used in department stores to read retail price tags by reflecting light on the printed characters.

Optical-mark recognition (OMR) is also called **mark sensing.** An OMR device senses the presence or absence of a mark, such as a pencil mark. OMR is often used to score multiple-choice tests such as the College Board's Scholastic Aptitude Test and the Graduate Record Examination.

Voice-Input Devices

Voice-input devices convert a person's speech into a digital code. (See Figure 6-15.) These input devices, when combined with the appropriate software, form **voice recognition systems.** These systems enable users to operate microcomputers and to create documents using voice commands.

Some of these systems must be "trained" to the particular user's voice. This is done by matching his or her spoken words to patterns previously stored in the computer. More advanced systems that can recognize the same word spoken by many different people have been developed. However, until recently the list of words has been limited. One voice recognition system, the Dragon Dictate, identifies over 30,000 words and adapts to individual voices. There are even systems that will translate from one language to another, such as from English to Japanese.

There are two types of voice recognition systems:

- **Continuous speech: Continuous speech recognition systems** are used to control a microcomputer's operations and to issue commands to special application programs. For example, rather than using the keyboard to save a spreadsheet file, the user could simply say "save the file." Two popular systems are Apple Computer's PlainTalk and IBM's Continuous Speech Series.

- **Discrete-word:** A common activity in business is preparing memos and other written documents. **Discrete-word recognition systems** allow users to dictate directly into a microcomputer using a microphone. The microcomputer stores the memo in a word processing file where it can be revised later or directly printed out. Two such systems are available from Kurzweil Applied Intelligence Inc. and IBM's Voice Type Dictation.

FIGURE 6-14
A wand reader: Recording product codes.

FIGURE 6-15
A voice-input device:
Dictating a letter.

Output: Monitors, Printers, Plotters, Voice

Output devices convert machine-readable information into people-readable form.

Data input to and then processed by the computer remains in machine-readable form until output devices make it people-readable. The output devices we shall describe for microcomputers are monitors, printers, plotters, and voice-output.

Monitors

Monitor standards indicate screen quality. Some monitors are used on the desktop, others are portable.

The most frequently used output device is the monitor, also known as the **display screen, video display, video display terminal,** and **VDT.** Two important characteristics of monitors are the number of colors that can be displayed and the clarity of images produced. Images are represented on monitors by individual dots or "picture elements" called **pixels.** A pixel is the smallest unit on the screen that can be turned on and off or made different shades. The *density* of the dots—that is, the number of rows and columns of dots—determines the images' clarity, the resolution.

Standards

To indicate a monitor's color and resolution capabilities, several standards have been created. The three most common are VGA, Super VGA and XGA. (See Figure 6-16.)

■ **VGA** stands for *V*ideo *G*raphics *A*rray. You can display 16 colors at a resolution of 640 by 480. Or, you can display 16 times as many colors—256 colors—with a resolution of 320 by 200. VGA has been a widely used monitor standard for general use.

FIGURE 6-16
Monitor standards.

STANDARD	PIXELS	COLORS
CGA	320 × 200	4
EGA	640 × 350	16
VGA	640 × 480	16
	320 × 200	256
Super VGA	800 × 600	256
	1024 × 768	256
XGA	1024 × 768	65,536

MONITORS

- **Super VGA** or **SVGA** stands for *Super Video Graphics Array*. SVGA has a higher resolution capability. It has a minimum of 800 by 600 resolution. Some higher-priced models have a 1600 by 1200 resolution. It is the most common standard today. SVGA is widely used in many applications, including industrial design, which requires precise measurements taken directly from the screen.

- **XGA** stands for *Extended Graphic Array* and has a resolution of up to 1024 by 768 pixels. It can display more than 18 million colors. XGA may become the next widely accepted standard. It is used primarily by experts in engineering design and in graphic arts.

Desktop Monitors

The most common type of monitor for the office and the home is the **desktop monitor.** (See Figure 6-17.) These monitors are typically placed directly on the system unit or on the top of the desk. Also called **cathode-ray tubes** or **CRTs,** these monitors are similar to the size and technology of televisions.

An important characteristic of desktop monitors is how the cathode-ray tube creates images on the screen. **Interlaced monitors** create images by scanning down the screen, skipping every other line. This technology can cause flickering and may lead to eye strain. **Noninterlaced monitors** avoid these problems by scanning each line.

Portable Monitors

Because CRTs are too bulky to be transported, portable monitors were developed. (See Figure 6-18.) This type of monitor is also known as a **flat-panel monitor** or **liquid crystal display (LCD).** Unlike the technology used in CRTs, portable monitors use liquid crystals.

FIGURE 6-17 A desktop monitor: SVGA display.

FIGURE 6-18 A portable monitor: Active matrix panel.

There are two basic types of portable monitors: *passive-matrix* and *active-matrix*. **Passive-matrix monitors** create images by scanning the entire screen. This type requires very little power, but the clarity of the images is not as sharp. **Active-matrix monitors** do not scan down the screen; instead, each pixel is independently activated. More colors with better clarity can be displayed. Active-matrix monitors are more expensive and require more power.

An exciting new development is the merger of microcomputers and television called **PC/TV.** This is becoming possible through the establishment of all-digital **high-definition television (HDTV).** HDTV delivers a much clearer and more detailed wide-screen picture. Additionally, because the output is digital, it enables users to readily freeze video sequences to create still images. These images can then be digitized and output as artwork or stored on laser disks. This technology will likely be very useful to graphic artists, publishers, and educators.

Cable operators like Time Warner Cable have recently introduced **ITV,** also known as **interactive TV,** to select markets. ITV provides viewers with videos on demand, video games, interactive shopping, and a dazzling array of entertainment and informational services. ITV uses normal telephone lines to transmit information, a terminal or microcomputer connected to the television to interpret information, and a supercomputer at a centralized site to coordinate the entire system. ITV promises to revolutionize the TV world.

Printers

Four kinds of printers used with microcomputer systems are dot-matrix, ink-jet, laser, and thermal.

The images output on a monitor are often referred to as **soft copy.** Information output on paper—whether by a printer or by a plotter—is called **hard copy.** Four popular kinds of printers used with microcomputers are dot-matrix, ink-jet, laser, and thermal. (See Figure 6-19.)

FIGURE 6-19
Microcomputer printers in 1996.

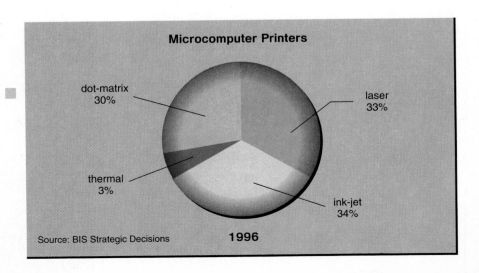

Microcomputer Printers

dot-matrix
30%

laser
33%

thermal
3%

ink-jet
34%

Source: BIS Strategic Decisions   **1996**

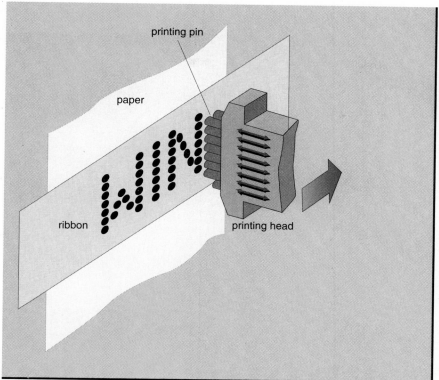

FIGURE 6-20
A dot-matrix printer: Epson ActionPrinter 5000+.

Dot-Matrix Printer

Dot-matrix printers can produce a page of text in less than 10 seconds and are highly reliable. These inexpensive printers were once the most widely used microcomputer printers. In general, they are used for tasks where a high-quality image is not essential. Thus, they are often used for documents that are circulated within an organization rather than shown to clients and the public. However, some dot-matrix printers print color and *are* used for advertising and promotional purposes.

The dot-matrix printer forms characters or images using a series of small pins on a print head. (See Figure 6-20.) The pins strike an inked ribbon and create dots that form an image on paper. Printers are available with print heads of 9, 18, or 24 pins. The pins print a character in a manner resembling the way individual lights spell out a number on a basketball scoreboard. One disadvantage of this type of printer is noise.

Ink-Jet Printer

An **ink-jet printer** sprays small droplets of ink at high speed onto the surface of the paper. This process not only produces a letter-quality image but also permits printing to be done in a variety of colors. (See Figure 6-21.) Ink-jet printers have recently become the most widely used printer. They are reliable, quiet, and inexpensive. Ink-jet printers are used wherever color and appearance are important, as in advertising and public relations.

FIGURE 6-21
An ink-jet printer: Hewlett-Packard PaintJet XL300.

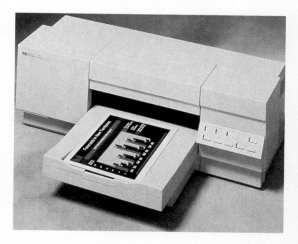

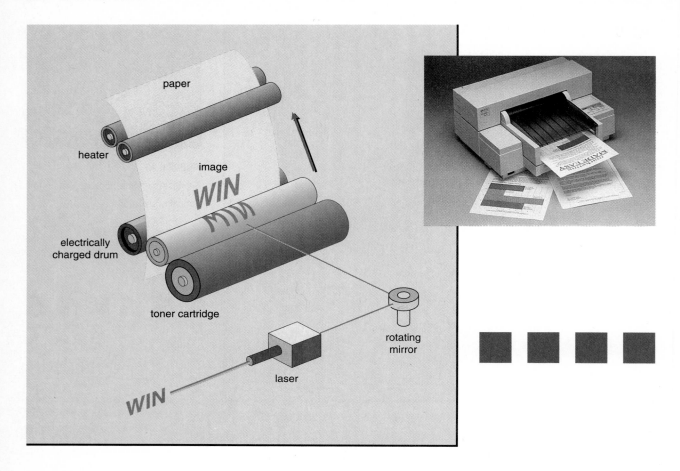

FIGURE 6-22

A laser printer: Hewlett-Packard LaserJet.

Laser Printer

The **laser printer** creates dotlike images (like a dot-matrix printer) on a drum, using a laser beam light source. (See Figure 6-22.) The characters are treated with a magnetically charged inklike toner and then are transferred from drum to paper. A heat process is used to make the characters adhere. This technology is similar to that of a photocopying machine.

The laser printer produces images with excellent letter and graphics quality. It is widely used in applications requiring high-quality output. This has made possible the whole new industry of desktop publishing. As we've mentioned earlier, desktop publishing software enables people to merge text and graphics. The publications produced have a polish that rivals the work of some professional typesetters and graphic artists.

There are two categories of laser printers. **Personal laser printers** are inexpensive and widely used by single users to produce black-and-white documents. They typically can print 4 to 6 pages a minute. **Shared laser printers** are more expensive and are used (shared) by a group of users to produce black-and-white documents. Some can produce color output. Shared laser printers typically print over 30 pages a minute.

Thermal Printer

A **thermal printer** uses heat elements to produce images on heat-sensitive paper. Originally these printers were used in scientific labs to record data. More recently, color thermal printers have been widely used to produce very high quality color artwork and text. (See Figure 6-23.)

Color thermal printers are not as popular because of their cost and the requirement of specifically treated paper. They are a more special use printer that produces near-photographic output. They are widely used in professional art and design work where very high quality color is essential.

Some of the important characteristics of the four most widely used microcomputer printers are summarized in the table in Figure 6-24.

FIGURE 6-23
A thermal printer: Tektronix's Phaser 200i.

PRINTERS

PRINTER	CHARACTERISTICS	TYPICAL USE
Dot-matrix	Reliable, inexpensive; forms text and graphics by dots; some color printing	In-house communications
Ink-jet	High color quality; sprays drops of ink on paper	Internal and external communications, advertising pieces
Laser	Very high quality; forms text and graphics by dots, using photocopying process	Desktop publishing, external documents
Thermal	Very high quality; uses heat elements on special paper	Art and design work

FIGURE 6-24
Four types of printers.

Other Printers

There are several other types of printers. Two are the daisy-wheel printer and the chain printer. Daisy-wheel printers produce very high quality, professional-looking correspondence. However, they are slower and less reliable than dot-matrix, ink-jet, and laser printers. Their sales have declined dramatically in the past few years.

You probably won't find a chain printer standing alone on a desk next to a microcomputer. This is because a chain printer is an expensive, high-speed machine originally designed to serve minicomputers and mainframes. However, you may see one in organizations that link several microcomputers together by a communications network.

Printer Features

Some general qualities to note about microcomputer printers are as follows:

- **Friction and tractor feed:** In a typewriter the paper is gripped by the roller (platen). Some printers use this method. It is called **friction feed.** In other microcomputer printers the paper is held in place by a **tractor feed** mechanism. This reduces the chance of the paper's getting out of alignment. The tractor feed has sprockets that advance the paper, using holes on the edges of continuous-form paper.

- **Type styles:** Some printers allow you to change type styles by changing the printing element. Others require you to do something with the software. Still others do not allow a change in type style.

- **Shared use:** Ink-jet, laser, and chain printers can be quite expensive. Thus, in organizations they are often found linked to several microcomputers through a communications network. Dot-matrix printers are quite often used to serve individual microcomputers.

- **Portability:** Some people (travelers, for instance) require not only a portable computer but also a portable printer. Rugged printers are available that are battery-powered and weigh less than 7 pounds. These printers typically are either dot-matrix or ink-jet. Such printers are recharged using a special connection that can be plugged into an AC outlet. Some can even be recharged through a car's cigarette lighter.

Plotters

Plotters are special-purpose drawing devices.

Plotters are special-purpose output devices for producing bar charts, maps, architectural drawings, and even three-dimensional illustrations. Plotters can produce high-quality multicolor documents and also documents that are larger in size than most printers can handle. There are four types of plotters: pen, ink-jet, electrostatic, and direct imaging.

Pen Plotter

Pen plotters (see Figure 6-25) create plots by moving a pen or pencil over drafting paper. (For some pen plotters, the paper moves and the pen remains stationary.) These plotters are the least expensive and easiest to maintain. Their major

FIGURE 6-25

A pen plotter.

limitations are speed and inability to produce solid fills and shading. They have been the most popular type of plotter.

Ink-Jet Plotter

Ink-jet plotters create line drawings and solid-color output by spraying droplets of ink onto paper. Their best features are their speed, high-quality output, and quiet operation. The major disadvantage of ink-jet plotters is that the spray jets can become clogged and require more maintenance. They are used by a wide variety of workers, including engineers and automotive designers.

Electrostatic Plotter

Whereas pen plotters use pens, **electrostatic plotters** use electrostatic charges to create images made up of tiny dots on specially treated paper. (See Figure 6-26.) The image is produced when the paper is run through a developer. Electrostatic plotters produce high-resolution images and are much faster than either pen or ink-jet plotters. These plotters, unfortunately, use expensive chemicals that are considered hazardous. Electrostatic plotters are used for applications that require high-volume and high-quality outputs such as in advertising and graphic arts design.

Direct Imaging Plotter

Direct-imaging plotters or thermal plotters create images using heat-sensitive paper and electrically heated pins. This type of plotter is comparably priced with electrostatic plotters, quite reliable, and good for high-volume work. However, direct-imaging plotters require expensive paper and typically create only two-color output. These plotters are typically used for very specific applications such as creating maps.

FIGURE 6-26
An electrostatic plotter.

Voice-Output Devices

Voice-output devices vocalize prerecorded sounds.

Voice-output devices make sounds that resemble human speech but actually are prerecorded vocalized sounds. With one Macintosh program, the computer speaks the synthesized words "We'll be right back" if you type in certain letters and numbers. (The characters are *Wiyl biy ray5t bae5k*—the numbers elongate the sounds.) Voice output is not anywhere near as difficult to create as voice input. In fact, there are many occasions when you will hear synthesized speech being used. Examples are found in soft-drink machines, on the telephone, and in cars.

For multimedia applications, the output device is typically a set of stereo speakers or headphones. (See Figure 6-27.) These devices are connected to a sound card in the system unit. The sound card is used to capture as well as play back recorded sounds.

Voice output is used as a reinforcement tool for learning, such as to help students study a foreign language. It is used in many supermarkets at the checkout counter to confirm purchases. Of course, one of the most powerful capabilities is to assist the physically challenged.

FIGURE 6-27
Stereo speakers: Bose
Mediamate Computer
Speakers.

A Look at the Future

Input and output devices are starting to look like us. Separate devices are being combined, and computers may be controlled by just looking at them.

We can expect some startling developments in input and output in the near future. The major trend is toward *natural* microcomputers or what some call *human-centered* technology. This is an extension or evolution of current devices. It integrates speech and handwriting recognition and other human-like and natural input and output devices. For example, IBM is developing a *conversational surrogate,* or an animated face, for the computer screen. You provide input by talking directly to the animated face that appears on your display screen. The animated face talks back to you, providing information and assistance.

Another trend is to combine individual input and output devices into a single unit. Sometimes called the *information appliance,* this "everything-but-the-kitchen-sink" approach is being used by QMS, Inc. QMS, Inc. has developed an all-in-one document-management system. This system combines a printer, scanner, copier, fax machine, and other capabilities into a single device. Rather than purchasing, installing, and maintaining each of these machines, you just have to keep track of one.

Even further down the road, you may be able to control a computer by blinking an eye or twitching a muscle. You may even be able to control a computer by just thinking about it. Using our bodies as an input device is called *biosignal processing.* BioControl Systems has developed a system that connects electrodes to the forehead and cheeks to measure eye movement. The eye movements are then used to control a mouse or robot.

KEY TERMS

active-matrix monitor (124)

bar codes (120)

bar-code reader (120)

cathode-ray tube (CRT) (123)

continuous speech recognition system (121)

cursor control keys (116)

dedicated fax machine (120)

desktop monitor (123)

digitizer (118)

digitizing tablet (118)

direct entry (117)

direct-imaging plotter (129)

directional arrow keys (116)

discrete-word recognition system (121)

display screen (122)

dot-matrix printer (125)

dumb terminal (116)

electrostatic plotter (129)

Enter (115)

facsimile transmission (fax) machine (120)

fax board (120)

fax/modem board (120)

flat-panel monitor (123)

friction feed (128)

function key (115)

hard copy (124)

high-definition television (HDTV) (124)

image scanner (119)

ink-jet plotter (129)

ink-jet printer (125)

intelligent terminal (117)

interactive TV (ITV) (124)

interlaced monitor (123)

laser printer (126)

light pen (118)

liquid crystal display (LCD) (123)

magnetic-ink character recognition
  (MICR) (120)

mark sensing (121)

mouse (117)

noninterlaced monitor (123)

numeric keypad (116)

numeric keys (116)

optical-character recognition (OCR)
  (120)

optical-mark recognition (OMR) (121)

passive-matrix monitor (124)

PC/TV (124)

pen plotter (128)

pen-based computer (119)

personal laser printer (126)

pixels (122)

platform scanner (115)

plotters (128)

point-of-sale (POS) terminal (115)

reader/sorter (120)

shared laser printer (126)

smart terminal (116)

soft copy (124)

source document (114)

special-purpose keys (116)

Super VGA, SVGA (123)

terminal (116)

thermal printer (127)

touch screen (118)

tractor feed (128)

typewriter keys (115)

VGA (122)

video display (122)

video display terminals (VDTs) (122)

voice recognition systems (121)

voice-input device (121)

voice-output device (129)

wand reader (115)

XGA (123)

REVIEW QUESTIONS

True/False

1. Input devices translate symbols that people understand into symbols that computers can process.

2. A plotter is a device that can be used to trace or copy a drawing or photograph.

3. Banks use a method called magnetic-ink character recognition (MICR) to automatically read and sort checks.

4. Laser printers are highly reliable but the quality of their output limits their use to rough drafts and in-house communications.

5. Plotters are special-purpose drawing devices.

Multiple Choice

1. Esc, Ctrl, Del, and Ins are _____ keys.
   a. function
   b. numeric
   c. directional arrow
   d. cursor control
   e. special-purpose

2. A device that converts images on a page to electronic signals that can be stored in a computer:
   a. monitor
   b. scanner
   c. plotter
   d. MICR
   e. POS

3. The type of portable monitor that can display more colors, with better clarity:
   a. active-matrix
   b. passive-matrix
   c. monochrome
   d. CGA
   e. VGA

4. The printer that can produce very high quality images using heat elements on heat-sensitive paper:
   a. dot-matrix
   b. laser
   c. ink-jet
   d. plotter
   e. thermal

5. The plotter that creates images using heat-sensitive paper and electrically heated pins:
   a. pen
   b. ink-jet
   c. direct imaging
   d. scanner
   e. electrostatic

Fill in the Blank

1. Another name for the mouse that has a ball that is controlled with the thumb is _____.

2. _____ machines are popular office machines because they can transfer documents at electronic speeds.

3. The _____ printer is a reliable, inexpensive printer that forms letters by a series of small pins on a print head.

4. A _____ feed printer has sprockets that advance the paper.

5. _____ devices make sounds that resemble human speech.

Open Ended

1. What are the differences between keyboard entry and direct entry as forms of input?

2. What is a POS terminal? What are two input devices on it that represent the two methods of inputting data?

3. Distinguish among the three kinds of terminals: dumb, smart, intelligent.

4. What are pixels? What do they have to do with screen resolution?

5. What are the differences between personal and shared lasers?

DISCUSSION QUESTIONS AND PROJECTS

1. *Evaluating laser printers:* When shopping for an inexpensive personal laser printer, you can't expect to get all of the fancy fonts. Nor can you expect the speedy, sophisticated paper handling more expensive printers offer. At the very least, you'd want crisp, professional-looking output and reasonably fast performance. Evaluate your printer needs in terms of the following criteria:
   a. Output quality
   b. Print speed
   c. Price
   d. Service and support
   e. Design and construction
   f. Font/graphics options
   g. Paper handling

2. *http://www.microsoft.com/advtech/InteractiveTelevision/mitvbroc.htm* An exciting development is ITV (Interactive TV). Imagine movies on demand and interactive shopping malls. To learn more about ITV, connect to Microsoft's home page using the Internet address given at the beginning of this question. Then expand your search for information on ITV by using other Internet resources. (Hint: Use the Every Student's Internet Resource Guide: Computer Science and Computer Technology—Entry Number: 01 and/or Entry Number: 02.)

Input and Output

Input devices translate symbols that people understand into symbols the computer can process. Two kinds of input are keyboard and direct entry.

INPUT

Keyboard entry may be categorized as keyboards and terminals.

Keyboards

In keyboard entry, data is typed. A keyboard consists of:

- **Typewriter keys,** for regular letters, numbers, etc., and **Enter** key to enter commands.
- **Function keys** (*F1, F2,* etc.), for special tasks.
- **Numeric keys,** for typing in numbers.
- **Special-purpose keys** (e.g., *Del* for Delete) and **cursor control (directional arrow) keys** (to move cursor).

Terminals

A **terminal** is an input/output device with keyboard, monitor, and communications link. Terminals are of three types:

- **Dumb**—sends and receives only; does no processing.
- **Smart**—allows some editing of data.
- **Intelligent**—has processing and primary and secondary storage and software for processing data.

Direct-entry devices may be categorized as pointing, scanning, or voice-input devices.

Pointing Devices

- **Mouse**—directs cursor on screen.
- **Touch screen**—touching your finger to the screen selects actions.
- **Light pen**—recognizes a spot on the screen as input.
- **Digitizer**—converts image to digital data. A **digitizing tablet** converts images using a stylus.
- **Pen-based computing**—computer with stylus to write on display screen.

Scanning Devices

- **Image scanner (bit-mapping device)**—converts an image to digital code.
- **Facsimile transmission (fax) machine**—converts images to electronic signals for sending over telephone lines. **Dedicated fax machines** are specialized devices. **Fax boards** may be inserted in microcomputers to send and receive images.

- **Bar-code reader**—scans zebra-striped **bar codes** on products to reveal their prices.
- Character and mark recognition devices include: **magnetic-ink character recognition (MICR),** used by banks to read magnetized-ink numbers on checks, which are sorted by a **reader/sorter** machine; **optical-character recognition (OCR),** used to read special preprinted characters (e.g., on utility bills); **optical-mark recognition (OMR),** which senses pencil marks (e.g., on College Board tests.).

Voice-Input Devices

Voice-input devices convert a person's spoken words to digital code. Combined with appropriate software, these devices are part of the **voice recognition system** that allows users to operate microcomputers using voice commands.

- **Continous speech recognition systems** control operations and issue commands for application packages.
- **Discrete-word recognition systems** convert and store dictation in a word processing file.

Output devices translate machine output to output that people can understand. Output devices include monitors, printers, plotters, and voice-output.

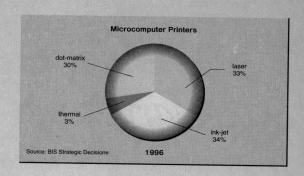

Microcomputer Printers

dot-matrix 30%
laser 33%
thermal 3%
ink-jet 34%

Source: BIS Strategic Decisions

1996

MONITORS

STANDARD	PIXELS	COLORS
CGA	320 × 200	4
EGA	640 × 350	16
VGA	640 × 200 320 × 200	I16 256
Super VGA	800 × 600 1024 × 768	256 256
XGA	1024 × 768	65,536rts

Monitors

Monitor **display screens** create images by individual dots ("picture elements") called **pixels.** The three most common monitor standards are shown above.

- **Desktop monitors** typically are placed on the system unit or desk. **Interlaced monitors** create images by scanning down and skipping every other line. They can cause eye strain. **Noninterlaced monitors** avoid problems by scanning down each line.
- **Portable monitors** are less bulky and flat. **Passive-matrix monitors** require little power but images not as sharp. **Active-matrix monitors** require more power, are more expensive, produce better images.

Printers

Output from display screens is called **soft copy.** Output from a printer is called **hard copy.** Four types of printers are:

- **Dot-matrix**—forms text and graphic images with a matrix of pins.
- **Ink-jet**—sprays droplets of ink on paper; it is good for color and provides very good quality.
- **Laser**—prints with light beam and magnetically charged toner. Lasers print high-quality text and graphics; **personal lasers** used by individual user; **shared lasers** used by many.
- **Thermal**—heat elements produce images on special heat-sensitive paper; expensive; produces very high quality art and design output.

Plotters

Plotters produce multicolor bar charts, maps, architectural drawings. Four types are:

- **Pen**—has been most popular and least expensive.
- **Ink-jet**—fastest and very good at producing solid color output.
- **Electrostatic**—electrostatic charges create high-quality and high-volume work on specially treated paper (shown).
- **Direct imaging**—electrically charged pins create two-color output on special heat-sensitive paper.

Voice-Output Devices

- **Voice-output devices** make sounds resembling human speech.

Secondary Storage

Data may be input, processed, and output as information. But one of the best features about using a computer is the ability to save—that is, store—information. Computers can save information permanently, after you turn them off. This way, you can save your work for future use, share information with others, or modify information already available. Secondary storage holds information external from the CPU. Secondary storage allows you to store programs, such as WordPerfect and Lotus 1-2-3. It also allows you to store the data processed by programs, such as text or the numbers in a spreadsheet.

What if you could buy a microcomputer and use your portable audiotape recorder to store programs and data? Actually, this was once advertised as a feature. In the early 1980s there were over 150 kinds of microcomputers being offered. Some inexpensive computers were advertised at that time that could store information on the tape in one's audiotape recorder.

To find a particular song on an audiotape, you may have to play several inches of tape. Finding a song on an audio compact disc, in contrast, can be much faster. You select the song, and the disc player moves directly to it. That, in brief, represents the two different approaches to external storage. The two approaches are called *sequential access* and *direct access*.

Magnetic tape is an example of **sequential access storage** media. Information is stored in sequence, such as alphabetically. You may have to search a tape past all the information from A to P, say, before you get to Q. This may involve searching several inches or feet, which takes time.

Generally speaking, disk storage falls in the category of **direct access storage.** That is, it is like selecting the song you want and then moving directly to it. This form of storage allows you to directly access information. Therefore, retrieving selected data and programs is much faster with disks than with tape.

Four Types of Secondary Storage

Microcomputer secondary storage may be on floppy disk, hard disk, optical disc, or magnetic tape.

We described random-access memory (RAM) in Chapter 5. This is the *internal* and *temporary* storage of data and programs in the computer's memory. Once the power is turned off or interrupted, everything in internal storage disappears. Such storage is therefore said to be **volatile.** Thus, we need *external, more permanent,* or **nonvolatile,** ways of storing data and programs. We also need external storage because users need much more capacity than is possessed by a computer's primary memory.

The most widely used external storage media are floppy disks, hard disks, optical discs, and magnetic tape. It is important for end users to understand the advantages, disadvantages, and typical uses for each.

Any particular microcomputer could use all of the different media. However, a typical system has a hard disk drive and one or two other drives. The hard disk drive is designated as the C drive and is typically used for storing system and application programs. Drives A and B are generally floppy disk drives used for data files. The D drive is typically a CD-ROM drive for programs and reference materials. (See Figure 7-1.)

FIGURE 7-1

Apple's Macintosh Performa 6200 CD with both floppy disk drive and optical drive.

Cover slides over
to expose disk.

FIGURE 7-2
A 3½-inch floppy disk.

Floppy Disks

Floppy disks are removable storage media that are inserted into disk drives.

Floppy disks, often called **diskettes** or simply **disks,** are flat, circular pieces of mylar plastic that rotate within a jacket. Data and programs are stored as electromagnetic charges on a metal oxide film coating the mylar plastic. Data and programs are represented by the presence or absence of these charges, using the ASCII or EBCDIC data representation codes. The two most popular sizes of floppy disks are 3½-inch diameter and 5¼-inch diameter. Larger and smaller sizes are also available, although they are not standard for most microcomputers.

Floppy disks are also called **flexible disks,** and **floppies.** This is because the plastic disk inside the diskette covers is flexible, not rigid. The 3½-inch standard is encased in a hard plastic jacket. (See Figure 7-2.)

The Disk Drive

The *disk drive* obtains stored data and programs from a floppy disk. It is also used to store data and programs on a floppy disk.

A disk drive consists of a box with a slot into which you insert the floppy disk. Often the slot is covered by a door, called the **drive gate.** A motor inside the drive rotates the floppy disk. As the floppy disk rotates, electronic heads can "read" data from and "write" data to it. As we stated earlier, *read* means that the disk drive *copies* data (stored as magnetic impulses) from the floppy disk. *Write* means that the disk drive *transfers* data, the electronic signals in the computer's memory, onto the floppy disk.

It's important to realize that reading makes a copy from the original data; it does not alter the original. Writing, in contrast, *writes over*—and replaces—any data that is already there. This is like recording a new song over an old one on a tape recorder. The same is true of programs on a floppy disk.

How a Disk Drive Works

A floppy disk is inserted into the slot in the front of the disk drive, and the drive gate is closed. (See Figure 7-3.) Closing the gate positions the floppy disk around a spindle and holds it so that it can revolve without slipping. When the drive is in motion, the floppy disk can turn at about 360 revolutions per minute, depending on the drive.

The magnetic data signals are transferred from floppy disk to computer (and computer to floppy disk) through **read-write heads.** (See Figure 7-3.) The read-write head is on an **access arm,** which moves back and forth over the floppy disk. To read or write on a particular part of the floppy disk, the access arm moves the read-write head on the floppy disk. This is called the **seek** operation. The drive then rotates the floppy disk to the proper position. This is called the **search** operation.

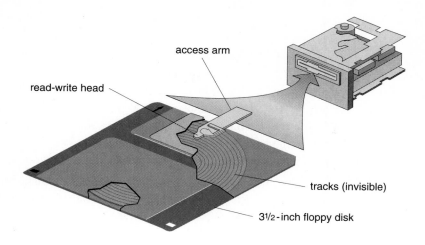

access arm

read-write head

tracks (invisible)

3½-inch floppy disk

FIGURE 7-3
**Reading from and writing
to a floppy disk.**

The Parts of a Floppy Disk

Both 3½-inch and 5¼-inch floppy disks work the same way in principle, although there are some differences.

Data is recorded on a floppy disk in rings called **tracks.** (See Figure 7-4.) These tracks are closed concentric circles, not a single spiral as on a phonograph record. Unlike a phonograph record, these tracks have no visible grooves. Looking at an exposed floppy disk, you would see just a smooth surface. Each track is divided into invisible wedge-shaped sections known as **sectors.**

Most disks are manufactured without tracks and sectors in place. Called **soft-sectored disks,** they must be adapted to the particular brand of microcomputer and disk drive you are using. Thus, you must put the tracks and sectors on yourself, using a process called *formatting,* or *initializing.*

Storage capacity of floppy disks can vary considerably. (See Figure 7-5.) For example, you will see boxes of 3½-inch disks labeled "DS, DD," which means "double-sided, double-density." A floppy disk of this sort can store 737,280 bytes or 720 KB—the equivalent of 450 typewritten pages. The more popular 3½-inch "DS,

FIGURE 7-4
**The parts of a 3½-inch
floppy disk.**

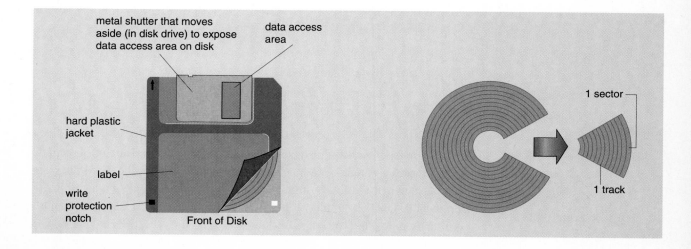

metal shutter that moves aside (in disk drive) to expose data access area on disk

data access area

hard plastic jacket

label

write protection notch

Front of Disk

1 sector

1 track

FLOPPY DISK CAPACITY

DESCRIPTION	CAPACITY
3½-inch	
Double-sided, double-density	720 KB
Double-sided, high-density	1.44 MB
Floptical	21 MB
5¼-inch	
Double-sided, double-density	360 KB
Double-sided, high-density	1.2 KB

FIGURE 7-5

Typical floppy disk capacities.

■ ■ ■ ■ ■ ■ ■ ■ ■

HD" ("double-sided, high density") disks have twice the capacity. Although not nearly as popular, floptical discs can store 21 MB by using optical technology.

The two most popular sizes of floppy disks have distinct differences in how the jacket and the write-protect notch are handled:

■ **3½-inch:** The 3½-inch version is the sturdier of the two. (Refer back to Figure 7-4.) The exterior **jacket** is made of hard plastic to protect the flexible disk inside. The **write-protect notch** is covered by a sliding shutter. When you open the shutter, the write-protect notch prevents the computer from accidentally writing over information on the disk that you want to keep.

■ **5¼-inch:** On the 5¼-inch version, the exterior jacket is made of flexible plastic or cardboard. The disk is protected by a paper envelope, or sleeve, when it is not in the disk drive. The write-protect notch can be covered with a removable tab, which comes with the disk when you buy it.

Taking Care of Floppy Disks

Taking care of floppy disks boils down to four rules:

1. *Don't bend the disks, put heavy weights on them, or use sharp objects on them.* For 5¼-inch disks, do not write on them with ballpoint pens. Use a felt-tip pen when writing on the index label.

2. *Don't touch anything visible through the protective jacket* (such as the data access area).

3. *Keep disks away from strong magnetic fields* (like motors or telephones). Also, *keep them away from extreme heat* (like a car trunk) *and chemicals* (such as alcohol and solvents). Keep 5¼-inch disks in their paper envelopes and store them in a file box when they are not in use.

4. *Store disks in a sturdy plastic storage box.* Even though the 3½-inch disks have a hard plastic jacket, they can be damaged.

Of course, the best protection is to make a *backup,* or duplicate, copy of your disk.

Despite these cautions, you will find floppy disks are actually quite durable. For instance, you can send them through the mail if you enclose them in cardboard or use special rigid mailing envelopes. They usually can also be put through the x-ray machines at airport security checkpoints without loss of data.

Hard Disks

Hard disks are of three types: internal hard disk, hard-disk cartridge, and hard-disk pack.

Hard disks consist of metallic rather than plastic platters. They are also tightly sealed to prevent any foreign matter from getting inside. Hard disks are extremely sensitive instruments. The read-write head rides on a cushion of air about 0.000001 inch thick. It is so thin that a smoke particle, fingerprint, dust, or human hair could cause what is known as a head crash. (See Figure 7-6.)

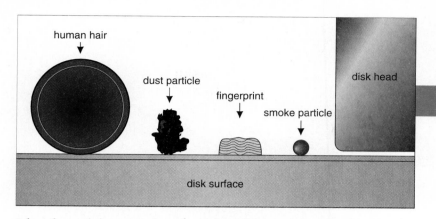

FIGURE 7-6

Materials that can cause a head crash.

A **head crash** happens when the surface of the read-write head or particles on its surface contact the magnetic disk surface. A head crash is a disaster for a hard disk. It means that some or all of the data on the disk is destroyed. Hard disks are assembled under sterile conditions and sealed from impurities within their permanent containers.

There are three types of hard disks: *internal hard disk, hard-disk cartridge,* and *hard-disk pack.*

Internal Hard Disk

An **internal hard disk** consists of one or more metallic platters sealed inside a container. The container includes the motor for rotating the disks. It also contains an access arm and read-write heads for writing data to and reading data from the disks. Like a floppy-disk drive, an internal hard-disk drive has a seek operation and a search operation for reading and writing data in tracks and sectors. From the outside of a microcomputer, an internal hard disk looks like part of a front panel on the system cabinet. Typically, inside is a 3½-inch metallic platter with an access arm that moves back and forth. (See Figure 7-7.)

Internal hard disks have two advantages over floppy disks: capacity and speed. A hard disk can hold many times the information of a similar size floppy disk. One 850-megabyte internal hard disk, for instance, can hold as much information as 590 3½-inch double-sided, high-density floppy disks. Some *external* hard-disk drives for microcomputers (drives that are not built into the system cabinet) can store thousands of megabytes. Moreover, access is faster: a hard disk spins 10 times faster than a floppy disk. For these reasons, almost all of today's powerful applications are designed to be stored and run from an internal hard disk. Adequate capacity or size of a microcomputer's internal hard disk is essential.

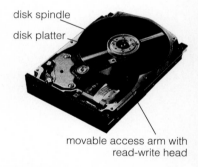

FIGURE 7-7

Inside of a hard-disk drive.

Hard-Disk Cartridges

The disadvantage of hard disks is that they have only a fixed amount of storage and cannot be easily removed. Hard-disk cartridges have the advantage of being as easy to remove as a cassette from a videocassette recorder. (See Figure 7-8.) They can give microcomputer systems fast access to very large quantities of data. The amount of storage available is limited only by the number of cartridges. For instance, the SyQuest removable hard-disk cartridge has a storage capacity of 200

FIGURE 7-8
Removable hard-disk
cartridge.

megabytes. While a regular hard-disk system has a fixed storage capacity, a removable hard-disk cartridge system is unlimited—you can just buy more removable cartridges. One removable 20-megabyte palm-sized hard disk available weighs only 7 ounces and may be moved easily from laptop to laptop.

Hard-Disk Packs

Microcomputers that are connected to other microcomputers, minicomputers, or mainframes often have access to external hard-disk packs. (See Figure 7-9.) Microcomputer hard-disk drives typically have only one or two disk platters and one or two access arms. In contrast, **hard-disk packs** consist of several *platters* aligned one above the other, thereby offering much greater storage capacity. These hard-disk packs resemble a stack of phonograph records. The difference is that there is space between the disks to allow the access arms to move in and out. (See Figure 7-10.) Each access arm has two read-write heads. One reads the disk surface above

FIGURE 7-9
Hard-disk packs.

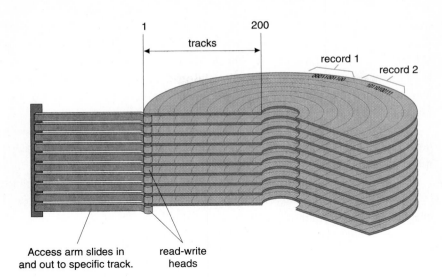

1   200

tracks

record 1

record 2

Access arm slides in
and out to specific track.

read-write
heads

FIGURE 7-10
How a disk pack works.

it; the other reads the disk surface below it. A disk pack with 11 disks provides 20 recording surfaces. This is because the top and bottom outside surfaces of the pack are not used.

All the access arms move in and out together. However, only one of the read-write heads is activated at a given moment. **Access time** is the time between the computer's request for data from secondary storage and the completion of the data transfer. Access time for most disk drives is under 25 milliseconds.

You may well use your microcomputer to gain access to information over a telephone or other communications line. (We show this in the next chapter.) Such information is apt to be stored on disk packs. One large information service (named Dialog), for example, has over 300 databases. These databases cover all areas of science, technology, business, medicine, social science, current affairs, and humanities. All of these are available through a telephone link with your desktop computer. There are more than 100 million items of information, including references to books, patents, directories, journals, and newspaper articles. Such an information resource may be of great value to you in your work.

Performance Enhancements

Three ways to improve the performance of hard disks are disk caching, data compression, and redundant arrays of inexpensive disks.

Disk caching improves hard-disk performance by anticipating data needs. It requires a combination of hardware and software. During idle processing time, frequently used data is read from the hard disk into memory (cache). When needed, the data is then accessed directly from memory. The transfer rate from memory is much faster than from hard disk. Thus, overall system performance is often increased by as much as 30 percent.

Data compression and **decompression** increase storage capacity by reducing the amount of space required to store data and programs. In data compression, entering data is scanned for ways to reduce the amount of required storage. One way is to search for repeating patterns. The repeating patterns are replaced with a token, leaving enough so that the original can be rebuilt or decompressed. Data compression and decompression can be accomplished through the use of special software and/or hardware. An example is add-on boards inserted into the computer's expansion slots. Many times the software is included in the operating system, as is the case with DOS 6.0. Also available are specialized programs. (See Figure 7-11.)

Data compression can regain or free as much as 80 percent of a microcomputer's hard disk. The major tradeoff is performance: A great deal of compression may slow down processing.

Redundant arrays of inexpensive disks (RAIDs) improve performance by expanding external storage. Groups of inexpensive hard-disk drives are related or grouped together using networks and special software. These grouped disks are treated as a single large-capacity hard disk. They can outperform single disks of comparable capacities.

Optical Discs

Optical discs are used for storing great quantities of data.

An **optical disc** can hold 650 megabytes of data—the equivalent of hundreds of floppy disks. (See Figure 7-12.) Moreover, an optical disc makes an immense amount of information available on a microcomputer. Optical discs are having a great impact on storage technology today, but we are probably only beginning to see their effects.

In optical-disc technology, a laser beam alters the surface of a plastic or metallic disc to represent data. To read the data, a laser scans these areas and sends the data to a computer chip for conversion. Optical discs are made in diameters of 3½, 4¾, 5¼, 8, 12, and 14 inches.

There are three kinds of optical discs available: *CD-ROM, CD-R,* and *erasable optical discs.*

FIGURE 7-11

Data compression software,

Stacker version 4.0.

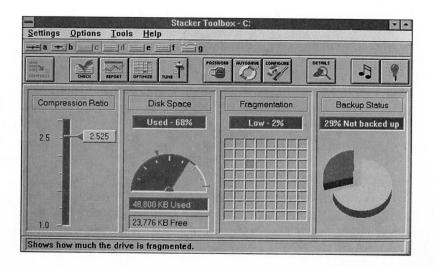

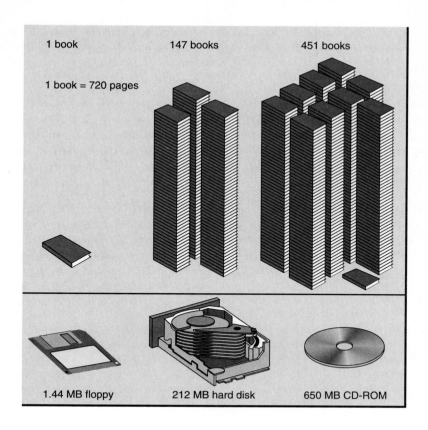

1 book

147 books

451 books

1 book = 720 pages

1.44 MB floppy   212 MB hard disk   650 MB CD-ROM

FIGURE 7-12
**Comparison of disk storage
capacities.**

CD-ROM

CD-ROM stands for *compact disc–read-only memory.* Industry sources estimate that half of the microcomputers sold in 1997 will contain a CD-ROM drive. And the number of installed CD-ROM drives will continue to increase every year. (See Figure 7-13.)

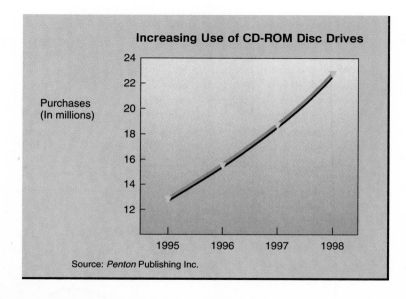

Increasing Use of CD-ROM Disc Drives

Purchases
(In millions)

Source: *Penton* Publishing Inc.

FIGURE 7-13
CD-ROM disc drive usage—
past, present, and future.

Unlike floppy and hard disks, which use magnetic charges to represent 1s and 0s, optical discs use reflected light. On a CD-ROM disc, 1s and 0s are represented by flat areas and bumpy areas (called "pits") on its bottom surface. The CD-ROM disc is read by a laser that projects a tiny beam of light on these areas. The amount of reflected light determines whether the area represents a 1 or a 0. (See Figure 7-14.)

Like a commercial CD found in music stores, a CD-ROM is a "read-only" disc. **Read-only** means it cannot be written on or erased by the user. Thus, you as a user have access only to the data imprinted by the publisher. CD-ROM discs are used to distribute large databases and references. An example is the *Grolier Electronic Encyclopedia,* a CD-ROM containing the *Academic American Encyclopedia,* with over 9 million words and 1500 pictures. (See Figure 7-15 for other CD-ROM titles.)

CD-ROMS are also used to distribute large software application packages. For example, Microsoft Office for Windows 95 is available on a single CD-ROM or on over twenty floppy disks. One advantage of the CD-ROM version is that installation from one CD-ROM to the internal hard disk is much faster and easier.

FIGURE 7-14
How a CD-ROM works.

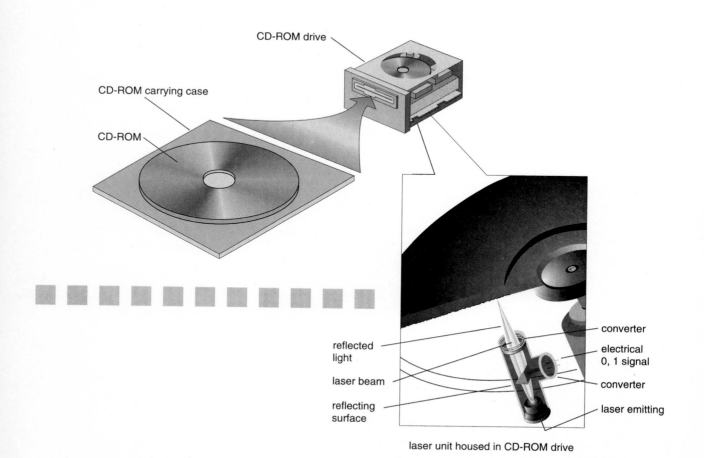

CD-ROM drive

CD-ROM carrying case

CD-ROM

reflected light

laser beam

reflecting surface

converter

electrical 0, 1 signal

converter

laser emitting

laser unit housed in CD-ROM drive

REFERENCE CD-ROMS

TITLE	DESCRIPTION
Grolier Electronic Encyclopedia	21 volumes of the Academic American Encyclopedia, with over 9 million words and 1500 pictures
Microsoft Bookshelf	8 complete reference books, including the American Heritage Dictionary, Roget's II Electronic Thesaurus, Bartlett's Familiar Quotations, and a ZIP code directory
U.S. History on CD-ROM	107 books on U.S. history, with over 1000 photos, maps, and tables
Compton's Multimedia Encyclopedia	Compton's Encyclopedia, including 15,000 illustrations and audio of speeches by Martin Luther King, Jr., and John F. Kennedy
Mammals: A Multimedia Encyclopedia	45 documentary video clips from National Geographic and animal audio sound tracks

FIGURE 7-15
Leading CD-ROM reference materials.

A single CD-ROM disc can store 650 megabytes of data. That is equivalent to 147 floppy disks. With that much information on a single disc, the time to retrieve or access the information is very important. An important characteristic of CD-ROM drives is their access rate. (See Figure 7-16.)

CD-R

CD-R stands for *CD-Recordable*. Also known as **WORM** or *write once, read many,* CD-R discs can be written to once. After that they can be read many times without deterioration and cannot be written on or erased. A typical 5¼-inch CD-R disc can store between 600 and 650 megabytes of data.

CD-ROM DRIVES

TYPE	DESCRIPTION
Single-speed	The original drive introduced in the mid 1980s; transfer rate of 150 KB per second; data retrieval was slow; poor sound and video capabilities
Double-speed	Introduced in 1991; transfer rate of 300 KB per second; widely used standard; acceptable data retrieval and sound production; video capabilities limited; too slow for most multimedia applications
Triple-speed	Introduced in 1993; transfer rate of 450 KB per second; also not quite fast enough for full-motion video
Quad-speed	Also introduced in 1993; transfer rate of 600 KB; acceptable for full-motion video
Six-speed	Recently introduced, with faster speeds expected soon

FIGURE 7-16
Access speeds for CD-ROM drives.

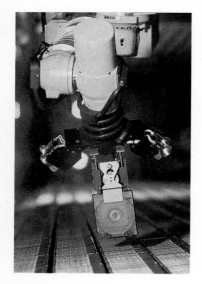

FIGURE 7-17

CD Jukebox.

OPTICAL DISCS	
DESCRIPTION	**CAPACITY**
CD-ROM	650 MB
CD-R	600–650 MB
Erasable	600–1000 MB

FIGURE 7-18

Typical capacities for optical discs.

■ ■ ■ ■ ■ ■ ■ ■ ■

Because the data cannot be erased, CD-R discs are ideal for use as archives to permanently store large amounts of important information. CD changers or CD Jukeboxes (see Figure 7-17) are used to give quick access to several CDs, allowing billions of bytes of data to be easily retrieved.

Erasable Optical Discs

Erasable optical discs, also known as **rewriteable optical discs,** are like CD-Rs except that they can be written to many times. That is, a disc that has been written on can be erased and used over and over again. The most viable disc of this type runs on a *magneto-optical* (MO) disc drive, which borrows from both magnetic and optical technologies. A typical 5¼-inch MO disc can store from 600 megabytes to 1000 megabytes (1 gigabyte) of data.

For a summary of optical disc storage capacities, see Figure 7-18.

Magnetic Tape

Magnetic tape streamers and magnetic tape reels are used primarily for backup purposes.

We mentioned the alarming consequences that can happen if a hard disk suffers a head crash. You will lose some or all of your data or programs. Of course, you can always make copies of your hard-disk files on floppy disks. However, this can be time-consuming and may require many floppy disks. Here is where magnetic tape storage becomes important. Magnetic tape falls into the category of sequential access storage and is therefore slower than direct access storage. However, it is an effective way of making a *backup,* or duplicate, copy of your programs and data.

There are two forms of tape storage. These are *magnetic tape streamers,* for use with microcomputers, and *magnetic tape reels,* for use with minicomputers and mainframes.

Magnetic Tape Streamers

Many microcomputer users with hard disks use a device called a **magnetic tape streamer** or a **backup tape cartridge unit.** (See Figure 7-19.) This enables you to duplicate or make a backup of the data on your hard disk onto a tape cartridge. Typical capacities of such tape cartridges are 120 megabytes to 5 gigabytes. Advanced forms of backup technology known as **digital audiotape (DAT) drives,** which use 2- by 3-inch cassettes, store 4 gigabytes or more. If your internal hard disk fails, you can have it repaired (or get another hard disk). You can restore all your lost data and programs in a matter of minutes from the backup tapes.

Magnetic Tape Reels

The cassette tapes you get for an audiotape recorder are only about 200 feet long. They record 200 characters to the inch. A reel of magnetic tape used with minicomputer and mainframe systems, by contrast, is ½-inch wide and ½-mile long.

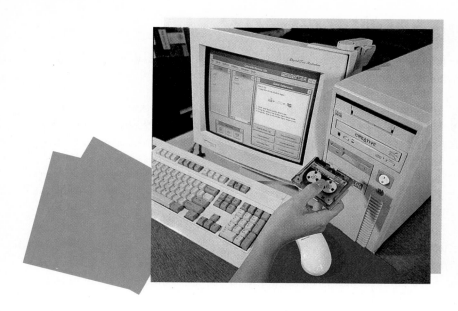

FIGURE 7-19
Backup software copying
files to magnetic tape.

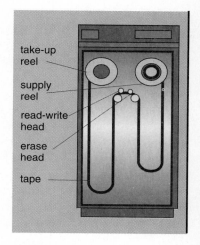

take-up reel

supply reel

read-write head

erase head

tape

FIGURE 7-20
Data is recorded on magnetic tape on tape reels.

It stores 1600 to 6400 characters to the inch. Such tapes are run on **magnetic tape drives** or **magnetic tape units.** (See Figure 7-20.) You may never actually see these devices yourself. However, as a microcomputer user sharing storage devices with others, you may have access to them through a minicomputer or mainframe.

For the typical microcomputer user, the four storage options—floppy disk, hard disk, optical disc, and magnetic tape—are complementary, not competing. Almost all microcomputers today have at least one floppy-disk drive and one hard-disk drive. For those users who need access to vast amounts of data, an optical drive is added. Lastly, for those who need to back up lots of data and programs, magnetic tape drives are added.

For a summary comparison of the four types of secondary storage, see Figure 7-21.

SECONDARY STORAGE

TYPE	ADVANTAGE	DISADVANTAGE	TYPICAL USE	COST/MEGABYTE
Floppy disk	Inexpensive, direct access, removable	Low capacity, slow access	Store files for word processors and spreadsheets	$1.00
Hard disk	Fast, direct access	Limited capacity	Store programs and data	$.40 to $.80
CD-ROM	High capacity, direct access	Slow access	Reference material	$.04 to $1.00
Magnetic tape	High capacity	Slow sequential data access	Backup programs and data	$.10 to $.40

FIGURE 7-21
Summary of storage options.

A Look at the Future

The future promises three storage technologies: wet disks, glass disks, and holograms.

The principal trend now in evidence—that of packing more and more data in less and less space—will doubtless continue. Three technologies that promise to greatly expand disk capacities are "wet" disks, glass disks, and holograms.

Wet disk technology replaces the air cushion between the disk and the drive head with a liquid. This allows the drive head to get closer to the disk and to read more closely packed data. Wet disks have approximately twice the capacity of today's disks; however, special liquid-resistant parts are required. The leader in developing this technology, Conner Peripherals Inc., recently introduced a wet-disk drive.

Traditional hard disks are made of aluminum. Developers have found that by replacing aluminum with glass, more data can be stored on a disk. Unfortunately, the cost to manufacture the glass disks is higher. But all that might change in the near future. An advantage over wet disks is that glass disks can be used with traditional hard disk drive technologies. Hewlett-Packard already has a commercial glass disk called Kittyhawk Personal Storage Module.

A bit further on the horizon is holographic storage, in which information is stored on holograms. Holograms, as you may know, are those shimmering, three-dimensional images often seen on credit cards and the like. Holographic systems store data equivalent to thousands of books in three dimensions inside a box made of special material the size of a sugar cube. Data stored in a holographic system is retrievable in 1 second. Tamarack Storage Devices expects to have a holographic drive available within the next few years.

KEY TERMS

access arm (138)

access time (143)

backup tape cartridge unit (148)

CD-R (147)

CD-ROM (145)

data compression (143)

data decompression (143)

digital audiotape (DAT) drive (148)

direct access storage (137)

disk (138)

disk caching (143)

diskette (138)

drive gate (138)

erasable optical disc (148)

flexible disk (138)

floppy (138)

floppy disk (138)

hard-disk pack (142)

head crash (140)

internal hard disk (141)

jacket (140)

magnetic tape drive (149)

magnetic tape streamer (148)

magnetic tape unit (149)

nonvolatile (137)

optical disc (144)

read-only (146)

read-write head (138)

redundant arrays of inexpensive disks
   (RAIDs) (144)

rewriteable optical disc (148)

search (138)

sector (139)

seek (138)

sequential access storage (136)

soft-sectored disk (139)

track (139)

volatile (137)

WORM (147)

write-protect notch (140)

REVIEW QUESTIONS

True/False

1. Secondary storage holds information within the CPU.
2. Floppy disks are also known as flexible disks and as floppies.
3. Sectors are wedge-shaped sections on a disk.
4. CD-R discs can be erased and used over and over again.
5. Laser beams are used to record data on optical discs.

Multiple Choice

1. Which of the following is exclusively a sequential access storage media?
   a. floppy disk
   b. hard disk
   c. magnetic tape
   d. CD-ROM
   e. WORM

2. On a floppy-disk drive, data signals are transferred to the computer through:
   a. read-write heads
   b. access arms
   c. drive gate
   d. drive A
   e. sectors

3. The disk with the greatest capacity:
   a. 5¼-inch double-sided, double-density
   b. 5¼-inch double-sided, high-density
   c. 3½-inch double-sided, double-density
   d. 3½-inch double-sided, high-density
   e. CD-ROM

4. The hard-disk type that has several platters aligned one above the other:
   a. internal hard disk
   b. hard-disk pack
   c. floppy-disk array
   d. hard-disk cartridge
   e. disk cache

5. The method of improving hard-disk performance by anticipating data needs is:
   a. disk compression
   b. disk caching
   c. disk decompression
   d. RAIDs
   e. virtual processing

Fill in the Blank

1. A _____ disc is read by a laser projecting a beam of light.
2. Data is recorded on a disk in rings called _____.
3. Internal hard disks have two advantages over floppy disks: _____ and speed.
4. Data _____ time measures how long it takes to move data from the hard-disk track to memory.
5. The two forms of tape storage are magnetic tape streamers and magnetic tape _____.

Open Ended

1. Explain the difference between direct access storage and sequential access storage. Which is more apt to be identified with magnetic disk and which with magnetic tape?
2. What are the four kinds of secondary storage? What are their relative advantages and disadvantages?
3. State the four primary rules about taking care of floppy disks.
4. What is so disastrous about a head crash?
5. What are the three types of hard-disk drives? Discuss their differences and similarities.

DISCUSSION QUESTIONS AND PROJECTS

1. *What type of storage system?* Suppose for the past few years you have owned a computer with two floppy-disk drives but no hard-disk drive. Your several file boxes of floppy disks include all kinds of research data comprising a college career. This is research that may be quite valuable later in college or in your career. You also have several disks containing important information about noncollege matters—for example, your family history, your music collection, and your personal finances.

Suppose that you're beginning to lose control and are no longer able to find things when you want them. A hard-disk drive would help. However, if a hard-disk drive suffers a head crash or other accident, you could lose all the programs and data on it. What kind of storage system should you get—hard disk, hard disk and magnetic tape backup (tape streamer), hard-disk cartridge, data-compression software and hardware, or optical disc?

2. *Looking for the right CD-ROM:* Perhaps you have had the difficulty of dealing with competing standards of media for something you want. Was a film you wanted to see available on Betamax but not on VHS videotape? Did a musical group have songs available on an LP or tape but not CD? Now you face a similar difficulty in evaluating the new storage medium of CD-ROM, for which competing versions exist. To help resolve the confusion, determine:

   a. How the CD-ROMs used for computer storage differ from those used as adjuncts to television sets, such as the CD-1 and CDTV.

   b. How the CD-ROMs normally associated with desktop computers differ from those used in the small electronic "book" players, such as the Data Discman put out by Sony.

   c. The difference between the CD-ROMs available for Macintosh and those available for IBM and IBM-compatible microcomputers.

3. *Obtaining a CD-ROM drive:* Suppose you have a microcomputer system that does not have a CD-ROM drive and that you would like to have one. You have three options: (1) purchase an external CD-ROM drive that connects to one of the ports in the back of your system unit; (2) purchase and install an internal CD-ROM directly into your system unit; or (3) purchase a new microcomputer system that has a CD-ROM drive.

   Research each of the three options and prepare a set of written guidelines that could be used to make the best choice.

4. *http://www.intergraph.com/stor.shtml* Large-capacity storage devices are sometimes referred to as mass storage devices. One manufacturer of these large-capacity devices is Intergraph. To learn more about mass storage, connect to Intergraph's home page using the Internet address given at the beginning of this question. Then expand your investigation on mass storage by using other Internet resources. (Hint: Use the Every Student's Internet Resource Guide: Computer Science and Computer Technology—Entry Number: 01.)

Secondary Storage

Primary storage in microcomputers is **volatile**; some things disappear when the power is turned off. Secondary storage is **nonvolatile**; it stores data and programs even after the power is turned off.

SECONDARY STORAGE

TYPE	ADVANTAGE	DISADVANTAGE	TYPICAL USE	COST/MEGABYTE
Floppy disk	Inexpensive, direct access, removable	Low capacity, slow access	Store files for word processors and spreadsheets	$1.00
Hard disk	Fast, direct access	Limited capacity	Store programs and data	$.40 to $.80
CD-ROM	High capacity, direct access	Slow access	Reference material	$.04 to $1.00
Magnetic tape	High capacity	Slow sequential data access	Backup programs and data	$.10 to $.40

FLOPPY DISK

Cover slides over to expose disk.

Floppy disks (disks, diskettes) are circular plastic disks. Two principal types are 3½-inch and 5¼-inch.

FLOPPY DISK CAPACITY

DESCRIPTION	BYTES
3½-inch	
Double-sided, double-density	720 KB
Double-sided, high-density	1.44 KB
Floptical	21 MB
5¼-inch	
Double-sided, double-density	360 KB
Double-sided, high-density	1.2 KB

The Disk Drive

- A floppy disk is inserted through a **drive gate** into a *disk drive*, which has an **access arm** equipped with **read-write heads** that move on the disk (**seek** operation), which is rotated to the proper position (**search** operation).
- The read-write head *reads* (obtains) data or programs from the disk and sends it to the CPU or *writes* (transfers) data from the CPU to the disk.

Parts of Floppy Disk

- Data is recorded on a disk's **tracks** (rings) and **sectors** (sections). In **soft-sectored disks,** tracks and sectors must be adapted to particular microcomputers by *formatting (initializing).*
- A disk is protected by the **jacket** (liner), paper envelope, and **write-protect notch** (covered by tab or shutter).

HARD DISK

Hard Disk

A **hard disk** is an enclosed disk drive that contains one or more metallic disks. Enclosing the disk in a sealed container prevents material entering that causes a **head crash.** Hard disks come in three forms:

- An **internal hard disk** has one or more metallic platters sealed inside a container. Hard disks have far more capacity than a floppy disk does.
- **Hard-disk cartridges** can be removed when they are filled or transported.
- Mini- and mainframe computers use **hard-disk packs,** which are hard disks consisting of several platters in a stack.

Performance Enhancements

- **Disk caching**—anticipates data needs by reading from hard disk to memory to reduce transfer rate of needed data.
- **Data compression (decompression)**—reduces amount of space required to store data and programs.
- **Redundant arrays of inexpensive disks (RAIDs)**—expands external storage by networking hard disks and grouping them so that they may be treated as a single large-capacity hard disk.

CD-ROM DRIVES

TYPE	FUNCTION
Single-speed	The original drive introduced in the mid 1980s; transfer rate of 150 KB per second; data retrieval was slow; poor sound and video capabilities
Double-speed	Introduced in 1991; transfer rate of 300 KB per second; widely used standard; acceptable data retrieval and sound production; video capabilities limited; too slow for most multimedia applications
Triple-speed	Introduced in 1993; transfer rate of 450 KB per second; also not quite fast enough for full motion video
Quad-speed	Also introduced in 1993; transfer rate of 600 KB; acceptable for full-motion video
Six-speed	Recently introduced, with faster speeds expected soon

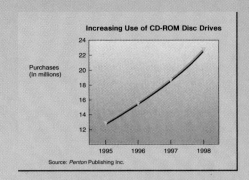

Increasing Use of CD-ROM Disc Drives

Purchases (In millions)

Source: *Penton* Publishing Inc.

OPTICAL DISCS

OPTICAL DISCS

DESCRIPTION	CAPACITY
CD-ROM	650 MB
CD-R	600–650 MB
Erasable	600–1000 MB

Optical Discs

An **optical disc** is a metallic disc that uses a laser beam for reading and writing. Three kinds are:

- **CD-ROM** (compact disc–read-only memory)—cannot be written on or erased by user **(read-only).**

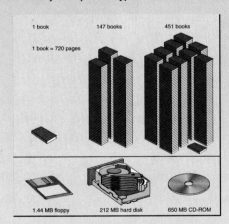

1 book   147 books   451 books

1 book = 720 pages

1.44 MB floppy   212 MB hard disk   650 MB CD-ROM

- **CD-R** (CD-recordable) or **WORM** (write once, read many)—can be written to one time, after which it cannot be erased by users but can be read many times without deterioration.
- **Erasable optical discs**—can be written on and erased and reused.

MAGNETIC TAPE

Magnetic Tape

Magnetic tape storage is mainly used to back up (duplicate) programs and data on disks. Two forms are:

- **Magnetic Tape Streamers (backup tape cartridge units)** consist of tape cartridges used to back up microcomputer hard disks.
- **Magnetic Tape Reels,** used to back up mini- and mainframe computer storage, run on **magnetic drives (magnetic tape units).**

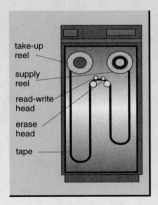

take-up reel

supply reel

read-write head

erase head

tape

Communications and Connectivity

A familiar instrument—the telephone—has extended our uses for the microcomputer enormously. With the telephone or other kinds of communications equipment, you can connect your microcomputer to other people and to other, larger computers. As we've mentioned earlier, this *connectivity* puts the power of a mainframe on your desk. The result is increased productivity—for you as an individual and for the groups and organizations of which you are a member. Connectivity has become particularly important in business, where individuals now find themselves connected in networks to other individuals and departments.

COMPETENCIES

After you have read this chapter, you should be able to:

1. Describe available communications resources and online services.

2. Describe the National Information Highway, the Internet, and the most common Internet applications.

3. Describe communications hardware, such as types of modems.

4. Describe the cable and air communications channels—telephone, coaxial, and fiber-optic cables; microwave relays; and satellites.

5. Discuss bandwidth, serial versus parallel transmission, direction of flow, modes of transmission, and protocols.

6. Explain network architecture—configurations and strategies.

7. Describe local area, metropolitan area, and wide area networks.

Imagine: You are a real estate salesperson, and the telephone in your car rings. It is a client who is on the phone in his car across town. He asks you about a certain property, and you agree to meet him there. After you go back to look at the property, you connect your laptop computer to your car phone. You then dial the multiple listing service and get information on the property. This is an example of the use of communications to expand computer capabilities.

In Chapter 2, you learned about communications software. In this chapter, you will learn about communications systems. **Data communications systems** are the electronic systems that transmit data over communications lines from one location to another. You might use data communications through your microcomputer to send information to a friend using another computer. You might work for an organization whose computer system is spread throughout a building, or even throughout the country or world. That is, all the parts—input and output units, processor, and storage devices—are in different places and linked by communications. Or you might use *telecommunications* lines—telephone lines—to tap into information located in an outside data bank. You could then transmit it to your microcomputer for your own reworking and analysis.

Data communications is now considered essential in business. As we will see, an important part of communications is the *network,* a system connecting two or more computers. A popular form of network is the *local area network (LAN).* In a LAN, computers are connected together within a limited area, such as within the same building. In one survey, over 80 percent responded that there was a local area network within their company or organization. There are many occasions when you and coworkers need a network to gain access to one another's information. Such information may be on sales, customers, prices, schedules, or products. The list is nearly endless.

Communications and Connectivity

With communications capability, microcomputer users can transmit and receive data and gain access to electronic information resources.

You may have a desktop microcomputer next to a telephone. You may (or may someday) have a laptop microcomputer and a cellular phone in your car. Or you may have a microcomputer that is directly connected to other computers without telephone lines at all. Whatever the case, communications systems present many opportunities for transmitting and receiving information, giving you access to many resources. This brings up the important revolution represented by this chapter, that of connectivity.

Connectivity means you can connect your microcomputer by telephone or other telecommunications links to other computers and information sources almost anywhere. With this connection, you are linked to the world of larger computers. This includes minicomputers and mainframes and their large storage devices, such as disk packs, and their enormous volumes of information. Thus, computer competence becomes a matter of knowing not only about microcomputers. You should also know something about larger computer systems and their information resources.

Let us consider the options that connectivity makes available to you. These include *fax machines, electronic bulletin boards, electronic mail, voice-messaging systems, shared resources,* and *online services.* (See Figure 8-1.)

FIGURE 8-1
Connectivity options.

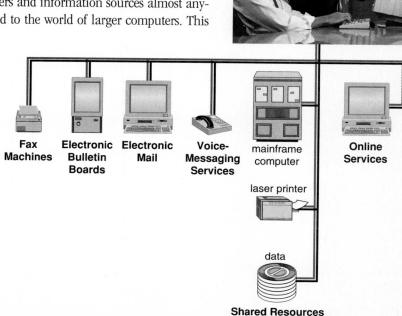

Fax Machines   Electronic Bulletin Boards   Electronic Mail   Voice-Messaging Services   mainframe computer   Online Services

laser printer

data

Shared Resources

Fax Machines

Fax machines—facsimile transmission machines—have become essential machines in almost all offices. (See Figure 8-2.) As we mentioned earlier, these devices scan the image of a document. They convert the image to signals that can be sent over a telephone line to a receiving machine. This machine prints the image out on paper. Microcomputers, using fax/modem circuit boards, can be used to send and receive fax messages.

Sending a document by fax is certainly faster—it arrives immediately—than any delivery service. It also is often cheaper than overnight delivery, unless you're sending more than 50 pages of a document. Almost every fax machine can exchange messages with every other fax machine. All you need is the receiving machine's phone number. It can transmit photographs and other artwork, as well as text in various typefaces.

If you are in the business of meeting deadlines—as most people are—a fax machine can be invaluable. Construction engineers can get cost estimates to major contractors. Lawyers can get contracts to other lawyers. Advertising people can get prospective ad layouts to their clients. Just as important, because people often respond better to pictures than to text, fax can get a picture to them quickly.

Electronic Bulletin Board Systems

This is an activity you can utilize yourself if you have access to a microcomputer and the necessary telephone links. **Electronic bulletin board systems (BBS)** are like public bulletin boards. You can post and read messages. These messages can be personal or intended for a group. The difference is that all the messages are electronic, and you need a microcomputer, telephone connection, and the electronic bulletin board's telephone number. The board's number connects you to a computer that receives messages, posts messages, and handles the details of administering the BBS. Such bulletin boards have been popular with microcomputer hobbyists and enthusiasts for many years. They are rapidly gaining favor with other people, too.

Bulletin boards exist for almost any subject. Many are concerned with new developments and problems related to particular brands of microcomputers. Others have to do with hobbies, such as rock music, science fiction, or genealogy. Still others serve special interests, such as political causes, or professional groups, such as lawyers. Finally, some companies offer bulletin boards as a means by which customers can get advice from other customers. They can also get advice from the company itself regarding a particular service or product. Finally, some companies use bulletin boards to communicate with employees working at home.

Electronic Mail

Also called **e-mail, electronic mail** resembles bulletin boards. (See Figure 8-3.) Often it uses a special communications line rather than a telephone line. In addition, electronic mail offers confidentiality. A **user name** and **password**—special number or letter sequences that limit access—are required to get into the

FIGURE 8-2
A fax machine.

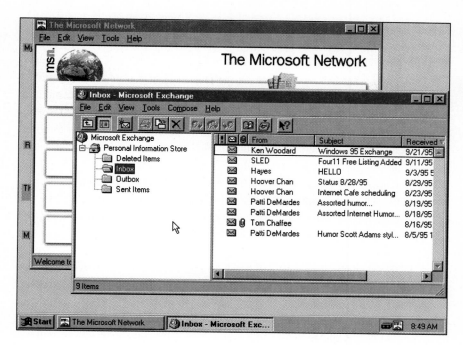

FIGURE 8-3
Microsoft Network's In-box.

"mailbox." The mailbox is simply a file stored on a computer system. Passwords are not limited to electronic mail. They are widely used to control access and use of restricted data and resources.

To send an electronic message, you dial the special number, specify the user name, password, and mailbox number, and type the message. You can also put the same message in several mailboxes at the same time. To access your own mailbox, dial the number of the e-mail system and type in your user name and password. You can look through the list of file names and transmission times of the messages. You then transfer to your own computer the messages you want to keep.

Electronic mail is used within companies to help employees exchange memos, set up meetings, and the like. It may also be used between companies. Sometimes outside electronic bulletin board services are used for these business purposes. We will further discuss electronic mail in the Internet Guide.

Voice-Messaging Systems

Voice-messaging systems are computer systems linked to telephones that convert the human voice into digital bits. They resemble conventional answering machines and also resemble electronic mail systems. However, they can receive large numbers of incoming calls and route them to the appropriate "voice mailboxes." They can deliver the same message to many people. They allow callers to leave "voice mail"—recorded voice messages. They can forward calls to your home or hotel, if you wish. When you check for your messages, you can speed through them or slow them down. You can dictate replies into the phone, and the system will send them out.

Shared Resources

An important aspect of connectivity is that it lets microcomputer users share expensive hardware. We have mentioned many of these: laser printers, chain printers, disk packs, and magnetic tape storage. Only in rare instances would a single microcomputer user need the use of, say, a disk pack. However, several microcomputers linked in a network make this option not only feasible but in many cases even essential. Communications networks also permit microcomputer users to share workstations, minicomputers, and mainframes. This is why we have stressed that it's important to know what these machines are.

Another important aspect of connectivity is the ability to share data. As we saw in Chapter 2, with a microcomputer you can have your own personal database. An example of such a database might be a collection of names and addresses. A *database,* as we mentioned, is a collection of integrated data. By "integrated," we mean the data consists of logically related files and records.

Your personal database might consist of data that only you use. However, it may also be data you share with others. The data might be stored on your microcomputer's hard disk. Or it might be located somewhere else. That is, you might use a shared database, like one a company might provide its employees so they can share information. This could be information stored on disk packs and accessible from the company's mainframe. You could gain access by using your microcomputer linked to your telephone and **downloading** selected data. That is, you could transfer the data from the larger computer to your microcomputer. Then you could process and manipulate the data as you chose. The reverse is **uploading**—transferring from your microcomputer to a mainframe or minicomputer. For example, a salesperson could record daily sales on a portable computer and upload monthly sales data to the company's mainframe.

Online Services

Several businesses offer services specifically for microcomputer users. Four well-known service providers are America Online, CompuServe, Microsoft Network, and AT&T Interchange. (See Figure 8-4.)

- **Teleshopping:** You dial into a database listing prices and descriptions of products such as appliances and clothes. You then order what you want and charge the purchase to a credit card number. The merchandise is delivered later by a package delivery service.

- **Home banking:** If you arrange it with your bank, you may be able to use your microcomputer to pay some bills. Such bills include those owed to big department stores and utility companies. You can also make loan payments and transfer money between accounts.

- **Investing:** You can get access to current prices of stocks and bonds and enter buy and sell orders.

- **Travel reservations:** Just like a travel agent, you can get information on airline schedules and fares. You can also order tickets, charging the purchase to your credit card.

See Figure 8-5 for a summary of the many connectivity options.

FIGURE 8-4
CompuServ's Basic Services.

FIGURE 8-5
Summary of connectivity options.

CONNECTIVITY OPTIONS

OPTION	FUNCTION
Fax machines	Convert images to signals and send them over telephone lines to receiving fax machines
Electronic bulletin boards	Provide forums on a variety of subjects available to telephone-linked microcomputer users
Electronic mail	Systems resembling bulletin boards but are restricted in access by passwords
Voice–mail systems	Convert a voice message to digital bits and distribute to many locations over telephone lines
Shared resources	Microcomputer users may share expensive hardware, data, and information
Online services	Provide wide range of activities including teleshopping, home banking, investments, and travel reservations services

National Information Highway and Internet

Internet is the foundation for future communication networks. Four applications: transfer electronic mail, participate in public discussions, copy files, and run programs. Two Internet utilities: Gopher and World Wide Web.

The **National Information Highway (NIH)** is also known as the **National Information Infrastructure (NII)** and as the **information superhighway.** These popular phrases are used to describe the future of communication networks and computers. Legislation proposed and championed by Vice President Gore has laid the foundation for this billion-dollar project. Because of this legislation, Congress is now encouraging private investment, competition, and two-way universal access for the NIH. Such access would make computing resources available to everyone.

Internet

At the forefront of today's NIH is the **Internet.** It is a huge computer network available to nearly everyone who has a microcomputer and a means to connect to it. Once on the Internet it seems like you are on a single giant computer that branches all over the world. It is an unprecedented resource for information about an infinite number of topics. Also, it connects people as close as the next office and as far as halfway around the world. (See Figure 8-6.)

FIGURE 8-6
Internet connections around the world.

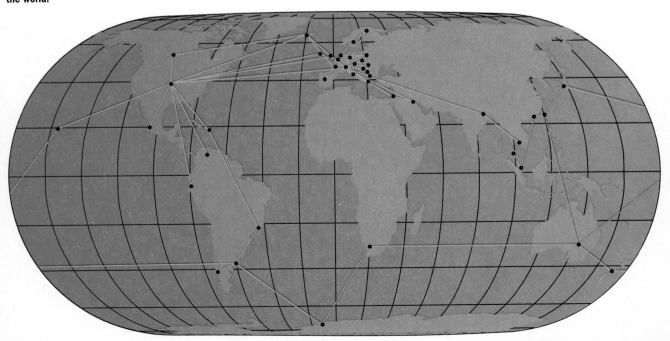

Technically, the Internet is a network connecting thousands of other networks and millions of computers; however, it represents much more. It is today's means to access and share knowledge. It is also tomorrow's foundation for a global community of users.

Applications

There are any number of uses for the Internet. The four most common applications are transferring electronic mail (e-mail), participating in public discussion groups, copying files, and running programs on a remote computer.

- **Electronic mail:** Sending and receiving e-mail is the most popular Internet service. You can send e-mail to anyone in the world if you know their e-mail address and have access to the Internet. You can even send and receive e-mail from other commercial service networks like America Online.

- **Public discussion groups:** You can join and listen to discussions and debates on a wide variety of topics on the Internet. This application is a variation of e-mail that uses a system called **UseNet.** This system creates an electronic forum of interested parties in a particular subject known as a *newsgroup.* There is an enormous number of newsgroups. They range from general interest topics such as current events and movie reviews, to specialized forums like computer trouble-shooting and Star Trek.

- **Files from remote databases:** The Internet service called **FTP** (file transfer protocol) lets you look at the names of files and copy files from other computers on the Internet. There are over 1500 FTP sites that have access to millions of publicly available files. These files can be downloaded to your microcomputer. FTP allows access to a large number of databases, from stock market quotations to personal income census data.

- **Programs on remote computers:** The Internet service called **Telnet** makes your computer a terminal for other computers on the Internet. It enables you to run selected programs from other computers. For example, you could access the NASA SPACElink computer. This Telnet link was originally designed for science teachers and is now available to the general public through the Internet. With it, you can learn about NASA's history, read about many exploration plans, view animated clips, and perform other space-related activities. Of course, not all Telnet connections are free. Medline, for example, is a fee-based application containing over 4000 medical journals and publications. You may have access to this application and others through a library or university near you.

See Figure 8-7 for a summary of Internet applications.

Utilities

Fortunately, there are several programs or utilities available to help you locate and use the Internet resources. Two of the most widely used Internet utility programs are gopher and World Wide Web.

- **Gopher: Gophers** are programs that help individuals on the Internet access other computers on the Internet. There are two types of gopher programs. One type, called the gopher client, runs on the computer requesting access. This program

INTERNET APPLICATIONS

APPLICATION	DESCRIPTION
Electronic mail	Send and receive e-mail worldwide
Public discussion	Participate in discussions and debates using UseNet newsgroups
File transfer	Locate and copy selected files using FTP
Run programs	Allow terminal access to locate and run programs using Telnet

FIGURE 8-7
Summary of common Internet applications.

uses Telnet to request access. Once access is granted, the second type—the *gopher server*—displays a menu system allowing access to the computer's available resources. There are hundreds of public computer systems on the Internet that can be accessed using gopher software.

■ **World Wide Web:** The **World Wide Web** is also known as **WWW, W3,** and the **Web.** Like gopher, WWW helps users search for and retrieve information on the Internet. It uses clients and servers to provide menus to access a computer's resources. However, WWW goes one step further by providing **hypertext links** that allow users to effortlessly jump from one computer's resources to another computer's resources. This is accomplished using special software called **browsers.** Three well-known browsers are Lynx, Mosaic, and Netscape.

User Connection

Microcomputers require modems to send and receive messages over telephone lines.

A great deal of computer communications is over telephone lines. However, because the telephone was originally designed for voice transmission, telephones typically send and receive **analog signals.** (See Figure 8-8.) Computers, in contrast, send and receive **digital signals.** These represent the presence or absence of an electronic pulse—the on/off binary signals we mentioned in Chapter 5. To convert the digital signals of your microcomputer to analog and vice versa, you need a modem.

Modems

The word *modem* is short for *"modulator-demodulator."* **Modulation** is the name of the process of converting from digital to analog. **Demodulation** is the process of converting from analog to digital. The modem enables digital microcomputers to communicate across analog telephone lines. Both voice communications and data communications can be carried over the same telephone line.

The speed with which modems transmit data varies. Communications speed is often measured in **baud rate.** Baud rate represents the number of changes in the electrical state in the line per second. Unfortunately, this measure can be misleading. At low speeds, baud rate is equivalent to *bits per second (bps).* However, at higher speeds, baud rate is not equal to bits per second. For this reason, most communications professionals prefer to measure modem speed in bits per second.

FIGURE 8-8
Analog versus digital signals.

■ ■ ■ ■ ■ ■ ■ ■

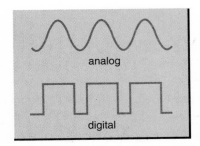

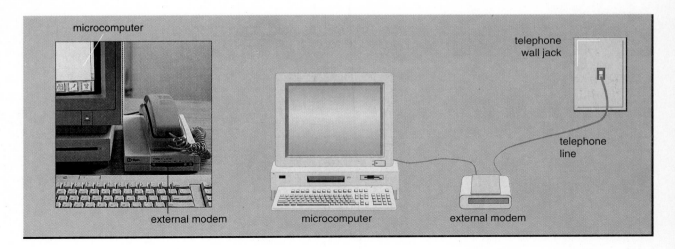

microcomputer

telephone wall jack

telephone line

external modem

microcomputer

external modem

FIGURE 8-9
An external direct-connect modem.

The most popular microcomputer speeds are 9600, 14,400, and 28,800 bps. The higher the speed, the faster you can transmit a document—and therefore the cheaper your line costs. For example, transmitting a 20-page single-spaced report could take nearly 1½ minutes at 9600 bps and less than 30 seconds at 28,800 bps.

Types of Modems

The four types of modems are external, internal, wireless, and fax.

■ The **external modem** stands apart from the computer and is connected by a cable to the computer's serial port. Another cable connects the modem to the telephone wall jack. (See Figure 8-9.) Some modems weigh as little as 3 ounces, making them practical for use with portable computers.

■ The **internal modem** consists of a plug-in circuit board inside the system unit. A cable directly connects the computer's serial port to the telephone wall jack. Internal modems are frequently used in portable computers where uploading and downloading files is common. They are generally less expensive than external modems.

■ The **wireless modem** is very similar to the external modem. (See Figure 8-10.) It connects to the computer's serial port. Unlike an external modem, it does not connect to telephone lines. Rather, wireless modems receive through the air. This is a new type of modem using new technology. Although not as fast as the other modems, wireless modems are becoming popular with users of portable computers.

■ A **fax modem** is a special modem that allows you to send and/or receive faxes. With the other modems, signals represent bits—0s and 1s combined to signify letters and numbers typically using an ASCII code. A fax modem uses the signals to represent a graphic image of a page. When a fax is received, the data is stored on the hard disk. The fax can be viewed on the screen or printed out.

FIGURE 8-10
A wireless modem.

Not all computer communications require a modem to convert from digital to analog and back. Computer systems connected by coaxial or fiber-optic cables can transmit digital data directly through these channels.

FIGURE 8-11
Comparing cable size and capacity.

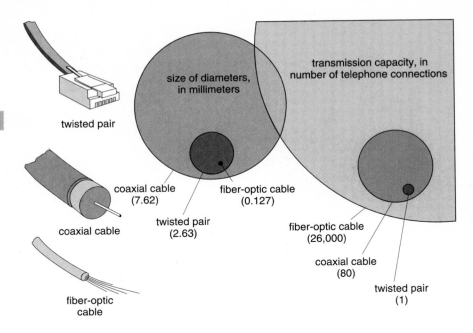

twisted pair

coaxial cable

fiber-optic cable

size of diameters, in millimeters

transmission capacity, in number of telephone connections

coaxial cable (7.62)

fiber-optic cable (0.127)

twisted pair (2.63)

fiber-optic cable (26,000)

coaxial cable (80)

twisted pair (1)

Communications Channels

Data may flow through five kinds of communications channels: telephone lines, coaxial cable, fiber-optic cable, microwave, and satellite.

The two ways of connecting microcomputers with each other and with other equipment are through the cable and through the air. Specifically, five kinds of technology are used to transmit data. These are telephone lines (twisted pair), coaxial cable, fiber-optic cable, microwave, and satellite. The diameters and transmission capacities of the three kinds of cable are compared in Figure 8-11.

Telephone Lines
Most telephone lines you see strung on poles consist of cables made up of hundreds of copper wires, called **twisted pairs.** A single twisted pair culminates in a wall jack into which you can plug your phone. Telephone lines have been the standard transmission medium for years for both voice and data. However, they are now being phased out by more technically advanced and reliable media.

Coaxial Cable
Coaxial cable, a high-frequency transmission cable, replaces the multiple wires of telephone lines with a single solid copper core. In terms of number of telephone connections, a coaxial cable has 80 times the transmission capacity of twisted pair. Coaxial cable is often used to link parts of a computer system in one building.

Fiber-Optic Cable
In **fiber-optic cable,** data is transmitted as pulses of light through tubes of glass. In terms of number of telephone connections, fiber-optic cable has 26,000 times the transmission capacity of twisted pair. (See Figure 8-11.) However, it is signifi-

cantly smaller. Indeed, a fiber-optic tube can be half the diameter of a human hair. Although limited in the distance they can carry information, fiber-optic cables have several advantages. Such cables are immune to electronic interference, which makes them more secure. They are also lighter and less expensive than coaxial cable and are more reliable at transmitting data. They transmit information using beams of light at light speeds instead of pulses of electricity, making them far faster than copper cable. Fiber-optic cable is rapidly replacing twisted-pair telephone lines.

Microwave

In this communications channel, the medium is not a solid substance but rather the air itself. **Microwaves** are high-frequency radio waves that travel in straight lines through the air. Because the waves cannot bend with the curvature of the earth, they can be transmitted only over short distances. Thus, microwave is a good medium for sending data between buildings in a city or on a large college campus. For longer distances, the waves must be relayed by means of "dishes," or antennas. These can be installed on towers, high buildings, and mountaintops, for example. (See Figure 8-12.)

FIGURE 8-12
Microwave transmission.

Satellites

Orbiting about 22,000 miles above the earth, **satellites** are also used as microwave relay stations. Many of these are offered by Intelsat, the *In*ternational *Tel*ecommunications *Sat*ellite Consortium, which is owned by 114 governments and forms a worldwide communications system. Teledesic Corporation announced plans to launch 840 satellites with the capability of linking 95 percent of the earth's surface. Satellites rotate at a precise point and speed above the earth. This makes them appear stationary so they can amplify and relay microwave signals from one transmitter on the ground to another. (See Figure 8-13.) Thus, satellites can be used to send large volumes of data. Their only drawback is that bad weather can sometimes interrupt the flow of data.

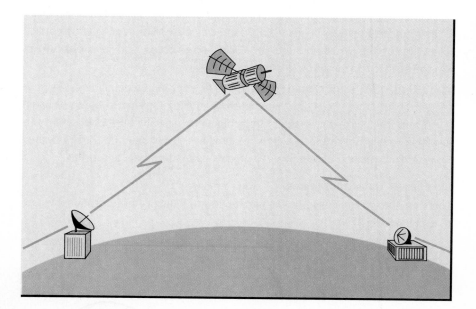

FIGURE 8-13
Satellite relaying microwave signals from earth.

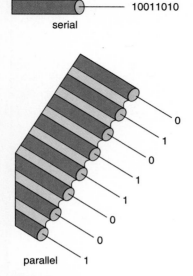

serial

10011010

0

1

0

1

1

0

0

parallel 1

FIGURE 8-14
Serial versus parallel
transmission.

Data Transmission

**Several technical matters affect data communications. They are
bandwidth, serial versus parallel transmission, direction of flow, modes of
transmission, and protocols.**

Several factors affect how data is transmitted. They include speed or bandwidth, serial or parallel transmission, direction of data flow, modes of transmitting data, and protocols.

Bandwidth

The different communications channels have different data transmission speeds. This bits-per-second transmission capability of a channel is called its **bandwidth.** Bandwidth may be of three types:

- **Voiceband: Voiceband** is the bandwidth of a standard telephone line and used often for microcomputer transmission; typical speeds are 9600 to 28,800, although with special equipment much higher speeds are possible.

- **Medium band:** The **medium band** is the bandwidth of special leased lines used mainly with minicomputers and mainframe computers; the bps is 56,000—264 million.

- **Broadband:** The **broadband** is the bandwidth that includes microwave, satellite, coaxial cable, and fiber-optic channels. It is used for very high speed computers whose processors communicate directly with each other. It is in the range of 56,000—30 billion bps.

Serial and Parallel Transmission

Data travels in two ways: serially and in parallel. (See Figure 8-14.)

- In **serial data transmission,** bits flow in a series or continuous stream, like cars crossing a one-lane bridge. Serial transmission is the way most data is sent over telephone lines. Thus, the plug-in board making up the serial connector in a microcomputer's modem is usually called a *serial port.* More technical names for the serial port are **RS-232C connector** and **asynchronous communications port.**

- With **parallel data transmission,** bits flow through separate lines simultaneously. In other words, they resemble cars moving together at the same speed on a multilane freeway. Parallel transmission is typically limited to communications over short distances and is not used over telephone lines. It is, however, a standard method of sending data from a computer's CPU to a printer.

Direction of Data Transmission

There are three directions or modes of data flow in a data communications system. (See Figure 8-15.)

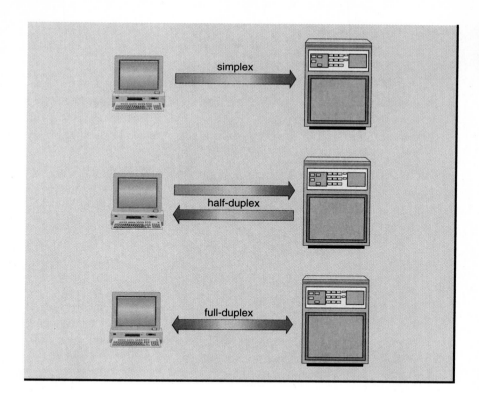

FIGURE 8-15
Simplex, half-duplex, and full-duplex communication.

- **Simplex communication** resembles the movement of cars on a one-way street. Data travels in one direction only. It is not frequently used in data communications systems today. One instance in which it is used may be in point-of-sale (POS) terminals in which data is being entered only.

- In **half-duplex communication,** data flows in both directions, but not simultaneously. That is, data flows in only one direction at any one time. This resembles traffic on a one-lane bridge. Half-duplex is very common and is frequently used for linking microcomputers by telephone lines to other microcomputers, minicomputers, and mainframes. Thus, when you dial into an electronic bulletin board through your microcomputer, you may well be using half-duplex communication.

- In **full-duplex communication,** data is transmitted back and forth at the same time, like traffic on a two-way street. It is clearly the fastest and most efficient form of two-way communication. However, it requires special equipment and is used primarily for mainframe communications. An example is the weekly sales figures and delivery schedules that a supermarket or regional office sends and receives from its corporate headquarters in another state.

Modes of Transmitting Data

Data may be sent by asynchronous or synchronous transmission. (See Figure 8-16.)

■ In **asynchronous transmission,** the method frequently used with microcomputers, data is sent and received one byte at a time. Asynchronous transmission is often used for terminals with slow speeds. Its advantage is that the data can be transmitted whenever convenient for the sender. Its disadvantage is a relatively slow rate of data transfer.

■ **Synchronous transmission** is used to transfer great quantities of information by sending several bytes or a block at a time. For the data transmission to occur, the sending and receiving of the blocks of bytes must occur at carefully timed intervals. Thus, the system requires a synchronized clock. Its advantage is that data can be sent very quickly. Its disadvantage is the cost of the required equipment.

Protocols

For data transmission to be successful, sender and receiver must follow a set of communication rules for the exchange of information. These rules for exchanging data between computers are known as the line **protocol.** A communications software package like Crosstalk helps define the protocol, such as speeds and modes, for connecting with another microcomputer.

When different types of microcomputers are connected in a network, the protocols can become very complex. Obviously, for the connections to work, these network protocols must adhere to certain standards. The first commercially available set of standards was IBM's Systems Network Architecture (SNA). This works for IBM's own equipment, but other machines won't necessarily communicate with them.

The International Standards Organization has defined a set of communications protocols called the Open Systems Interconnection (OSI). The purpose of the OSI model is to identify functions provided by any network. It separates each network's

FIGURE 8-16
Asynchronous and synchronous communication.

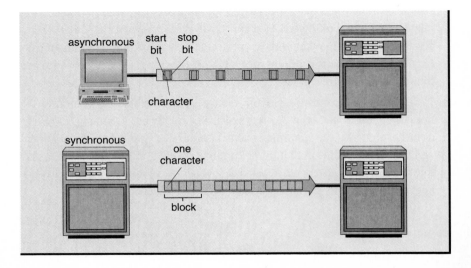

functions into seven "layers" of protocols, or communication rules. When two network systems communicate, their corresponding layers may exchange data. This assumes that the microcomputers and other equipment on each network have implemented the same functions and interfaces.

Network Architecture

Network architecture describes how a computer network is configured and what strategies are used.

Communications channels can be connected in different arrangements, or *networks,* to suit different users' needs. A *computer network* is a communications system connecting two or more computers that work together to exchange information and share resources. **Network architecture** describes how the network is arranged and how the resources are coordinated and shared.

Terms

There are a number of specialized terms that describe computer networks. Some terms often used with networks are:

- **Node:** A node is any device that is connected to a network. It could be a computer, printer, or data storage device.

- **Client:** A client is a node that requests and uses resources available from other nodes. Typically, a client is a user's microcomputer.

- **Server:** A server is a node that shares resources with other nodes. Depending on the resources shared, it may be called a file server, printer server, communication server, or database server.

- **Network Operating System (NOS):** Microcomputer operating systems like DOS and Windows interact with an application and a computer. On the other hand, network operating systems control and coordinate the activities between computers on a network. These activities include electronic communication and the sharing of information and resources.

- **Distributed processing:** In a distributed processing system, computing power is located and shared at different locations. This type of system is common in decentralized organizations where divisional offices have their own computer systems. The computer systems in the divisional offices are networked to the organization's main or centralized computer.

- **Host computer:** A host computer is a large centralized computer, usually a minicomputer or a mainframe.

A network may consist only of microcomputers, or it may integrate microcomputers or other devices with larger computers. Networks can be controlled by all nodes working together equally or by specialized nodes coordinating and supplying all resources. Networks may be simple or complex, self-contained or dispersed over a large geographical area.

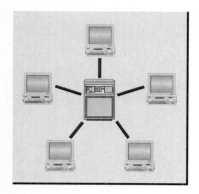

FIGURE 8-17
Star network.

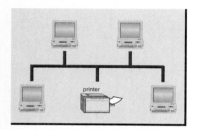

FIGURE 8-18
Bus network.

Configurations

A network can be arranged or configured in several different ways. This arrangement is called the network's **topology.** The four principal network topologies are star, bus, ring, and hierarchical.

In a **star network,** a number of small computers or peripheral devices are linked to a central unit. (See Figure 8-17.) This central unit may be a *host computer* or a *file server.*

All communications pass through this central unit. Control is maintained by **polling.** That is, each connecting device is asked ("polled") whether it has a message to send. Each device is then in turn allowed to send its message.

One particular advantage of the star form of network is that it can be used to provide a **time-sharing system.** That is, several users can share resources ("time") on a central computer. The star is a common arrangement for linking several microcomputers to a mainframe that allows access to an organization's database.

In a **bus network,** each device in the network handles its own communications control. There is no host computer. All communications travel along a common connecting cable called a **bus.** (See Figure 8-18.) As the information passes along the bus, it's examined by each device to see if the information is intended for it.

The bus network is typically used when only a few microcomputers are to be linked together. This arrangement is common in systems for electronic mail or for sharing data stored on different microcomputers. The bus network is not as efficient as the star network for sharing common resources. (This is because the bus network is not a direct link to the resource.) However, a bus network is less expensive and is in very common use.

In a **ring network,** each device is connected to two other devices, forming a ring. (See Figure 8-19.) There is no central file server or computer. Messages are passed around the ring until they reach the correct destination. With microcomputers, the ring arrangement is the least frequently used of the four networks. However, it often is used to link mainframes, especially over wide geographical areas. These mainframes tend to operate fairly autonomously. They perform most or all of their own processing and only occasionally share data and programs with other mainframes.

A ring network is useful in a decentralized organization because it makes possible a *distributed data processing system.* That is, computers can perform processing tasks at their own dispersed locations. However, they can also share programs, data, and other resources with each other.

The **hierarchical network**—also called a **hybrid network**—consists of several computers linked to a central host computer, just like a star network. However, these other computers are also hosts to other, smaller computers or to peripheral devices. (See Figure 8-20.)

Thus, the host at the top of the hierarchy could be a mainframe. The computers below the mainframe could be minicomputers, and those below, microcomputers. The hierarchical network allows various computers to share databases, processing power, and different output devices.

A hierarchical network is useful in centralized organizations. For example, different departments within an organization may have individual microcomputers connected to departmental minicomputers. The minicomputers in turn may be connected to the corporation's mainframe, which contains data and programs accessible to all.

Strategies

Every network has a strategy or way of coordinating the sharing of information and resources. The most common network strategies are terminal, peer-to-peer, and client/server systems.

In a **terminal network system,** processing power is centralized in one large computer, usually a mainframe. The nodes connected to this host computer are terminals with little or no processing capabilities. The star and hierarchical networks are typical configurations with UNIX as the operating system.

Most airline reservation systems are terminal systems. A large central computer maintains all the airline schedules, rates, seat availability, and so on. Travel agents use terminals to connect to the central computer and use it to schedule reservations. Although the tickets may be printed along with travel itineraries at the agent's desk, nearly all processing is done at the central computer.

Some of the advantages of terminal network systems are centralized location and control of technical personnel, software, and data. One disadvantage is the lack of control and flexibility for the end user. Another disadvantage is that terminal systems do not use the processing power available with microcomputers. Once very popular, most new systems do not use the terminal strategy.

In a **peer-to-peer network system,** nodes can act as both servers and clients. For example, one microcomputer can *obtain* files located on another microcomputer and can also *provide* files to other microcomputers. A typical configuration for a peer-to-peer system is the bus network. Commonly used network operating systems are Artisoft LANtastic, Apple's Macintosh Peer-to-Peer LANs, Novell's NetWare Lite, and Microsoft's Windows for Workgroups.

There are several advantages to using this type of strategy. The networks are inexpensive and easy to install, and they usually work well for smaller systems with less than ten nodes. As the number of nodes increases, however, the performance of the network declines. Another disadvantage is the lack of powerful management software to effectively monitor a large network's activities. For these reasons, peer-to-peer networks are typically used by small networks.

Client/server network systems use one powerful computer to coordinate and supply services to all other nodes on the network. The server provides access to centralized resources such as databases, application software, and hardware. This strategy is based on specialization. Server nodes coordinate and supply specialized services, and client nodes request the services. Commonly used network operating systems are Novell's NetWare, IBM's LAN Server, Banyan Vines, and Microsoft's LAN Manager and Windows NT.

One advantage of client/server network systems is their ability to handle very large networks efficiently. Another advantage is the powerful network management software that monitors and controls the network's activities. The major disadvantages are the cost of installation and maintenance.

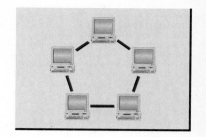

FIGURE 8-19
Ring network.

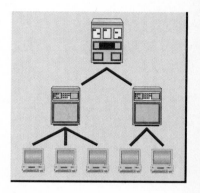

FIGURE 8-20
Hierarchical network.

Computer networks in organizations have evolved over time. Most large organizations have a wide range of different network configurations, operating systems, and strategies. These organizations are moving toward integrating or connecting all of these networks together. That way, a user on one network can access resources available throughout the company. This is called **enterprise computing.**

Network Types

Communications networks differ in geographical size. Three important types are LANs, MANs, and WANs.

Clearly, different types of channels—cable or air—allow different kinds of networks to be formed. Telephone lines, for instance, may connect communications equipment within the same building. In fact, many new buildings—called *smart buildings*—have coaxial or fiber-optic cable installed inside the walls. This makes it easy to form communications networks.

Networks may also be citywide and even international, using both cable and air connections. Here let us distinguish among three types: *local area networks, metropolitan area networks,* and *wide area networks.*

Local Area Networks

Networks with computers and peripheral devices in close physical proximity—within the same building, for instance—are called **local area networks (LANs).** Linked by cable—telephone, coaxial, or fiber-optic—LANs often use a bus form of organization.

Our illustration shows an example of a LAN. (See Figure 8-21.) This typical arrangement has two benefits. People can share different equipment, which lowers the cost of equipment. For instance, here the four microcomputers share the laser printer and the file server, which are expensive pieces of hardware. (Individual microcomputers many times also have their own less expensive printers, such as the dot-matrix printer shown in our illustration.) Other equipment may also be added to the LAN—for instance, mini- or mainframe computers or optical-disc storage devices.

Note that the LAN shown in our illustration also features a **network gateway.** A LAN may be linked to other LANs or to larger networks in this manner. With the gateway, one LAN may be connected to the LAN of another office group. It may also be connected to others in the wider world, even if their configurations are different. Alternatively, a network bridge would be used to connect networks with the same configurations.

Experts predict great growth of microcomputer LANs. (See Figure 8-22.)

Metropolitan Area Networks

The next step up from the LAN might be the **MAN**—the **metropolitan area network.** These networks are used as links between office buildings in a city. *Cellular phone systems* expand the flexibility of MANs by allowing links to car phones and portable phones.

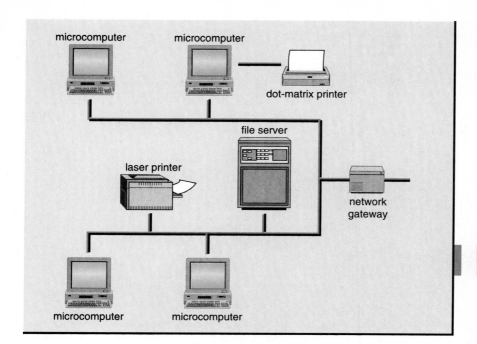

FIGURE 8-21
A local area network that includes a file server and network gateway.

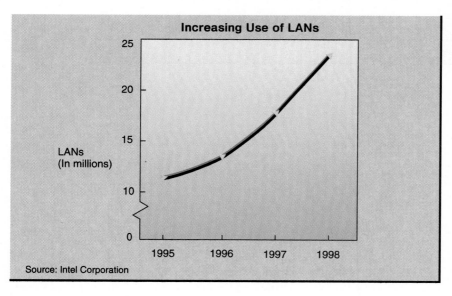

FIGURE 8-22
Local area network usage— past, present, and future.

Wide Area Networks

Wide area networks (WANs) are countrywide and worldwide networks. Among other kinds of channels, they use microwave relays and satellites to reach users over long distances—for example, from Los Angeles to Paris. (See Figure 8-23.) One of the most widely used WANs is the Internet, which allows users to connect to other users and facilities worldwide.

The primary difference between a LAN, MAN, and WAN is the geographical range. Each may have various combinations of hardware, such as microcomputers, minicomputers, mainframes, and various peripheral devices.

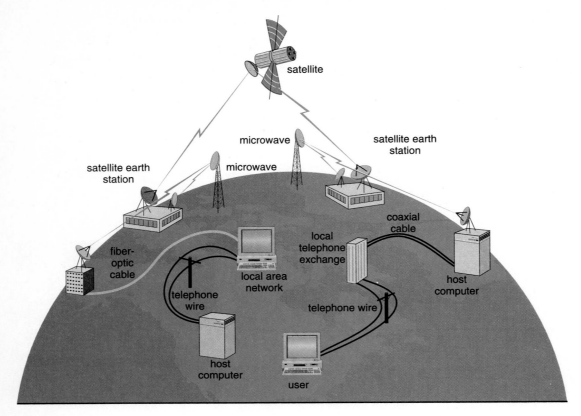

FIGURE 8-23
Wide area network.

A Look at the Future

New developments in hardware, the telephone system, and the National Information Highway suggest new trends: fewer "standalone computers," the era of the portable office, and downsized applications.

The next decade will see phenomenal changes in the area of communications. Two important developments will be the expansion of the Integrated Services Digital Network (ISDN) and Asynchronous Transfer Mode (ATM). In use in the United States since 1988, ISDN utilizes a set of technologies and international-exchange standards that will completely digitize today's telephone system. ATM extends ISDN's capability by providing even faster data transfer using public telephone lines. In early 1994, long distance telephone providers U.S. West and Sprint agreed to supply ATM services countrywide. These developments promise to support data, voice, and video transmission across the country. ATM is expected to be widely used by multimedia specialists. ISDN is expected to have more general use in smaller organizations and home offices.

What do these trends suggest? First, the "standalone" computer—one that isn't connected to any network—will become a thing of the past. Second, we have arrived at the era of the *portable office*. Hooking a portable computer or fax machine to a network while you are traveling makes you more efficient. Third, we are clearly at the point of so-called *downsized applications.* That is, many applications that were once available only on mainframes and minicomputers are now possible on network-linked microcomputers.

KEY TERMS

analog signal (164)

asynchronous communications port (168)

asynchronous transmission (170)

bandwidth (168)

baud rate (164)

broadband (168)

browser (164)

bus (172)

bus network (172)

client/server network system (173)

coaxial cable (166)

data communications system (156)

demodulation (164)

digital signal (164)

downloading (160)

electronic bulletin board system (158)

electronic mail (158)

e-mail (158)

enterprise computing (174)

external modem (165)

fax machine (158)

fax modem (165)

fiber-optic cable (166)

FTP (163)

full-duplex communication (169)

gopher (163)

half-duplex communication (169)

hierarchical network (172)

hybrid network (172)

hypertext link (164)

information superhighway (162)

internal modem (165)

Internet (162)

local area network (LAN) (174)

medium band (168)

metropolitan area network (MAN) (174)

microwave (167)

modulation (164)

National Information Highway (NIH) (162)

National Information Infrastructure (NII) (162)

network architecture (171)

network gateway (174)

parallel data transmission (168)

password (158)

peer-to-peer network system (173)

polling (172)

protocol (170)

ring network (172)

RS-232C connector (168)

satellite (167)

serial data transmission (168)

simplex communication (169)

star network (172)

synchronous transmission (170)

Telnet (163)

terminal network system (173)

time-sharing system (172)

topology (172)

twisted pair (166)

uploading (160)

UseNet (163)

user name (158)

voiceband (168)

voice-messaging system (159)

wide area network (WAN) (175)

wireless modem (165)

World Wide Web, WWW, W3, the Web (164)

REVIEW QUESTIONS

True/False

1. A local area network connects two or more computers within a limited area, such as within the same building.
2. Modems are used to convert data on a CD-ROM to an internal hard disk.
3. Frequently, computer communications over telephone lines require a modem.
4. In half-duplex communication, data flows in both directions at the same time.
5. In a client/server system, each node on the network has equal responsibility for coordinating the network's activities.

Multiple Choice

1. A special sequence of numbers or letters that limits access to electronic mail boxes is a:
   a. combination   d. password
   b. code   e. modem
   c. fax
2. Transferring data from a larger computer to your microcomputer is called:
   a. a LAN   d. networking
   b. time-sharing   e. uploading
   c. downloading
3. What communications channel transfers data as pulses of light?
   a. telephone lines   d. microwave
   b. coaxial cable   e. satellite
   c. fiber-optic cable
4. Rules for exchanging data on a network:
   a. protocol
   b. asynchronous transmission
   c. configuration
   d. channel
   e. serial transmission
5. A system frequently used in decentralized organizations in which computing power is located and shared at different sites:
   a. client/server   d. mainframe
   b. ring   e. distributed
   c. centralized

Fill in the Blank

1. _____ systems are computer systems linked to telephones that convert the human voice into digital bits.

2. Transferring data from your microcomputer to a minicomputer or mainframe is called _____.

3. Because _____ travel in straight lines through the air and cannot bend with the curvature of the earth, they can transmit data only over short distances.

4. A _____ _____ system controls and coordinates the activities on a network.

5. _____ are countrywide and worldwide networks that connect users over long distances.

Open Ended

1. What are electronic bulletin boards? How do they differ from electronic mail systems?

2. List and describe the five kinds of communications channels.

3. What are the differences between a terminal, a peer-to-peer, and a client/server system?

4. Describe the difference between simplex, half-duplex, and full-duplex communication.

5. Discuss the four basic network configurations.

DISCUSSION QUESTIONS AND PROJECTS

1. *Electronic bulletin boards:* Unquestionably there is an area of personal interest to you that is available on an electronic bulletin board. A glance at one local microcomputer publication shows bulletin boards available on such subjects as sports, restaurants, politics, religion, business opportunities, music, mental health, drug recovery, alternative lifestyles, and many other topics.

   What kind of electronic bulletin board would be of interest to you? See if you can find a printed list of bulletin boards in a local microcomputer publication. Or try contacting a users' group for help. Users' groups are clubs or volunteer organizations. Their members meet to help each other solve problems or share interests regarding particular personal computers.

2. *http://sunsite.nus.sg/pub/slip*   One of the most common ways to gain access to the Internet is through a provider who has a direct connection to the Internet. This type of connection requires special software called SLIP or PPP. Use the Internet to learn more about SLIP and PPP. Start with the Internet address above and then expand your search using other Internet resources. (Hint: Use the Every Student's Internet Resource Guide: Computer Science and Computer Technology—Entry Number: 01 and/or Entry Number: 02.)

Communications and Connectivity

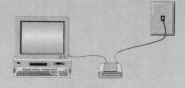

Data communications systems are the electronic systems that transmit data over communications lines from one location to another.

NATIONAL INFORMATION HIGHWAY AND INTERNET

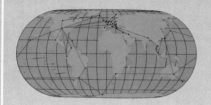

Internet

At the **Internet** is a worldwide computer network that is at the forefront of the **National Information Highway (NIH).**

Internet Applications

INTERNET APPLICATIONS

APPLICATION	DESCRIPTION
Electronic mail	Send and receive e-mail worldwide
Public discussion	Participate in discussions and debates using UseNet newsgroups
File transfer	Locate and copy selected files using FTP
Run programs	Allow terminal access to locate and run programs using Telnet

Utilities

Two widely known and used Internet utility programs:

- **Gophers** are programs to access computers on the Internet. **Gopher clients** request access. **Gopher servers** provide access by displaying menus.
- **Archies** are programs to help locate and copy files from **Archie servers.**

USER CONNECTION

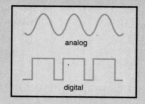

analog

digital

Telephones typically send and receive **analog signals.** Computers send and receive **digital signals.**

Modems and Communications Speeds

- A *modem* ("*mo*dulator *dem*odulator") converts digital to analog and vice versa. **Modulation**—digital to analog. **Demodulation**—analog to digital.
- Popular speeds are 2400 and 9600 bits per second.

Types of Modems

- **External modem**—outside system cabinet and connected by cable.
- **Internal modem**—plug-in circuit board inside system unit.
- **Wireless modem**—does not connect to telephone line, receives data through the air.
- **Fax modem**—unlike other modems, fax modems send and receive signals that represent graphic images.

COMMUNICATIONS CHANNELS

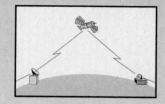

Data may be transmitted by:

Telephone Lines

Most phone lines have consisted of copper wires called **twisted pairs.**

Coaxial Cable

Coaxial cable is high-frequency, solid core cable.

Fiber-Optic Cable

Fiber-optic cable transmits data as pulses of light through tubes of glass.

Microwave

Microwaves are high-frequency radio waves that travel in a straight line.

Satellites

Satellites act as microwave relay stations rotating above the earth.

CONNECTIVITY OPTIONS

OPTION	FUNCTION
Fax machines	Convert images to signals and send them over telephone lines to receiving fax machines
Electronic bulletin boards	Provide forums on a variety of subjects available to telephone-linked microcomputer users
Electronic mail	Systems resembling bulletin boards but are restricted in access by passwords
Voice–mail systems	Convert a voice message to digital bits and distribute to many locations over telephone lines
Shared resources	Microcomputer users may share expensive hardware, data, and information
Online services	Provide wide range of activities including teleshopping, home banking, investments, and travel reservations services

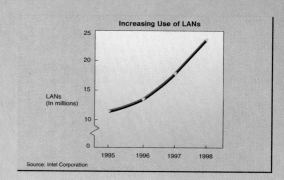

Increasing Use of LANs

LANs (In millions)

Source: Intel Corporation

DATA TRANSMISSION

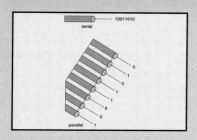

Data transmission factors:

Bandwidth

Bandwidth may be **voiceband, medium band,** or **broadband.**

Serial and Parallel Transmission

With **serial data transmission,** bits flow in a continuous stream. With **parallel data transmission,** bits flow through separate lines simultaneously.

Direction of Data Transmission

Three directions of data flow are **simplex communication**—one direction only, **half-duplex communication**—both directions but not simultaneously, and **full-duplex communication**—both directions at the same time.

Modes of Transmitting Data

Two modes are **asynchronous**—data is sent and received one byte at a time—and **synchronous**—several bytes (a block) are sent at one time.

Protocols

A **protocol** defines rules by which senders and receivers may exchange information.

NETWORK ARCHITECTURE

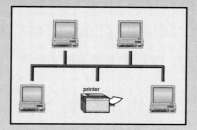

Network architecture describes how a computer network is configured and what strategies are used.

Configurations

Networks can be arranged or configured in several different ways. Four principal ways:

- **Star network**—small computers or peripheral devices are linked to a central unit.
- **Bus network**—each device handles its own communications.
- **Ring network**—each device is connected to two other devices, forming a ring.
- **Hierarchical network**—several computers are linked to a central host.

Strategy

Every network has a strategy for coordinating and sharing. The three most common are:

- With **terminal networks,** power is centralized in one large computer.
- With **peer-to-peer networks,** each node acts as both a server and a client.
- With **client/server networks,** one node coordinates and supplies services to all other nodes.

NETWORK TYPES

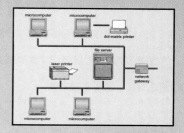

Three types of geographical networks are:

Local Area Networks

Local Area Networks (LANs) are computers and peripheral devices close together (for example, in same building). Linked by telephone, coaxial, or fiber-optic cable, LANs often take bus form. LANs may be linked to other LANs or networks by a **network gateway.**

Metropolitan Area Networks

A **metropolitan area network (MAN)** consists of citywide networks, often using cellular phones.

Wide Area Networks

Wide area networks (WANs) are countrywide and worldwide networks, often using microwave relays and satellites.

Files and Databases

Like a library, the purpose of secondary storage is to store information. How is such information organized? What are files and databases, and why know anything about them? Perhaps the answer is: To become competent at making use of information in the Information Age, you have to know how to *find* that information.

COMPETENCIES

After you have read this chapter, you should be able to:

1. Describe how data is organized: characters, fields, records, and files.
2. Understand the difference between batch processing and real-time processing.
3. Describe the difference between master files and transaction files.
4. Define and describe the three types of file organization: sequential, direct, and index sequential.
5. Describe the advantages of a database.
6. Describe the two essential parts of a database management system (DBMS).
7. Describe three ways of organizing a DBMS: hierarchical, network, and relational.
8. Distinguish among individual, company, distributed, and proprietary databases.
9. Discuss some issues of productivity and security.

At one time, it was not important for microcomputer users to have to know much about files and databases. However, the recent arrival of very powerful microcomputer chips and their availability to communications networks has changed that. To attain true computer competency, you need to know how to gain access to the files and databases on your personal computer. You also need to be able to access those available from other sources. Communications lines extend the reach of your microcomputer well beyond the desktop.

Files

Understanding how files work means understanding data organization, key fields, batch versus real-time processing, master versus transaction files, and file organization.

Y̲ou want to know your final grades for the semester. You call your school's registrar after your last semester exams to find out your grade point average. Perhaps you are told, "Sorry, that's not in the computer yet." Why can't they tell you? How is the school's computer system different from, say, your bank's, where deposits and withdrawals seem to be recorded right away?

Data Organization

To be processed by the computer or stored in secondary storage, data is typically organized into groups or categories. Each group is more complex than the one before:

- **Character:** A character is a single letter, number, or special character such as a punctuation mark or $.
- **Field:** A field contains a set of related characters. On a college registration form or a driver's license, a person's first name is a field. Last name is another field, street address another field, city yet another field, and so on.
- **Record:** A record is a collection of related fields. Everything on a person's college registration form or driver's license, including identification number, is a record.
- **File:** A file is a collection of related records. All the driver's licenses issued in one county could be a file.
- **Database:** A database is a collection of related files. All the driver's license files for the state could be a database.

An example of how data is organized is shown in the illustration. (See Figure 9-1.) Note that a student's name is not one field, but three: first name, middle initial, and last name.

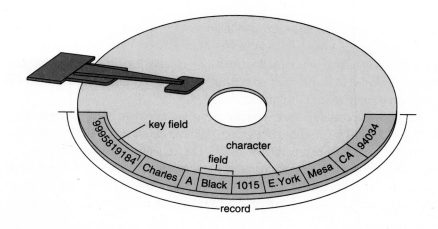

FIGURE 9-1
How data is organized.

The Key Field

Our illustration also shows the student's identification number. Is such a number really necessary? Certainly most people's names are different enough that at a small college, say, you might think identification numbers wouldn't be necessary. However, as anyone named John Smith or Linda Williams knows, there are plenty of other people around with the same name. Sometimes they even have the same middle initial. This is the reason for the student identification number: The number is unique, whereas the name may not be.

This distinctive number is called a *key field*. A **key field** is the particular field of a record that is chosen to uniquely identify each record. The key may be a social security number, employee identification number, or part number.

Batch Versus Real-Time Processing

Traditionally data is processed in two ways. These are *batch processing,* what we might call "later," and *real-time processing,* what we might call "now." These two methods have been used to handle common record-keeping activities such as payroll and sales orders.

- **Batch processing:** In **batch processing,** data is collected over several hours, days, or even weeks. It is then processed all at once—as a "batch." If you have a bank credit card, your bill probably reflects batch processing. That is, during the month, you buy things and charge them to your credit card. Each time you charge something, a copy of the transaction is sent to the credit card company. At some point in the month, the company's data processing department puts all those transactions (and those of many other customers) together. It then processes them at one time. The company then sends you a single bill totaling the amount you owe.

- **Real-time processing:** Totaling up the sales charged to your bank credit card is an example of batch processing. You might use another kind of card—your bank's automatic teller machine (ATM) card—for the second kind of processing. **Real-time processing** occurs when data is processed at the same time the transaction occurs. As you use your ATM card to withdraw cash, the system automatically computes the balance remaining in your account.

At one time, only tape storage, and therefore only sequential access storage (as we discussed in Chapter 7), was available. All processing then was batch processing and was done on mainframe computers. Even today, a great deal of mainframe time is dedicated to this kind of processing. Many smaller organizations, however, use microcomputers for this purpose.

Real-time processing is made possible by the availability of disk packs and direct access storage (as we described in Chapter 7). Direct access storage enables the user to quickly go directly to a particular record. (In sequential access storage, by contrast, the user must wait for the computer to scan several records one at a time. It continues scanning until it comes to the one that's needed.) Not long ago, specialized terminals were used to enter data and perform real-time processing. Today, however, more and more microcomputers are being used for this purpose. As we have stated, microcomputers have become increasingly more powerful. Thus, smaller companies and departments of large companies use these machines by themselves for many real-time processing needs. That is, they use them without connecting to a mainframe.

Master Versus Transaction Files

Two types of files are commonly used to update data—a *master file* and a *transaction file.*

- The **master file** is a complete file containing all records current up to the last update. An example is the data file used to prepare your last month's telephone bill or credit card bill.

- The **transaction file** contains *recent* changes to records that will be used to update the master file. An example could be a temporary "holding" file that accumulates telephone charges or credit card charges through the present month.

File Organization

File organization may be of three types: *sequential, direct,* and *index sequential.*

- **Sequential file organization:** The simplest organization is **sequential file organization,** in which records are stored physically one after another in predetermined order. This order is determined by the key field on each record, such as a student identification number. (See Figure 9-2.)

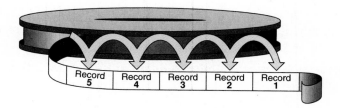

FIGURE 9-2
Sequential file organization.

This organization is very efficient whenever all or a large portion of the records need to be accessed—for example, when final grades are to be mailed out. There is also an equipment cost advantage because magnetic tapes and tape drives can be used. Both are less expensive than disks and disk drives. One disadvantage is that the records must be ordered in a specific way, and that can be time-consuming.

The major disadvantage, however, is that access to a particular record can be very slow. For example, to find the record about a particular student, the registrar's office would sequentially search through the records. It would search them one at a time until the student's number was found. If the number is 4315, the computer will start with record number 0000. It will go through 0001, 0002, and so on until it reaches the student's number.

FIGURE 9-3
Direct file organization.

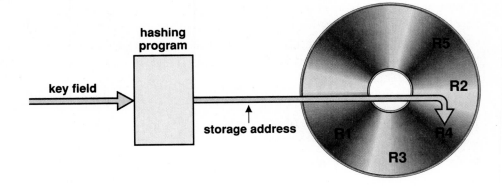

- **Direct file organization:** To obtain particular records, **direct file organization** is much better. Records are not stored physically one after another. Rather, they are stored on a disk in a particular address or location that can be determined by their key field. This address is calculated by a technique known as **hashing.** Hashing programs use mathematical operations to convert the key field's numeric value to a particular storage address. These programs are used to initially store records and later to relocate them. (See Figure 9-3).

    Unlike sequential access files, which are stored on either magnetic tape or disk, direct files can only be stored on disk. The primary advantage is that direct file organization can locate specific records very quickly. If your grades were stored in a direct file, the registrar could access them quickly using only your student identification number.

    The disadvantage of direct file organization is cost. It needs more storage space on disk. It also is not as good as sequential file organization for large numbers of updates or for listing large numbers of records.

- **Index sequential file organization: Index sequential file organization** is a compromise between sequential and direct file organizations. It stores records in a file in sequential order. However, an index sequential file also contains an index. The index lists the key to each group of records stored and the corresponding disk address for that group. When the user seeks a particular record, the computer starts searching sequentially by looking at the beginning of the record group. (See Figure 9-4.) Note: The disk addresses listed in Figure 9-4 represent the actual locations, which are identified by specific track and sector locations.

    For example, the college registrar could index certain ranges of student identification numbers—0000 to 1999, 2000 to 3999, and so on. For the computer to find your number (for example, 4315), it would first go to the index. The index would give the location of the range in which your number appears on the disk (for example, 4000 to 4999). The computer would then search that range (A4) sequentially to find your number.

    Index sequential file organization requires disks or other direct access storage devices. It is faster than sequential but not as fast as direct access. It's best used when large batches of transactions must occasionally be updated, yet users also

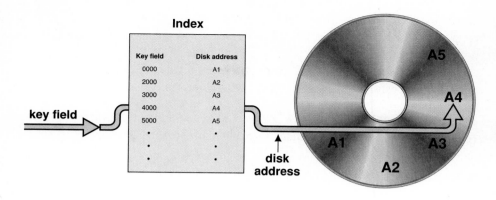

FIGURE 9-4
Index sequential file organization.

want frequent, quick access to data. For example, every month a bank will update bank statements to send to its customers. However, customers and bank tellers need to be able to have up-to-the-minute information about checking accounts.

See Figure 9-5 for a summary of the advantages and disadvantages of each type of file organization.

Database

Databases integrate data. DBMS create, modify, and access databases using data dictionaries and query languages.

Many organizations have multiple files on the same subject or person. For example, records for the same customer may appear in different files in the sales department, billing department, and credit department. If the customer moves, then the address in each file must be updated. If one file is overlooked, it can cause embarrassments. For example, a product ordered might be sent to the new address, but the bill might be sent to the old address.

Moreover, data spread around in different files is not as useful. The marketing department, for instance, might want to do special promotions to customers who

FILE ORGANIZATION

TYPE	ADVANTAGES	DISADVANTAGES
Sequential	Efficient access to all or large part of records, cost	Slow access to specific records
Direct	Fast access to specific records	Inefficient access to all or large part of records, cost
Index sequential	Faster than sequential, more efficient than direct	Not quite as efficient as sequential, not quite as fast as direct, cost

FIGURE 9-5
Summary of the three types of file organization.

order large quantities of merchandise. However, they may be unable to do so because that information is in the billing department. A database can make the needed information available.

A *database* is defined as a collection of integrated data. By "integrated," we mean the data consists of logically related files and records.

The Need for Databases

For both individuals and organizations, there are many advantages to having databases:

- **Sharing:** In organizations, information from one department can be readily shared with others, as we saw in the example above.

- **Security:** Users are given passwords or access only to the kind of information they need to know. Thus, the payroll department may have access to employees' pay rates, but other departments would not.

- **Fewer files:** With several departments having access to one file, there are fewer files. Excess storage, or what is called "data redundancy," is reduced. Microcomputers linked by a network to a file server, for example, could replace the hard disks located in several individual microcomputers.

- **Data integrity:** Older filing systems many times did not have "integrity." That is, a change made in the file in one department might not be made in the file in another department. As you might expect, this can cause serious problems and conflicts when data is used for important decisions affecting both departments.

Software for a Database Management System

In order to create, modify, and gain access to the database, special software is required. This software is called a *database management system,* which is commonly abbreviated DBMS.

Some DBMSs, such as dBASE, are designed specifically for microcomputers. Other DBMSs are designed for minicomputers and mainframes. Once again, increased processing power and the wide use of communications networks linked to file servers are changing everything. Now microcomputer DBMSs have become more like the ones used for mainframes—and vice versa.

DBMS software is made up of a data dictionary and a query language.

Data Dictionary

A **data dictionary** contains a description of the structure of the data used in the database. For a particular item of data, it defines the names used for a particular field. It defines what type of data that field is (alphabetic, numeric, alphanumeric, date, time, or logic). It also specifies the number of characters in each field and whether that field is a key field. An example of a data dictionary appears in the illustration. (See Figure 9-6.)

Query Language

Access to most databases is accomplished with a **query language.** This is an easy-to-use language understandable to most users. The most widely used query language is **SQL** or **Structured Query Language.**

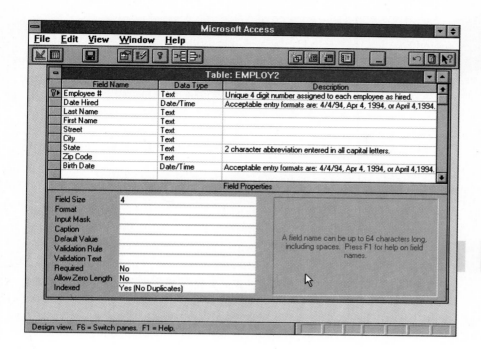

FIGURE 9-6

Data dictionary: Access for Windows 3.1, version 2.0.

Query languages have commands such as DISPLAY, ADD, COMPARE, LIST, SELECT, and UPDATE. For example, imagine you wanted the names of all salespeople in an organization whose sales were greater than their sales quotas. You might type the statement "DISPLAY ALL FOR SALES > QUOTA."

DBMS Organization

The three principal DBMS organizations are hierarchical, network, and relational.

The purpose of a database is to integrate individual items of data—that is, to transform isolated facts into useful information. We saw that files can be organized in various ways (sequentially, for example) to best suit their use. Similarly, databases can also be organized in different ways to best fit their use. Although other arrangements have been tried, the three most common formats are *hierarchical, network,* and *relational.*

The Hierarchical Database

In a **hierarchical database,** fields or records are structured in **nodes.** Nodes are points connected like the branches of an upside-down tree. Each entry has one **parent node,** although a parent may have several **child nodes.** This is sometimes described as a one-to-many relationship. To find a particular field you have to start at the top with a parent and trace down the tree to a child.

The nodes farther down the system are subordinate to the ones above, like the hierarchy of managers in a corporation. An example of a hierarchical database for part of a nationwide airline reservations system is shown in our illustration. (See

Figure 9-7.) The parent node is the "departure" city, Los Angeles. This parent has four children, labeled "arrival." New York, one of the children, has three children of its own. They are labeled "flight number." Flight 110 has three children, labeled "passenger."

The problem with a hierarchical database is that if one parent node is deleted, so are all the subordinate child nodes. Moreover, a child node cannot be added unless a parent node is added first. The most significant limitation is the rigid structure: one parent only per child, and no relationships or connections between the child nodes themselves.

The Network Database

A **network database** also has a hierarchical arrangement of nodes. However, each child node may have more than one parent node. This is sometimes described as a many-to-many relationship. There are additional connections—called **pointers**—between parent nodes and child nodes. Thus, a node may be reached through more than one path. It may be traced down through different branches.

An example of the use of a network organization is that shown in our illustration for students taking courses. (See Figure 9-8.) If you trace through the logic of this organization, you can see that each student can have more than one teacher. Each teacher can also teach more than one course. Students may take more than a single course. This demonstrates how the network arrangement is more flexible and in many cases more efficient than the hierarchical arrangement.

The Relational Database

The most flexible type of organization is the **relational database.** In this structure, there are no access paths down a hierarchy to an item of data. Rather, the data elements are stored in different tables, each of which consists of rows and columns. A table is called a **relation.**

FIGURE 9-7

Example of a hierarchical database.

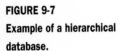

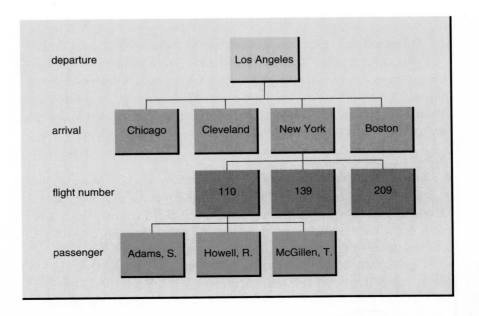

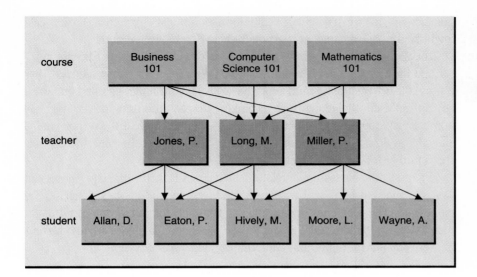

FIGURE 9-8
Example of a network database.

An example of a relational database is shown in our illustration. (See Figure 9-9.) The address table contains the names, drivers' license numbers, and addresses for all registered drivers in a particular state. Within the table, a row resembles a record—for example, information about one driver. A column entry resembles a field. The driver's name is one field; the driver's license number is another field. All related tables must have a *common data item* (a key field). Thus, information

FIGURE 9-9
Example of a relational database.

Address Table

Name	License Number	Street Address	City	State	Zip
Aaron, Linda	FJ1987	10032 Park Lane	San Jose	CA	95127
Abar, John	D12372	1349 Oak St	Lakeville	CA	94128
Abell, Jack	LK3457	95874 State St	Stone	CA	95201

key fields linked — key fields linked

Owner's Table

Name	Plate Number
Abell, Jack	ABK241
Abrams, Sue	LMJ198
Abril, Pat	ZXA915

Outstanding Citation Table

License Number	Citation Code	Violation
T25476	00031	Speed
D98372	19001	Park
LK3457	89100	Speed

stored on one table can be linked with information stored on another. One key field might be a person's name. Another might be a driver's license number.

Thus, police officers who stop a speeding car can radio the driver's license number and the car's license plate number to the department of motor vehicles. They can use the driver's license number as the key field. With it they can find out about any unpaid traffic violations (such as parking tickets). Also using the license plate number they can obtain the car owner's name and address. If the owner's name and address do not match the driver who has been stopped, the police officer may check further for a stolen vehicle.

The most valuable feature of relational databases is their simplicity. Entries can be easily added, deleted, and modified. The hierarchy and network databases are more rigid. The relational organization is common for microcomputer DBMSs, such as Access, Paradox, dBASE, and R:Base. Relational databases are also becoming very popular for mainframe- and minicomputer-based systems.

Types of Databases

There are four kinds of databases: individual, company, distributed, and proprietary.

Databases may be small or large, limited in accessibility or widely accessible. Databases may be classified into four types: *individual, company* (or shared), *distributed,* and *proprietary.*

The Individual Database

The **individual database** is also called a **microcomputer database.** It is a collection of integrated files primarily used by just one person. Typically, the data and the DBMS are under the direct control of the user. They are stored either on the user's hard-disk drive or on a LAN file server.

There may be many times in your life when you will find this kind of database valuable. If you are in sales, for instance, a microcomputer database can be used to keep track of customers. If you are a sales manager, you can keep track of your salespeople and their performance. If you're an advertising account executive, you can keep track of what work and how many hours to charge each client.

The Company, or Shared, Database

Companies, of course, create databases for their own use. The **company database** may be stored on a mainframe and managed by a computer professional (known as a database administrator). Users throughout the company have access to the database through their microcomputers linked to local area networks or wide area networks. Company databases are of two types:

- The **common operational database** contains details about the operations of the company, such as inventory, production, and sales. It contains data describing the day-to-day operations of the organization.

- The **common user database** contains selected information both from the common operational database and from outside private (proprietary) databases. Managers can tap into this information on their microcomputers or terminals and use it for decision making.

As we will see in the next chapter, company databases are the foundation for management information systems. For instance, a department store can record all sales transactions in the database. A sales manager can use this information to see which salespeople are selling the most products. The manager can then determine year-end sales bonuses. Or the store's buyer can learn which products are selling well or not selling and make adjustments when reordering. A top executive might combine overall store sales trends with information from outside databases about consumer and population trends. This information could be used to change the whole merchandising strategy of the store.

The Distributed Database

Many times the data in a company is stored not in just one location but in several locations. It is made accessible through a variety of communications networks. The database, then, is a **distributed database.** That is, it is located in a place or places other than where users are located. Typically, database servers on a client/server network provide the link between users and the distant data.

For instance, some database information can be at regional offices. Some can be at company headquarters, some down the hall from you, and some even overseas. Sales figures for a chain of department stores, then, could be located at the various stores. But executives at district offices or at the chain's headquarters could have access to these figures.

The Proprietary Database

A **proprietary database** is generally an enormous database that an organization develops to cover certain particular subjects. It offers access to this database to the public or selected outside individuals for a fee. Sometimes proprietary databases are also called *information utilities* or *data banks*. An example is CompuServe, which sells a variety of consumer and business services to microcomputer users. (See Figure 9-10.)

Some important proprietary databases are the following:

- **CompuServe:** Offers consumer and business services, including electronic mail.
- **Dialog Information Services:** Offers business information, as well as technical and scientific information.
- **Dow Jones News Retrieval:** Provides world news and information on business, investments, and stocks.
- **Prodigy:** Offers news and information on business and economics, as well as leisure services.

There are also specialized proprietary databases for investors and financial analysts, such as Chase Econometric Associates.

FIGURE 9-10
Proprietary database:
CompuServe's Consumer
Reports.

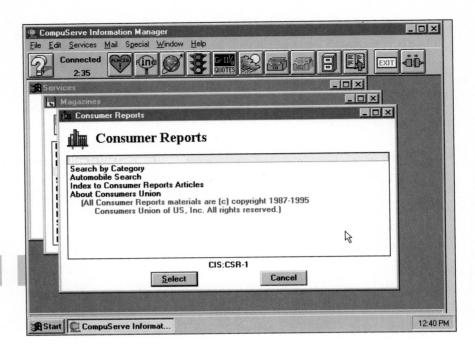

Costs

If you have a microcomputer, modem, and phone at home, many of these proprietary databases are available to you. Usually you pay a start-up fee, an hourly charge for searching the database, and the phone company or telecommunications line charges.

As you might expect, fees and charges are high during the normal nine-to-five business hours. However, proprietary databases often offer cheaper after-hours rates. Dialog Information Services, for example, offers The Knowledge Index nights and weekends for (as of this writing) a start-up fee of $9.95 through CompuServe. An online search charge (which includes telecommunications line costs) is $28.80 an hour. This service offers comprehensive coverage of journals, abstracts, research reports, reviews, news, tax information, and bibliographies. Topics covered range from agriculture to social science.

See Figure 9-11 for a summary of the four types of databases.

FIGURE 9-11
Summary of the four types of
databases.

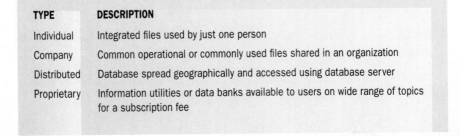

TYPES OF DATABASES

TYPE	DESCRIPTION
Individual	Integrated files used by just one person
Company	Common operational or commonly used files shared in an organization
Distributed	Database spread geographically and accessed using database server
Proprietary	Information utilities or data banks available to users on wide range of topics for a subscription fee

Database Uses and Issues

Databases help users keep current and plan for the future, but keeping them secure is important. Databases may be supervised by a database administrator.

D atabases offer great opportunities for productivity. In fact, in corporate libraries, electronic databases are now considered more valuable than books and journals. However, maintaining databases means users must make constant efforts to keep them from being tampered with or misused.

Data for Strategic Uses

Databases help users keep up to date and plan for the future. Among the hundreds of databases available to help users with both general and specific business purposes are the following:

- *Business directories* providing addresses, financial and marketing information, products, and trade and brand names.
- *Demographic data,* such as county and city statistics, current estimates on population and income, employment statistics, census data, and so on.
- *Business statistical information,* such as financial information on publicly traded companies, market potential of certain retail stores, and other business data and information.
- *Text databases* providing articles from business publications, press releases, reviews on companies and products, and so on.

Importance of Security

Precisely because databases are so valuable, their security has become a vital issue. One concern is that personal and private information about people stored in databases will be used for the wrong purposes. For instance, a person's credit history or medical records might be used to make hiring or promotion decisions.

Another concern is with preventing unauthorized users from gaining access to a database. For example, there have been numerous instances in which a **computer virus** has been launched into a database or network. Computer viruses are hidden instructions that "migrate" through networks and operating systems and become embedded in different programs and databases. Some are relatively harmless, but others may destroy data. Computer viruses and other security issues are discussed in detail in Chapter 13.

Security can require putting guards on company computer rooms and checking the identification of everyone admitted. Some security systems electronically check fingerprints. (See Figure 9-12.) Security concerns are particularly important to organizations using WANs. Violations can occur without actually entering secured areas.

The Database Administrator

Librarians have had to be trained in the use of electronic databases so that they can help their corporate users. However, corporate databases of all sorts—not just

FIGURE 9-12
Security: Electronic finger-print pads.

those in the library—have become extremely important. Hence, many large organizations employ a **database administrator (DBA).** He or she helps determine the structure of the large databases and evaluates the performance of the DBMS. For shared databases, the DBA also determines which people have access to what kind of data; these are called **processing rights.** In addition, the DBA is concerned with such significant issues as security, privacy, and ethics.

A Look at the Future

Large databases give us everything from specialty phone books to census maps. Risks are increased compromises of privacy and security. Products are available to sift information.

The collection and use of data are sure to get more and more sophisticated. Microcomputer users now, for instance, can get computerized *specialty phone books* loaded with corporate names, telephone numbers, and other data. A database project of awesome proportions is the huge national computer map developed by the U.S. Census Bureau. Known as *TIGER* (for *T*opologically *I*ntegrated *G*eographic *E*ncoding and *R*eference system), it will have 23 million street intersections. TIGER can be coupled with statistics that provide a numerical or income profile of every block in the United States. *Taxi* is a recently developed software package that uses a computer map database for six major cities. Users are provided with detailed maps including individual street addresses, and hotel and restaurant locations.

Global Positioning Systems (GPS) combine databases like *TIGER* with satellite communications. A GPS allows a vehicle to be precisely tracked as it travels to its destination. Oldsmobile is offering a GPS navigation system in the Los Angeles area.

Big databases have not only great potential payoffs in productivity but also great risks for privacy and security. Your name probably passes through 50 different databases in a day. One worry is that corporations and governments may use them to create unnecessary or dangerous confidential files (dossiers) about private citizens. People also worry about disasters disrupting a local communications or computer system. A fire, earthquake, computer virus, or sabotage could have nationwide or worldwide effects on such a computer system.

Finally, the mountains of information generated by databases have now created a new industry. We now have products that sift the information to give us what we really want to know. These products range from personal newsletters to filtering technology that scans data for key words specified by the user.

KEY TERMS

batch processing (184)

child node (189)

common operational database (192)

common user database (193)

company database (192)

computer virus (195)

data dictionary (188)

database administrator (DBA) (196)

direct file organization (186)

distributed database (193)

hashing (186)

hierarchical database (188)

index sequential file organization (186)

individual database (192)

key field (184)

master file (185)

microcomputer database (192)

network database (190)

nodes (189)

parent node (189)

pointer (190)

processing rights (196)

proprietary database (190)

query language (188)

real-time processing (184)

relation (190)

relational database (190)

sequential file organization (185)

Structured Query Language (SQL) (188)

transaction file (185)

REVIEW QUESTIONS

True/False

1. A record is a collection of related files.

2. In batch processing, data is processed at the same time the transaction occurs.

3. A data dictionary describes the structure of the data in a database.

4. A distributed database has data located in more than one location.

5. Processing rights are typically determined by the database administrator to specify which people have access to what kind of data.

Multiple Choice

1. A collection of related fields:
   a. byte
   b. word
   c. character
   d. record
   e. file

2. A temporary file containing recent changes to records:
   a. master
   b. data
   c. transaction
   d. indexed
   e. batch

3. The database organization in which fields and records are structured in nodes with each child node having only one parent.
   a. hierarchical
   b. network
   c. proprietary
   d. relational
   e. individual

4. The type of database that is sometimes called an information utility or a data bank:
   a. individual
   b. common operational
   c. common user
   d. distributed
   e. proprietary

5. Hidden instructions that "migrate" through networks and operating systems:
   a. file servers
   b. viruses
   c. nodes
   d. relation
   e. pointer

Fill in the Blank

1. The _____ field uniquely identifies each record.
2. _____ file organization is best for locating specific records.
3. A database is a collection of _____ data.
4. _____ databases are more flexible and easier to use than hierarchical and network databases.
5. Large organizations employ database _____ to help determine database structures and evaluate database performance.

Open Ended

1. Describe how data is organized and give an example.
2. What are the differences between sequential, direct, and index sequential file organizations?
3. What are databases, and why are they needed?
4. Discuss the three principal ways of organizing a database.
5. Describe each of the four types of database.

DISCUSSION QUESTIONS

1. *Useful information utilities:* What is your major or prospective major? What kinds of information are you apt to be required to obtain for research papers, projects, and assignments? If you're in the health field, you may be required to learn about diet, exercise, drug recovery, and the like. If you're in marketing, you may need to know about sales forecasting and product marketing.

   Take a few minutes to list the areas of information required in your field. Then go to the library and look up which information utilities or data banks would be most valuable to you. Examples are CompuServe, Dialog or The Knowledge Index, Dow Jones News Retrieval, and Prodigy.

2. *Your school's database:* Almost all organizations keep information about their employees and customers in databases. Surely your college or university does also. Without conducting extensive research, respond to each of the following:

   a. What information about you do you think is stored in your school's database?

   b. How do you suppose the data is organized? Specifically, give an example of a database, file, record, field, and character.

   c. Which type of file organization do you think is used, and why?

   d. Which type of DBMS organization is likely used, and why?

3. *http://www.soonet.ca/eliris/prodserv.htm*   Global Positioning Systems, Geographic Information Systems, and Desktop Mapping Systems use computers linked to satellites to provide fast and accurate locational information. They are used for navigation on the land and sea and in the air. Eliris Inc., one of the organizations that sell these systems, has a home page on the Internet. To learn more about these technologically advanced systems, connect to Eliris's home page using the Internet address given at the beginning of this question. Then expand your search to other vendors and applications using other Internet resources. (Hint: Use the Every Student's Internet Resource Guide: Computer Science and Computer Technology—Entry Number: 02.)

Files and Databases

Through communication lines, users can gain access to files and databases.

FILE ORGANIZATION

TYPE	ADVANTAGES	DISADVANTAGES
Sequential	Efficient access to all or large part of records, cost	Slow access to specific records
Direct	Fast access to specific records	Inefficient access to all or large part of records, cost
Index sequential	Faster than sequential, more efficient than direct	Not quite as efficient as sequential, not quite as fast as direct, cost

---

FILES

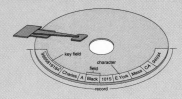

Understanding how files work means understanding:

Data Organization

- **Character**—letter, number, special character.
- **Field**—set of related characters.
- **Record**—collection of related fields.
- **File**—collection of related records.
- **Database**—collection of related files.
- **Key field**—unique identifier for each record in a file.

Batch Versus Real-Time Processing

Two methods of processing:

- **Batch processing**—transactions are collected over time, then processed all at once.
- **Real-time processing**—data is processed at the same time transactions occur.

Master Versus Transaction Files

- **Master file**—complete file, current to the last update.
- **Transaction file**—temporary "holding file" used to update the master file.

Three types of file organization:

Sequential

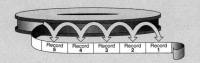

- **Sequential**—records are stored one after the other in ascending or descending order. This method is often used with magnetic tape.

Direct

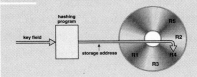

- **Direct**—records are stored in order by a key field such as a special number. This method is often used with magnetic disk.

Index Sequential

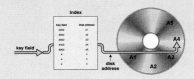

- **Index sequential**—a compromise organization with records stored sequentially with an index for near direct access. Used with magnetic disk storage.

DATABASE

A *database* is a collection of integrated data—logically related files and records.

The Need for Databases

Advantages of databases:

- **Sharing**—users may share with others.
- **Security**—access is restricted to authorized people.
- **Fewer files**—a company avoids multiple files on the same subject.
- **Database integrity**—changes in one file are made in other files as well.

Software for a DBMS

A **database management system (DBMS)** is the software for creating, modifying, and gaining access to the database. A DBMS consists of:

- **Data dictionary**—describes the structure of the database.
- **Query language**—language to get access to the database.

Relational databases use **tables** where rows resemble records. Related tables have a **common data element** (key field). Table entries can be easily added, deleted, and modified.

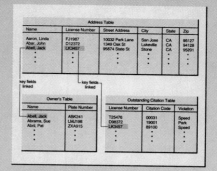

DBMS ORGANIZATION

Three principal DBMS organizations are:

Hierarchical Database

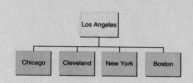

In a **hierarchical database**, fields and records are structured in **nodes**, points connected like tree branches. An entry may have a **parent** node with several **child** nodes. A node may be reached by only one path.

Network Database

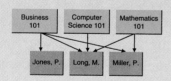

In a **network database**, nodes are arranged hierarchically, but a child node may have more than one parent. There are additional connections called **pointers**. A node may be reached by several paths.

Relational Database

In a **relational database,** data is stored in tables consisting of rows and columns; data items are found by means of an index.

TYPES OF DATABASE

Four types of databases are:

Individual Database

The **individual database** is a collection of integrated files useful mainly to just one person.

Company, or Shared, Database

Two types of **company (shared) database** are:

- **Common operational database**—contains data on company operations.
- **Common user database**—contains data from common operational database and from outside private databases.

Distributed Database

The **distributed database** is spread out geographically and is accessible by communications links.

Proprietary Database

A **proprietary database** is available by subscription to customers.

DATABASE USES AND ISSUES

Databases offer increased productivity but also risks to security.

Data for Strategic Uses

Databases help users keep current and plan for the future.

Importance of Security

Two security concerns are illegal use of data and unauthorized access. **Computer viruses** are hidden instructions that "migrate" into programs and databases.

The Database Administrator

The **database administrator (DBA)** is a specialist who sets up and manages the database and determines **processing rights**—which people have access to what kind of data.

The Internet Guide:

How to Surf the Net

Want to communicate with a friend across town, in another state, or even in another country? Perhaps you would like to send a drawing, a photo, or just a letter. Looking for travel or entertainment information? Perhaps you're researching a term paper or exploring different career paths. Where do you start? For these and other information-related activities, try the Internet. It is the 20th-century information resource designed for all of us to use.

The Internet is like a giant highway that connects you to millions of other people and organizations. Unlike typical highways that move people and things from one location to another, the Internet moves your *ideas* and *information*. Rather than moving through geographic space, you move through **cyberspace**—the space of electronic movement of ideas and information. In this guide, we describe the Internet, how you can get onto it, and how you can use it.

The Internet

The Internet is a giant computer network. Four applications: electronic mail, discussion groups, run programs, and transfer files. Two Utilities: Gopher and World Wide Web.

The Internet is a giant worldwide network. It connects computer systems located throughout the world that are willing to share their resources. The Internet has created a cooperative society that forms a virtual community stretching from one end of the globe to the other. (See Figure 1.)

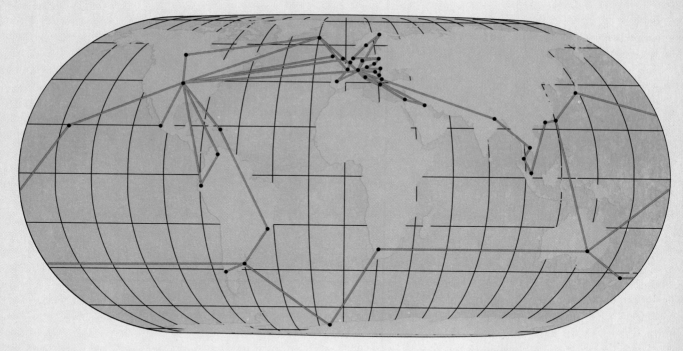

FIGURE 1
Internet connections around
the world.

The Internet's origin can be traced back to 1969, when the United States government funded a major research project on computer networking. A national computer network called **ARPANET (Advanced Research Project Agency Network)** was developed. It was used by government and military agencies to communicate and share computer resources with researchers working on national security projects.

From these military and research beginnings, the Internet has evolved as a tool for all of us to use in our daily lives. In 1995 over 4 million computers in 156 countries were connected to the Internet with over 30 million users. By the year 2000, 100 million computers in every country in the world are expected to be connected to over a billion users. (See Figure 2.)

To access the Internet, you connect to one of the computer systems already on it. After you connect to one, you can easily connect to another. You move electronically from one computer system to another, from one site to another, and often from one country to another—all within seconds. What makes the Internet so remarkable is the incredible speed and efficiency with which these connections are made. Once you are on the Internet it seems like you are on a single giant computer that branches all over the world.

FIGURE 2

Internet use—past, present, and future.

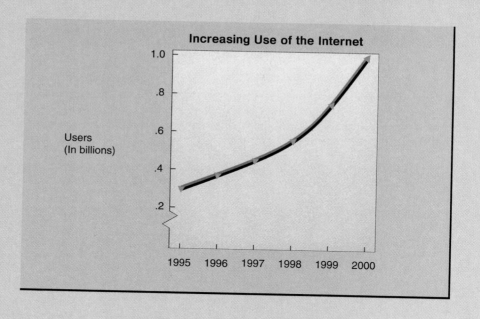

Internet Applications

What Can You Do on the Internet? There are any number of uses for the Internet. The four most common are sending and receiving electronic mail (e-mail), participating in public discussions, running programs on a remote computer, and transferring files.

- **Electronic mail:** Sending and receiving e-mail is the most popular Internet service. If you know their addresses and have access to the Internet, you can send to and receive e-mail from your friends and family located almost anywhere in the world.

- **Discussion groups:** You can join and listen to discussions and debates on a wide variety of special-interest topics. There are thousands of special-interest groups, ranging from physical fitness to job hunting.

- **Run programs:** You can even run selected programs from other computers. These programs range from games like DOOM to educational programs from NASA.

- **Transfer files:** You can copy or transfer files from one computer to another. There are thousands of free programs and games available on the Internet.

Internet Utilities

How Do You Surf the Net? The Internet provides access to a tremendous amount of information. How to find the information that you really need, however, can be challenging. Fortunately, there are several Internet utilities or programs designed to help you to navigate, or surf, the Internet. The two most widely used are gopher and World Wide Web (WWW).

- **Gopher:** Many computers on the Internet run gopher programs to provide a menu or list of their available resources. For example, many college and university libraries provide access to their card catalogs.

- **WWW:** Like gophers, WWW helps users search for and retrieve information from a specific computer system. WWW goes one step further by using a more graphical interface and providing information about resources available from other computer systems on the Internet. Additionally, direct links to those computers are provided.

Where should you begin to learn more about how to use and to surf the Internet? First, you should gain access to or get onto the Internet. Then, explore the applications and use the available Internet utilities. The following sections of this guide will help you do just that.

Access

Providers give access to the Internet. Internet connections are either direct, SLIP and PPP, or dial-up. Protocols are rules for exchanging information between computers.

The Internet and the telephone system are similar—you can connect to the Internet much like you connect a phone to the telephone system. Once you are on the Internet, your computer becomes an extension of what seems like a giant computer—a computer that branches all over the world.

Providers

The most common way to access the Internet is through a **provider** or **host computer.** The providers are already connected to the Internet and provide a path or connection for individuals to access the Internet. There are two widely used providers.

- **College and universities:** Another source is through colleges and universities. Many provide free access to the Internet through their local area networks. You may be able to access the Internet through your school or through other local colleges and universities. Check with the computer services department at your school as well as other nearby schools.

- **Service providers:** A widely used source for access is through online commercial service providers, discussed in Chapter 8. They provide access to the Internet and numerous other electronic services for a fee. The best-known service providers are America Online, CompuServe, Prodigy, Microsoft Network, and AT&T Interchange. (See Figure 3.)

Connections

To gain access to the Internet, you must have a connection. This connection can be made either directly to the Internet or indirectly through a provider. There are three types of connections:

FIGURE 3
Microsoft Network.

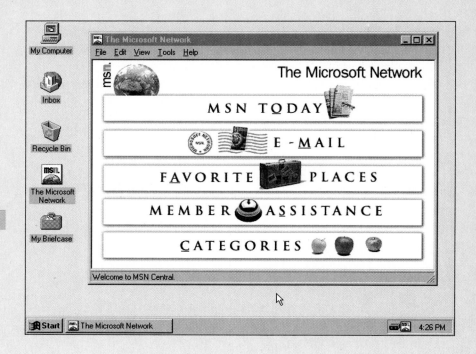

■ **Direct or dedicated:** To have access to all the functions on the Internet, you need a direct or dedicated link. This requires a special high-speed communication line that is either owned or leased. Individuals rarely have direct connections because they are quite expensive. However, many organizations such as colleges, universities, service providers, and corporations do have direct links.

The primary advantages of a direct link are complete access to Internet functions, ease of connection for individual users, and fast response and retrieval of information. The primary disadvantage is cost.

■ **SLIP and PPP:** Using a high-speed modem and standard telephone lines, you can connect to a provider that has a direct connection to the Internet. This type of connection requires special software such as **SLIP (serial line internet protocol)** or **PPP (point to point protocol).** Using this type of connection, your computer becomes part of a client/server network. The provider or host computer is the server providing access to the Internet. Your computer is the client. Using special client software, your computer is able to communicate with server software running on the provider's computer and on other Internet computers.

This type of connection is widely used by end users to connect to the Internet. It provides a high level of service at a lower cost than a direct or dedicated connection. Of course, it is somewhat slower and may not be as convenient.

■ **Dial-up:** Another way to access the Internet using a high-speed modem and standard telephone lines is called a **dial-up** or **terminal connection.** Using this type of connection, your computer becomes a part of a terminal network. Unlike a SLIP or PPP connection, your computer's operations are very limited. It operates as a terminal that simply displays the communication that occurs between the provider and the other computers on the Internet. Compared to a SLIP or PPP connection, dial-up is less expensive but not as fast or as convenient.

For a summary of the costs and typical users of the three types of connections, see Figure 4.

TCP/IP

When information is sent over the Internet, it usually travels through numerous interconnected networks. Before a message is sent, it is broken down into small parts called **packets.** Each packet is then sent separately over the Internet, possibly traveling different routes to one common destination. At the receiving end, the packets are reassembled into the correct order. Protocols control how the messages are broken down, sent, and reassembled. They govern how and when computers talk to one another. The standard protocol for the Internet is called **TCP/IP (transmission control protocol/internet protocol).**

E-Mail

An e-mail message has three basic elements. Internet addresses use the domain name system. E-mail etiquette is called netiquette.

E-mail is a way of sending an electronic letter or message between individuals or computers. It is like an answering machine in that you can receive messages even when you are not home. Unlike an answering machine, e-mail can contain text, graphics, and images as well as sound. E-mail can also be used to communicate with more than one person at a time, to conveniently schedule meetings, to keep current on important events, and much more.

Sending and receiving e-mail is by far the most common Internet activity. You can communicate with anyone in the world who has an Internet address or e-mail

USERS AND CONNECTION COSTS

CONNECTION	USER	COST
Direct/Dedicated	Medium to large company	$4,000 to $15,000 per year
SLIP/PPP	Individual or small company	$250 to $750 per year plus hourly charges
Dial-up	Individual	$0 to $250 per year

FIGURE 4
Typical user and connection costs.

account with a system connected to the Internet. E-mail programs such as Pine, Elm, and Eudora automate the process of creating, sending, reading, and receiving messages.

Suppose that you have a friend, Chris James, who is going to an out-of-state school. You and Chris have been calling back and forth at least once a week for the past month. Unfortunately, your telephone bill has skyrocketed. Fortunately, you both have Internet e-mail accounts through your schools. To save money, you and Chris agree to communicate via the Internet instead of the telephone. After exchanging e-mail addresses, you are ready to send your first Internet e-mail message to Chris.

Basic Elements

A typical e-mail message has three basic elements: header, message, and signature. (See Figure 5.) The header appears first and typically includes the following information.

■ **To line:** The e-mail address for the person that is to receive the letter.

■ **From line:** The address of the person sending the e-mail follows the To line.

■ **Subject line:** A one-line description of the message is used to present the topic of the message. Subject lines typically are displayed when a person checks his or her mailbox.

■ **Attachment line:** Many e-mail programs allow you to attach files such as documents and worksheets. If a message has an attachment, the file name appears on the attachment line.

FIGURE 5

Basic elements of an e-mail message.

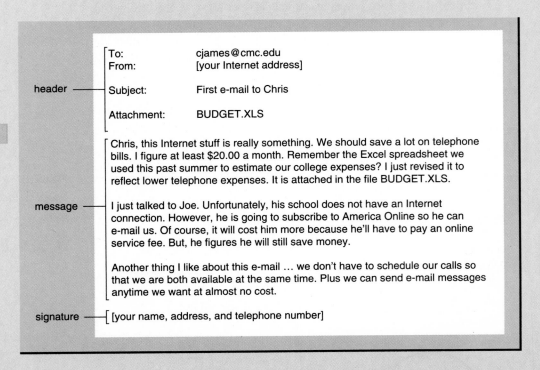

header —

To:	cjames@cmc.edu
From:	[your Internet address]
Subject:	First e-mail to Chris
Attachment:	BUDGET.XLS

message —

Chris, this Internet stuff is really something. We should save a lot on telephone bills. I figure at least $20.00 a month. Remember the Excel spreadsheet we used this past summer to estimate our college expenses? I just revised it to reflect lower telephone expenses. It is attached in the file BUDGET.XLS.

I just talked to Joe. Unfortunately, his school does not have an Internet connection. However, he is going to subscribe to America Online so he can e-mail us. Of course, it will cost him more because he'll have to pay an online service fee. But, he figures he will still save money.

Another thing I like about this e-mail … we don't have to schedule our calls so that we are both available at the same time. Plus we can send e-mail messages anytime we want at almost no cost.

signature —

[your name, address, and telephone number]

The letter or message comes next. It is typically short and to the point. Finally, the signature line provides additional information about the sender. Typically, this information includes the sender's name, address, and telephone number. This information is automatically "stamped" onto all e-mail sent out.

Addresses

One of the most important elements of an e-mail message is the address of the person who is to receive the letter. The Internet uses an addressing method known as the **domain name system (DNS)** to assign names and numbers to people and computers. This system divides an address into three parts. (See Figure 6.)

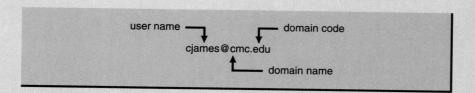

FIGURE 6
Parts of an Internet address.

Internet addresses typically are read backwards. The last part of the address is the **domain code,** which identifies the geographical description or organizational identification. For example, *edu* in Figure 6 indicates an address at an educational and research institution. (See Figure 7.)

Separated from the domain code by a dot (.) is the **domain name.** It is a reference to the particular organization. In this case, *cmc* represents Claremont McKenna College. Separated from the domain name by an "at" (@) symbol, the **user name** identifies a unique person or computer at the listed domain. The address shown in Figure 6 is for Chris James (cjames) at Claremont McKenna College (cmc), which is an education and research institution (edu).

Netiquette

Netiquette refers to the etiquette you should observe when using e-mail. Remember that you are communicating with people, not computers—these people have the same feelings and sensibilities that you do. (See Figure 8.)

ORGANIZATIONAL IDENTIFICATIONS

DOMAIN	IDENTIFICATION
com	Commercial organizations
edu	Educational and research institutions
gov	Non-military government agencies
mil	Military agencies
net	Major network support centers
org	Other organizations

FIGURE 7
Commonly used Internet organizational identifications.

FIGURE 8

E-mail etiquette.

NETIQUETTE

1. Don't send abusive, threatening, harassing, or bigoted messages. You could be held criminally liable for what you write.

2. DO NOT TYPE YOUR MESSAGES IN ALL UPPERCASE CHARACTERS! This is called shouting and is perceived as very harsh. Use a normal combination of upper- and lowercase characters. Sometimes all lowercase is perceived as too informal or timid.

3. Keep line length to 60 characters or less so your messages can be comfortably displayed on most monitors.

4. Before sending a message, carefully check the spelling, punctuation, and grammar. Also think twice about the content of your message. Once it is sent, you can't get it back.

Discussion Groups

Mailing lists send e-mail to all members. Newsgroups use the Usenet. Lurk before you contribute.

You can also use e-mail to communicate with people you do not know but with whom you wish to share ideas and interests. You can participate in discussions and debates that range from general topics like current events and movies to specialized forums like computer troubleshooting and Star Trek.

Mailing Lists

Mailing lists are one type of discussion group available on the Internet. Members of a mailing list communicate by sending messages to a **list address.** Each message is then copied and sent via e-mail to every member of the mailing list.

There are thousands of different mailing lists. To participate in one, you must first subscribe by sending an e-mail request to the mailing list **subscription address.** (See Figure 9.) Once you are a member of a list, you can expect to receive e-mail from others on the list. You may find the number of messages to be overwhelming. If you want to cancel a mailing list, send an e-mail request to "unsubscribe" to the subscription address.

FIGURE 9

Five popular mailing lists.

MAILING LISTS

MAILING LIST	SUBSCRIPTION ADDRESS	DESCRIPTION
Harleys	harleys-request@think.age.on.ca	For people who love motorcycles
Info-Aids	info-aids@rainbow.uucp	A clearinghouse for information and discussion about AIDS
Luckytown	luckytown-request@netcom.com	For fans of Bruce Springsteen
Musicals	musicals-request@world.std.com	For fans of musical theater
Outdoor-l	outdoor-l@ulkyum	For those who love the outdoors

Newsgroups

Newsgroups are the most popular type of discussion group. Unlike mailing lists, **newsgroups** use a special network of computers called the **UseNet.** Each of these computers maintains the newsgroup listing. The newsgroups are organized into major topic areas that are further subdivided into hierarchies.

This hierarchy system is similar to the Domain Name System. For example, the newsgroup specializing in motion picture discussions is categorized under the major topic REC (for "recreational"), then the subtopic ARTS, and then the further subdivision CINEMA. (See Figure 10.)

Contributions to a particular newsgroup are sent to one of the computers on the UseNet. This computer saves the messages on its system and periodically shares all its recent messages with the other computers on the UseNet. Unlike mailing lists, a copy of each message is not sent to each member of a list. Rather, interested individuals check contributions to a particular newsgroup, reading only those of interest.

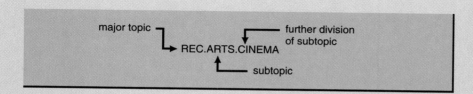

FIGURE 10
Newsgroup hierarchy.

There are thousands of newsgroups covering a wide variety of topic areas. (See Figure 11.)

Lurking

Before you submit a contribution to a discussion group, it is recommended that you observe or read the communications from others. This is called **lurking.** (See Figure 12.)

By lurking, you can learn about the culture of a discussion group. For example, you can observe the level and style of the discussions. You may decide that a particular discussion group is not what you were looking for—in which case, unsubscribe. If the discussions are appropriate and you wish to participate, try to fit into the prevailing culture. Remember that your contributions will likely be read by hundreds of people.

NEWSGROUPS

NEWSGROUP	DESCRIPTION
clari.biz.finance	Financial news
misc.fitness	Discussion about physical fitness
misc.jobs.offered	Online job hunting
rec.travel	Discussion for those who love to travel
soc.women	Discussions of women's issues

FIGURE 11
Five popular newsgroups.

FIGURE 12
Selected discussion group
terms.

■ ■ ■ ■ ■ ■ ■ ■ ■

DISCUSSION GROUP TERMS

TERM	DESCRIPTION
Lurking	Reading news but not joining in to contribute
FAQ	Frequently asked question
Flaming	Insulting, putting-down, or attacking
RFD	Request for discussion
Saint	Someone who aids new users by answering questions
Thread	A sequence of ongoing messages on the same subject
Wizard	Someone who has comprehensive knowledge about a subject

Telnet and FTP

Telnet runs programs on remote computers. FTP transfers files.

Telnet

Many computers on the Internet will allow you to connect to them and to run selected programs on them. **Telnet** is the Internet service that allows you to dial another computer (host) on the Internet and log on to that computer as if you were a terminal in the next room. There are hundreds of computers on the Internet that you can connect to. Some allow limited free access and others charge fees for their use.

The NASA SPACElink computer, located in Huntsville, Alabama, allows free public access. The Internet address for this computer is spacelink.msfc.nasa.gov. This Telnet link was originally designed for science teachers and is now available to the general public through the Internet. With it you can learn about NASA's history, read about exploration plans, view animated clips, and participate in a variety of other space-related activities. (See Figure 13.)

Medline is an example of a fee-based Telnet link. Medline is the National Library of Medicine database. This database is not universally available to the public. It is a commercial database that charges for its services and controls its Telnet access. Medline contains millions of articles from more than 4000 medical journals. It is an excellent medical research tool. Many university and public libraries license Medline, so you may have access to it without incurring special fees.

FTP

FTP (file transfer protocol) is an Internet service for transferring files. Many computers on the Internet allow you to copy files to your computer. This is called **downloading.** Using FTP you can also copy files from your computer to another computer on the Internet. This is called **uploading.**

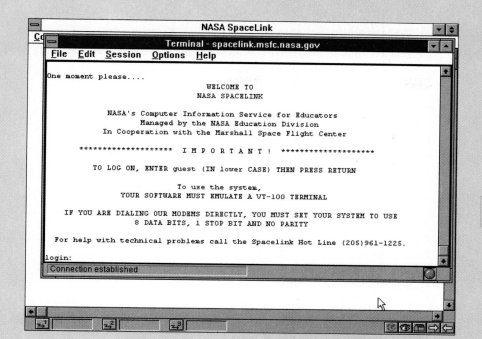

FIGURE 13
NASA SPACElink.

FTP and Telnet are not the same. Telnet allows you to run programs from remote computers but does not support copying of files. FTP allows copying of files but does not support running of programs from another computer.

Computers on the Internet that allow copying of their files are called **FTP sites.** There are more than 1500 separate FTP sites that allow access to millions of publicly available files. FTP allows access to a large number of databases, from stock market quotations to personal income census data.

With all the information that is available on the Internet, finding a particular file can be difficult. Fortunately, specialized search programs are available to help locate information on the Internet. One of the best known is called **Archie.** It is a program that automatically checks FTP sites at least once every month to see what files are publicly available. Archie notes file names, locations, and descriptions (if available). Computers on the Internet that run Archie are called **Archie servers.**

To locate information on specific topics, you can connect to an Archie server. There are more than forty Archie servers located throughout the world. Although some of these servers are fee-based, **public Archie servers** are free. (See Figure 14.)

PUBLIC ARCHIE SERVERS

LOCATION	INTERNET ADDRESS (LOG IN AS ARCHIE)
Maryland	archie.sura.net
Nebraska	archie.unl.edu
New York	archie.ans.net
Australia	archie.au
Japan	archie.wide.ad.jp

FIGURE 14
Five public Archie servers.

Gophers

Gophers provide menus for each gopher site. Veronica provides custom menus for many gopher sites. WAIS looks into documents.

L ooking for information on the Internet is called "surfing the net." It can be quite enjoyable when you have the time. But, it can be pretty frustrating if you need some specific information in a timely manner.

FIGURE 15

Gopher menu.

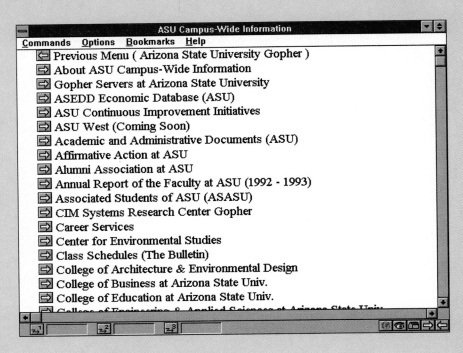

There are millions of public files available on host computers all around the world. How can you find what you're looking for? How can you effectively surf the net? A good way is to use Internet search tools. One widely used tool is called *gopher.*

Menus

Gopher is a software application that provides menu-based search and retrieval functions for a particular computer site. It was originally developed at the University of Minnesota in 1991. Internet **gopher sites** are computers that provide menus describing their available resources and direct links to the resources. Essentially, these menus are a "table of contents" for organizing and locating information. In addition, these sites typically handle transferring of files (FTP) and connecting to other computers (Telnet). (See Figure 15.)

Public Gophers

There are thousands of gophers on the Internet that provide free access. These free gopher sites are called **public gophers.** (See Figure 16.)

To search for information, you would likely begin at one of the public gophers, search its available resources, and then move to another gopher site and continue this process. Gophers are used to search for a wide variety of different types of information. They can find e-mail addresses, locate mailing lists and newsgroups, and research specific topics.

Veronica

Veronica is typically one of the options available from a gopher menu. It is a software application that makes searching for information with gophers much more efficient. Veronica periodically checks with a large number of gopher sites and

PUBLIC GOPHERS

LOCATION	INTERNET ADDRESS (LOG IN AS GOPHER)
Illinois	ux1.cso.uiuc.edu
Michigan	gopher.msu.edu
Virginia	ecosys.drdr.virginia.edu
England	info.brad.ac.uk
Europe	gopher.edbone.net

FIGURE 16

Five public gopher sites.

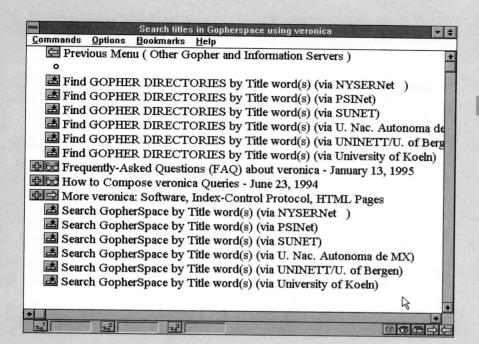

FIGURE 17
Veronica menu.

maintains a list of the menus at each site. Upon request, Veronica will search this list for a specific word or topic. It will then display a custom-menu listing each gopher menu that contains the word or topic. The user can then select from the Veronica menu to connect directly to the topic area. (See Figure 17.)

WAIS

Another search tool, **WAIS (wide area information server)** (pronounced "wayz"), extends the search capabilities of gopher and Veronica. Veronica creates its list of available resources by investigating menu options from various gopher sites. WAIS goes one step further by examining individual documents and maintaining an extensive list of key words and phrases. A WAIS search on a topic is more thorough and provides more specific references. There are hundreds of WAIS sites available. Each site generally maintains information on a single subject. (See Figure 18.)

WAIS SITES

LOCATION	INTERNET ADDRESS	LOG IN
California	quake.think.com	wais
California	swais.cwis.uci.edu	swais
North Carolina	sunsite.unc.edu	swais
Massachusetts	nnsc.nsf.net	swais
Finland	info.funet.fi	wais

FIGURE 18
Five WAIS sites.

World Wide Web

WWW uses hypertext to jump from document to document and from computer to computer. Browsers are software programs to access the WWW.

One of the newest Internet search tools is **World Wide Web,** also known as **WWW, W3,** and the **Web.** It was introduced in 1992 at CERN, the Center for European Nuclear Research in Geneva, Switzerland. Like gopher, WWW provides a search and retrieval system that conveniently handles transferring of files (FTP) and connecting to other computers on the Internet (Telnet). But WWW takes gopher one step further by using hypertext.

Hypertext

A **hypertext** document contains more than information. It also contains references and links to other documents that contain related information. These documents may be located on a nearby computer system or one located halfway around the world. These references are similar to traditional footnotes or bibliographies.

The references appear as highlighted text in the hypertext document. To access the references material, all you do is click on the highlighted text. A link is automatically made to the computer containing the material, and the referenced material appears.

These linked information sources are called **pages.** Any one page may contain many hypertext links to related information—text files, graphic images, movies, audio, or video clips. WWW allows you to jump from one page to another in a nonsequential manner. (See Figure 19.)

FIGURE 19
WWW page with hypertext links.

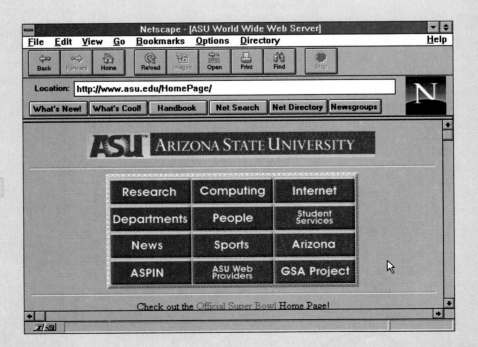

Browsers

The WWW is typically accessed by using special software known as **browsers.** This software connects to remote computers, opens and transfers files, displays text and images, and provides in one tool an uncomplicated interface to the Internet and WWW documents. Three well-known browsers are Lynx, Mosaic, and Netscape. (See Figure 20.)

See Figure 21 for a summary of Internet search tools.

FIGURE 20

Netscape.

FIGURE 21

Four Internet search tools.

INTERNET SEARCH TOOLS

TOOL	DESCRIPTION
Gopher	Provides a menu of available information resources from a particular computer
Veronica	Lists available information resources at several computer sites by searching each site's gopher menu
WAIS	Searches individual documents available at several computer sites for specific key words and phrases
WWW	Uses hypertext to link information resources on different computers

A Look at the Future

The Internet is making the world smaller, providing a foundation for the NIH, and creating global villages in cyberspace.

I s the world getting smaller? It is in the sense that we can share ideas and resources with people halfway around the world just as though they were in the next room. Many have compared the Internet to a superhighway of information and ideas for the 20th century.

The Internet is the foundation for a large project called the **National Information Highway (NIH),** also known as the **National Information Infrastructure (NII)** and as the **information superhighway.** These popular phrases are used to describe the future of communication networks and computers. Legislation proposed and championed by Vice President Gore has laid the foundation for this billion-dollar project. Because of this legislation, Congress is now encouraging private investment, competition, and two-way universal access for the NIH.

We are just at the forefront of this rapidly evolving area. Sociologists suggest that the most significant advances will develop from the so-called global village. Unlike a normal village where members are located near one another, the global village is not constrained by geographic space. It is constrained only by cyberspace, or communication links with computers. Members will likely develop close relationships without ever seeing one another. In fact, they may live in different parts of the world with widely varying cultures and backgrounds.

What is the future of the Internet and the information superhighway? No one knows for certain, but the clear consensus is that they will provide a wide-open highway from your home and future office to the rest of the world.

KEY TERMS

Archie (IG12)

Archie server (IG12)

ARPANET (IG2)

browser (IG16)

cyberspace (IG1)

dial-up connection (IG6)

domain code (IG8)

domain name (IG8)

domain name system (DNS) (IG8)

downloading (IG11)

e-mail (IG6)

FTP (file transfer protocol) (IG11)

FTP site (IG12)

gopher (IG13)

gopher site (IG13)

host computer (IG4)

hypertext (IG15)

information superhighway (IG17)

list address (IG9)

lurking (IG10)

mailing list (IG9)

National Information Highway (NIH) (IG17)

National Information Infrastructure (NII) (IG17)

newsgroup (IG10)

packet (IG6)

page (IG15)

PPP (point to point protocol) (IG5)

provider (IG4)

public Archie server (IG12)

public gopher (IG13)

SLIP (serial line internet protocol) (IG5)

subscription address (IG9)

TCP/IP (transmission control protocol/ internet protocol) (IG6)

Telnet (IG11)

terminal connection (IG6)

uploading (IG11)

UseNet (IG10)

user name (IG8)

Veronica (IG13)

WAIS (wide area information server) (IG14)

World Wide Web, WWW, W3, the Web (IG15)

The Internet Guide: How to Surf the Net

The Internet is the roadway for ideas and information through **cyberspace.** It is a giant world-wide computer network.

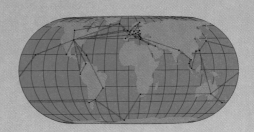

ACCESS

Providers

The most common access is through a **provider** or **host computer.** Three types of providers:

- **Free-Nets** are electronic towns that provide free access.
- **Colleges** and **universities** often provide free student access.
- **Online commercial service providers** provide access for a fee.

Connections

To access the Internet, you need to connect to a provider. Three types of connections:

- **Direct** or **dedicated** lines directly connect to the Internet through expensive high-speed lines.
- **SLIP** and **PPP** connections use high-speed modems. They are widely used by individuals.
- **Dial-up** connections also use high-speed modems but are not as fast or convenient as SLIP or PPP connections.

TCP/IP

TCP/IP (transmission control protocol/Internet protocol) is the standard protocol of the Internet.

IG19

E-MAIL

Basic Elements

An e-mail message has three basic elements:

- The **header** includes To, From, Subject, and Attachment lines
- The **message** is short and to the point
- The **signature** provides additional sender information

Addresses

The Internet uses the **domain name system (DNS)** addressing system.

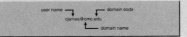

Netiquette

Netiquette is the accepted rules of etiquette when using the Internet.

DISCUSSION GROUPS

DISCUSSION GROUP TERMS

TERM	DESCRIPTION
Lurking	Reading news but not joining in to contribute
FAQ	Frequently asked question
Flaming	Insulting, a putting-down, or attacking
RFD	Request for discussion
Saint	Someone who aids new users by answswering questions
Thread	A sequence of ongoing messages on the same subject
Wizard	Someone who has comprehensive knowledge about a subject

Mailing Lists

Mailing lists, one type of **discussion group,** send all messages to each member of a **list address.** You can subscribe and unsubscribe to a list by sending a request to the **subscription address.**

Newsgroups

Newgroups are the most popular. Using a special network, UseNet, discussions are organized into topic areas and hierarchies. Interested individuals copy down only those contributions of interest.

Lurking

Lurking is a commonly used discussion group term that means to observe before contributing to a discussion.

TELNET AND FTP	GOPHERS	WWW

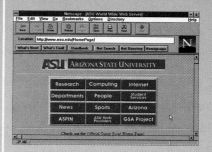

Telnet

Telnet allows you to connect to a host computer, log on to that computer, and run programs from that computer. Your microcomputer acts as a terminal.

FTP

FTP (file transfer protocol) allows transferring or copying files from a host computer to your microcomputer (**downloading**) and transferring from your computer to a host computer (**uploading**). **Archie servers** automatically check FTP sites monthly. **Archie public servers** are free.

PUBLIC ARCHIE SERVERS

LOCATION	INTERNET ADDRESS (LOG IN AS ARCHIE)
Maryland	archie.sura.net
Nebraska	archie. unl.edu
New York	archie.ans.net
Australia	archie.au
Japan	archie.wide.ad.jp

Menus

Gophers are programs that provide **menu**-based search and retrieval operations. These gophers run on host computers called **gopher sites** and provide access to that site's facilities.

Public Gophers

Public gophers allow free access to their facilities. Internet users seeking specific information typically begin at one public gopher and search its resources, then move to another and continue their search.

Veronica

One option on most gopher sites is **Veronica.** It is a program that searches other gopher sites, maintaining a list of the menus at these sites. Veronica can also search for a specific word or topic.

WAIS

WAIS (wide area information server) extends gopher and Veronica search capabilities. It examines individual documents located on host computers throughout the Internet. It maintains an extensive list of key words and phrases usually pertaining to a single subject.

The World Wide Web (WWW, W3, Web) is a search and retrieval system that handles FTP and Telnet operations. WWW takes gopher one step further by using hypertext.

Hypertext

Hypertext documents have highlighted text that identifies links to other **pages** of information. It allows WWW to nonsequentially jump from one page to another.

Browsers

Browsers are programs that provide an interface for the WWW. They connect, open, and transfer files as well as display text and graphs.

Three well-known browsers are Lynx, Mosaic, and Netscape.

IG20

The Buyer's Guide:

How to Buy Your Own Microcomputer System

Some people make snap judgments about some of the biggest purchases in their lives: cars, college educations, houses. People have been known to buy things based solely on an ad, a brief conversation, or a one-time look. And they may be making an impulsive decision about something costing thousands of dollars. Who is to blame, then, if they are disappointed later? They simply didn't take time to check it out.

The same concerns apply in buying a microcomputer system. You can make your choice on the basis of a friend's enthusiasm or a salesperson's promises. Or you can proceed more deliberately, as you would, say, in looking for a job.

Four Steps in Buying a Microcomputer System

The following is not intended to make buying a microcomputer an exhausting experience. Rather, it is to help you clarify your thinking about what you need and can afford.

The four steps in buying a microcomputer system are presented on the following pages. We divided each step into two parts on the assumption that your needs may change, but so may the money you have to spend on a microcomputer. For instance, later in your college career or after college graduation, you may want a far more powerful computer system than you need now. At that point you may have more money to spend. Or you may not need to spend money at all, if your employer provides you with a computer.

Step 1: What Needs Do I Want a Computer to Serve?

The trick is to distinguish between your needs and your wants. Sure, you *want* a cutting-edge system powerful enough to hold every conceivable record you'll ever need. And you want a system fast enough to process them all at the speed of light. But do you *need* this? Your main concern is to address the two-part question:

- What do I need a computer system to do for me today?
- To do for me in another year or two?

The questionnaire at the end of this guide will help you determine the answers to both questions.

Suggestions

The first thing to establish is whether you need a computer at all. Some colleges offer computer facilities at the library or in some dormitories. Or perhaps you can borrow a roommate's. The problem, however, is that when you are up against a term-paper deadline, many others may be also. Then the machine you want may not be available. To determine the availability of campus computers, call the computer center or the dean of students' office.

Another matter on which you might want advice is what type of computer is popular on campus. Some schools favor Apple Macintoshes, others favor IBMs or IBM-compatibles. If you own a system that's incompatible with most others on campus, you may be stuck if your computer breaks down. Ask someone knowledgeable who is a year or two ahead of you if your school favors one system over another.

Finally, look ahead and determine whether your major requires a computer. Business and engineering students may find one a necessity, physical education and drama majors less so. Your major may also determine the kind of computer that's best. A journalism major may want an IBM or IBM-compatible notebook that can be set up anywhere. An architecture major may want a powerful desktop Macintosh with a LaserWriter printer that can produce elaborate drawings. Ask your academic advisor for some recommendations.

Example

Suppose you are a college student beginning your sophomore year, with no major declared. Looking at the courses you will likely take this year, you decide you will probably need a computer mainly for word processing. That is, you need a system that will help you write short (10- to 20-page) papers for a variety of courses.

By this time next year, however, you may be an accounting major. Having talked to some juniors and seniors, you find that courses in this major, such as financial accounting, will require you to use elaborate spreadsheets. Or maybe you will be a fine arts or architectural major. Then you may be required to submit projects for which drawing and painting desktop publishing software would be helpful. Or perhaps you will be out in the job market and will be writing application letters and résumés. In that case, you'll want them to have a professional appearance.

Step 2: **How Much Money Do I Have to Spend on a Computer System?**

When you buy your first computer, you are not necessarily buying your last. Thus, you can think about spending just the bare-bones amount for a system that meets your needs while in college. Then you might plan to get another system later on. After all, most college students who own cars (quite often used cars) don't consider those the last cars they'll own. Or, if you can afford it, you can buy an expensive system. That way, your computer will handle any kind of work required in your major and even after graduation.

You know what kind of money you have to spend. Your main concern is to answer this two-part question:

- How much am I prepared to spend on a computer system today?
- How much am I prepared to spend in another year or two?

The questionnaire at the end of this guide asks you this.

Suggestions

You can probably buy a used computer of some sort for under $400 and a printer for under $100. On the other hand, you might spend $2000–$5000 on a new state-of-the-art system. When upgraded, this computer could meet your needs for the next 5 years.

There is nothing wrong with getting a used system, if you have a way of checking it out. For a reasonable fee, a computer-repair shop can examine it prior to your purchase. Look at newspaper ads and notices on campus bulletin boards for good buys on used equipment. Often the sellers will include a great deal of software and other items (disks, reference materials) with the package. If you stay with recognized brands such as Apple, IBM, Compaq, Dell, or Zeos, you probably won't have any difficulties. The exception may be with printers, which, since they are principally mechanical devices, may get a lot of wear and tear. This is even more reason to tell the seller you want a repair shop to examine the equipment before you buy.

If you're buying new equipment, be sure to look for student discounts. Most college bookstores, for instance, offer special prices to students. Mail-order houses also steeply discount their products. These firms run ads in such periodicals as *Computer Shopper* (sold on newsstands) and other magazines. However, using mail and telephone for repairs and support can be a nuisance. Often you can use the prices advertised by a mail-order house to get local retail computer stores to lower their prices.

Example

Perhaps you have access to a microcomputer at the campus student computing center, the library, or the dormitory. Or you can borrow a friend's. However, this computer isn't always available when it's convenient for you. Moreover, you're not only going to college but also working, so both time and money are tight. Having your own computer would enable you to write papers when it's convenient for you. Spending more than $500 might cause real hardship, so a new microcomputer system may be out of the question. You'll need to shop the newspaper classified ads or the campus bulletin boards to find a used but workable computer system.

Or, maybe you can afford to spend more now—say, between $1000 and $2000—but probably only $500 next year. By this time next year, however, you'll know your major and how your computer needs have changed. For example, if you're going to be a finance major, you need to have a lot more computer memory (primary storage). This will hold the massive amounts of data you'll be working with in your spreadsheets. Or maybe you'll be an architecture major or graduating and looking for a job. In that case, you'll need a laser printer to produce attractive-looking designs or application letters. Thus, whatever system you buy this year, you'll want to upgrade it next year.

Step 3: What Kind of Software Will Best Serve My Needs?

Most computer experts urge that you determine what software you need before you buy the hardware. The reasoning here is that some hardware simply won't run the software that is important to you. This is certainly true once you get into *sophisticated* software. Examples include specialized programs available for certain professions (such as certain agricultural or retail-management programs). However, if all you are interested in today are the basic tools of software—word processing, spreadsheet, and communications programs— these are available for nearly all microcomputers. The main caution to be aware of is that some more recent versions of application software won't run on older hardware. Still, if someone offers you a free computer, don't say no "because I have to decide what software I need first." You will no doubt find it sufficient for many general purposes, especially during the early years in college.

That said, you are better served if you follow step 3 after step 2—namely, finding the answers to the two-part question:

■ What kind of software will best serve my needs today?

■ What kind will best serve my needs in another year or two?

The questionnnaire at the end of this guide may help you determine your answers.

Suggestions

No doubt some kinds of application software are more popular on your campus— and in certain departments on your campus—than others. Are freshman and sophomore students mainly writing their term papers in Word, WordPerfect, or Ami Pro? Which spreadsheet is most often used by business students: Excel, Lotus 1-2-3, or Quattro Pro? Which desktop publishing program is most favored by graphic arts majors: PageMaker, Ventura Publisher, or First Publisher? Do many students use their microcomputers to access the Internet, and, if so, which communications software is the favorite? Do engineering and architecture majors use their own machines for CAD/CAM applications? Start by asking other students and your academic advisor.

Whatever word processing software you buy, you'll probably find the addition of an electronic spelling checker and built-in thesaurus helpful.

If you're looking to buy state-of-the-art software, you'll find plenty of advice in various computer magazines. Several of them rate the quality of newly issued programs. Such periodicals include *InfoWorld, PC World, PC/Computing,* and *MacWorld.*

Example

Suppose you determine that all you need is software to help you write short papers. In that case, nearly any kind of word processing program would do. You could even get by with some older versions or off-brand kinds of word processing software. This might happen if such software was included in the sale of a used microcomputer that you bought at a bargain price.

But will this software be sufficient a year or two from now? Looking ahead, you guess that you'll major in theater arts, and minor in screenwriting, which you may pursue as a career. At that point a simple word processing program won't do. You learn from juniors and seniors in that department that screenplays are written using special screenwriting programs. This is software that's not available for some computers. Or, as an advertising and marketing major, you're expected to turn word-processed promotional pieces into brochures. For this, you need desktop publishing software. Or, as a physics major, you discover you will need to write reports on a word processor that can handle equations. This requires a machine with a great deal of memory. In short, you need to look at your software needs not just for today but also for the near future. You especially want to consider what programs will be useful to you in building your career.

Step 4: What Kind of Hardware Will Best Serve My Needs?

A bare-bones hardware system might include a five-year-old desktop or portable computer with a 5¼-inch floppy disk drive and a hard disk drive. It may also include a monochrome monitor and a dot-matrix printer. With a newer system, the sky's the limit. On the one hand, as a student—unless you're involved in some very specialized activities—it's doubtful you'll need such things as voice-input devices, touch screens, scanners, and the like. On the other hand, you may need a 3½-inch floppy disk drive and a CD-ROM drive. The choices of equipment are vast.

As with the other steps, the main task is to find the answers to the two-part question:

- What kind of hardware will best serve my needs today?
- What kind will best serve my needs in another year or two?

There are several questions on the questionnaire at the end of this guide to help you determine answers to these concerns.

Suggestions

Clearly, you should let the software be your guide in determining your choice of hardware. Perhaps you've found that the most popular software in your department runs on a Macintosh rather than an IBM-compatible. If so, that would seem to determine your general brand of hardware.

Whether you buy IBM or Macintosh, a desktop or a portable, we suggest you get a 3½-inch floppy disk drive, a hard disk drive, and at least 4MB of memory. If you can afford a CD-ROM disc drive and more memory, so much the better. And, of course, you need some sort of printer.

As with software, several computer magazines not only describe new hardware but also issue ratings. See *InfoWorld, PC World,* and *MacWorld,* for example.

Example

Right now, let's say, you're mainly interested in using a computer to write papers, so almost anything would do. But you need to look ahead.

Suppose you find that WordPerfect seems to be the software of choice around your campus. You find that WordPerfect 5.0 will run well on a 386 machine with 4MB of memory and a 60-MB hard disk. A near-letter-quality dot-matrix printer will probably be acceptable for most papers. Although this equipment is now outdated, you find from looking at classified ads that there are many such used machines around. Plus, they cost very little—under $500 for a complete system.

If you're a history or philosophy major, maybe this is all the hardware and software you need. Indeed, this configuration may be just fine all the way through college. However, some majors, and the careers following them, may require more sophisticated equipment. Your choice then becomes: Should I buy an inexpensive system now that can't be upgraded, then sell it later and buy a better one? Or should I buy at least some of the components of a good system now and upgrade it over the next year or so?

As an advertising major, you see the value of learning desktop publishing. This will be a useful if not essential skill once you embark on a career. In exploring the software, you learn that Word includes some desktop publishing capabilities. However, the hardware you previously considered simply isn't sufficient. Morever, you learn from reading about software and talking to people in your major that there are better desktop publishing programs. Specialized desktop publishing programs like Ventura Publisher are considered more versatile than Word. Probably the best software arrangement, in fact, is to have Word as a word processing program and Ventura Publisher running under Windows for a desktop publishing program.

To be sure, the campus makes computers that will run this software available to students. If you can afford it, however, you're better off having your own. Now, however, we're talking about a major expense. A computer running a Pentium microprocessor, with 8 MB of memory, a 3½-inch disk drive, a CD-ROM disc drive, and an 850-MB hard disk, plus a modem, color monitor, and laser printer, could run in excess of $3000.

Perhaps the best idea is to buy now knowing how you would like your system to grow in the future. That is, you will buy a microcomputer with a Pentium microprocessor. But at this point, you will buy only an ink jet printer and not buy a CD-ROM drive. Next year or the following, you might sell off the less sophisticated peripheral devices and add a CD-ROM drive and a laser printer.

Developing a Philosophy About Computer Purchasing

It's important not to develop a case of "computer envy." Even if you bought the latest, most expensive microcomputer system, in a matter of months, something better will come along. Computer technology is still in a very dynamic state, with more powerful, versatile, and compact systems constantly hitting the marketplace. So what if your friends have the hottest new piece of software or hardware? The main question is: Do you need it to solve the tasks required of you or to keep up in your field? Or can you get along with something simpler but equally serviceable?

The Buyer's Guide: How to Buy Your Own
Microcomputer System

To help clarify your thinking about buying a microcomputer system, complete
the questionnaire below by checking the appropriate boxes.

NEEDS			BUDGET		

? What do I need a computer system to do for me today? In another year or two?

$ How much am I prepared to spend on a system today? In another year or two?

I wish to use the computer for:

	Today	1–2 years
Word processing—writing papers, letters, memos, or reports	❏	❏
Business or financial applications—balance sheets, sales projections, expense budgets, or accounting problems	❏	❏
Record-keeping and sorting—research bibliographies, scientific data, or address files	❏	❏
Graphic presentations— of business, scientific, or social science data	❏	❏
Online information retrieval— from campus networks, electronic bulletin boards, CompuServe, Prodigy, or the Internet	❏	❏
Publications, design, or drawing—for printed news-letters, architectural drawing, or graphic arts	❏	❏
Multimedia—for video games, viewing, creating, presenting, or research	❏	❏
Other—(Specify): _____	❏	❏

I can spend:

	Today	1–2 years
Under $500	❏	❏
Up to $1000	❏	❏
Up to $1500	❏	❏
Up to $2000	❏	❏
Up to $2500	❏	❏
Over $3000 (specify) _____	❏	❏

STEP	QUESTIONS	
1	**?**	*My Needs:* What do I need a computer system to do for me today? In another year or two?
2	**$**	*My Budget:* How much am I prepared to spend on a system today? In another year or two?
3	💾	*My Software:* What kind of software will best serve my needs today? In another year or two?
4	🖥	*My Hardware:* What kind of hardware will best serve my needs today? In another year or two?

SOFTWARE

💾 What kinds of software will best serve my needs today? In another year or two?

The application software I need includes:

	Today	1–2 years
Word processing—WordPerfect, Word, Ami Pro, or other (specify): _____	☐	☐
Spreadsheet—Lotus 1-2-3, Excel, Quattro Pro, or other (specify): _____	☐	☐
Database—dBASE, Paradox, Access, Approach, or other (specify): _____	☐	☐
Presentation Graphics— Harvard Graphics, PowerPoint, Freelance, or other (specify): _____	☐	☐
Communications—ProComm, Smartcom, Crosstalk, or other (specify): _____	☐	☐
Other—integrated packages, software suites, programming, multimedia, desktop publishing, CAD/CAM, other (specify): _____	☐	☐

The system software I need:

	Today	1–2 years
DOS	☐	☐
Windows	☐	☐
Windows 95	☐	☐
Windows NT	☐	☐
OS/2	☐	☐
Macintosh	☐	☐
Unix	☐	☐
Other (specify): _____	☐	☐

HARDWARE

🖥 What kinds of hardware will best serve my needs today? In another year or two?

The hardware I need includes:

	Today	1–2 years
Microprocessor—80486, Pentium, 68030, 68040, Power PC, other (specify): _____	☐	☐
Memory—(specify amount): _____	☐	☐
Monitor—monochrome, color, size, (specify): _____	☐	☐
Floppy disk drives—3½″ and/or 5¼″ (specify size of drive): _____	☐	☐
Optical disc drive—CD-ROM, WORM, erasable (specify type, speed, and capacity): _____	☐	☐
Hard disk drive—(specify capacity): _____	☐	☐
Portable computer—laptop, notebook, subnotebook, personal digital assistant (specify): _____	☐	☐
Printer—dot-matrix, ink-jet, laser, color (specify): _____	☐	☐
Other—modem, speakers, fax, surge protector (specify): _____	☐	☐

Glossary

Access arm: The arm that holds the read-write head and moves back and forth over the surface of a disk.

Access time: The period between the time the computer requests data from a secondary storage device and the time the transfer of data is completed.

Active-matrix monitor: Monitor in which each pixel is independently activated. More colors with better clarity can be displayed.

Adapter card: *See* Expansion board

Address: Location in main memory in which characters of data or instructions are stored during processing.

ALU: *See* Arithmetic-logic unit

American Standard Code of Information Interchange: *See* ASCII

Analog signal: Signal that represents a range of frequencies, such as the human voice.

Analysis tool: Program tools that help perform complicated what-if analyses.

Analytical graphics: Form of graphics used to put numeric data into forms that are easier to analyze, such as bar charts, line graphs, and pie charts.

Application software: Software that can perform useful work, such as word processing, cost estimating, or accounting tasks.

Archie: Internet utility used to locate and copy files.

Archie server: A computer on the Internet that runs Archie is called an Archie server.

Arithmetic-logic unit (ALU): The part of the CPU that performs arithmetic and logical operations.

Artificial intelligence(AI): A field of computer science that attempts to develop computer systems that can mimic or simulate human thought processes and actions.

Artificial reality: *See* Virtual reality

ASCII (American Standard Code for Information Interchange): Binary coding scheme widely used on all computers, including microcomputers.

Asynchronous communications port: *See* Serial port

Asynchronous transmission: Method whereby data is sent and received one byte at a time.

Backup: Duplicate copy of a disk or program.

Backup tape cartridge unit: *See* Magnetic tape streamer

Bandwidth: Bit-per-second transmission capability of a channel.

Bar code: Code consisting of vertical zebra-striped marks printed on product containers; read with a bar-code reader.

Bar-code reader: Photoelectric scanner that reads bar codes for processing.

Basic input-output system: Type of system software consisting of programs that interpret keyboard characters or transmit characters to monitor or disk.

Batch processing: Processing performed all at once on data that has been collected over several days.

Baud rate: Communication speed; the number of changes in the electrical state in the line per second. At low speeds, baud rate is equal to bits per second (bps), but at higher speeds it is not.

BBS: *See* Electronic bulletin board system

Binary system: Numbering system in which all numbers consist of only two digits—0 and 1.

Bit (binary digit): A 0 or 1 in the binary system.

Booting: Loading the operating system from hard or floppy disk into memory when the computer is turned on.

Bootstrap loader: Program that is stored permanently in the computer's electronic circuitry. When the computer is turned on, the bootstrap loader obtains the operating system from a hard or floppy disk and loads it into memory.

Broadband: Bandwidth that includes microwave, satellite, coaxial cable, and fiber-optic channels. It is used for very high-speed computers.

Browser: Special Internet software that allows users to effortlessly jump from one computer's resources to another computer's resources.

Bus (bus line): Electronic data roadway, connecting the parts of the CPU to each other and linking the CPU with other important hardware, along which bits travel. Also, the common connecting cable in a bus network.

Bus network: Network in which all communications travel along a common path. Each device in the network handles its own communications control. There is no host computer or file server.

Button bar: Bar located on the screen, typically below the menu bar. It contains icons or graphics representations for commonly used commands.

Byte: Unit consisting of eight bits. There are 256 possible bit combinations in a byte.

Cache memory: Area of random-access memory (RAM) set aside to store the most frequently accessed information. Acts as a temporary high-speed holding zone between memory and CPU.

Cathode-ray tube (CRT): Desktop-type monitor built in the same way as a television set.

CD-R: An optical disc that can be written to once. After that it can be read many times without deterioration and cannot be written on or erased.

CD-ROM (compact disc read-only memory): Form of optical disc that allows data to be read but not recorded.

Cell: Intersection of a row and a column in a spreadsheet. A cell holds a single unit of information.

Cell address: Position of a cell in a spreadsheet.

Cell pointer: Indicator for where data is to be entered or changed in a spreadsheet.

Central processing unit (CPU): Part of the computer that holds data and program instructions for processing the data. The CPU consists of the control unit and the arithmetic-logic unit. In a microcomputer, the CPU is on a single electronic component, the microprocessor chip.

Character-based interface: Arrangement in DOS in which users issue commands by typing or selecting items from a menu.

Child node: A node one level below the node being considered in a hierarchical database or network.

Chip: A tiny circuit board etched on a small square of sandlike material called silicon.

CISC (complex instruction set computer) chip: The most common type of microprocessor that has thousands of programs written specifically for it.

Client/server network system: Network in which one powerful computer coordinates and supplies services to all other nodes on the network. Server nodes coordinate and supply specialized services, and client nodes request the services.

Clip art: Graphics enhancement that enables the user to include available graphic images in a document.

Coaxial cable: High-frequency transmission cable that replaces the multiple wires of telephone lines with a single solid copper core.

Column headings: Labels across the top of the worksheet area of a spreadsheet.

Command line interface: *See* Character-based interface

Common operational database: Integrated collection of records that contain details about the operations of a company.

Common user database: Company database that contains selected information both from the common operational database and from outside (proprietary) databases.

Company database: Collection of integrated records shared throughout a company or other organization.

Computer: Electronic device that can follow instructions to accept input, process that input, and produce information.

Computer competent: Being able to use a computer to meet one's information needs.

Computer network: Communications system connecting two or more computers and their peripheral devices.

Computer program: *See* Software

Computer virus: Hidden instructions that migrate through networks and operating systems and become embedded in different programs. They may be designed to destroy data or simply to display messages.

Connectivity: Capability of the microcomputer to use information from the world beyond one's desk. Data and information can be sent over telephone or cable lines and through the air.

Context-sensitive help: Feature of most application software that locates and displays reference information directly related to the task the user is performing.

Continuous speech recognition system: Voice-recognition system used to control a microcomputer's operations and to issue commands to special application programs.

Controller card: *See* Expansion board

Control unit: Section of the CPU that tells the rest of the computer how to carry out program instructions.

Conventional memory: First 640K of RAM.

Copy: Duplicate. In word processing, moving selected portions of text from one location to another.

CPU: *See* Central processing unit

Cursor: Blinking symbol on the screen that shows where data may be entered.

Cursor control keys: Special keys that are used to move the cursor.

Custom-made software: Software designed by a professional programmer for a particular purpose.

Custom program: *See* Custom-made software

Cut: In word processing, this command removes a portion of highlighted text to be moved from the screen.

Cyberspace: The space of electronic movement of ideas and information.

Data: Raw, unprocessed facts that are input to a computer system.

Database administrator (DBA): Person in a large organization who determines the structure of the large databases and evaluates the performance of the database management system.

Database file: File containing highly structured and organized data.

Database management system (DBMS): *See* Database manager

Database manager: Software package used to set up, or structure, a database.

Data communications system: Electronic system that transmits data over communications lines from one location to another.

Data compression/decompression: Method of improving performance by reducing the amount of space required to store data and programs. In data compression, entering data is scanned for ways to reduce the amount of required storage. One way is to search for repeating patterns, which are replaced with a token, leaving enough so that the original can be rebuilt or decompressed.

Data dictionary: Dictionary containing a description of the structure of the data in a database.

DAT drive: *See* Digital audiotape (DAT) drive

DBA: *See* Database administrator

Dedicated fax machine: Specialized machine for sending and receiving images of documents over telephone lines.

Demodulation: Process performed by a modem in converting analog signals to digital signals.

Desktop computer: Computer small enough to fit on top or along the side of a desk and yet too big to carry around.

Desktop monitor: The most common type of monitor for the office and the home. These monitors are typically placed directly on the system unit or on the top of the desk.

Diagnostic routine: Program stored in the computer's electronic circuitry that starts up when the machine is turned on. It tests the primary storage, the CPU, and other parts of the system.

Dialog box: Box that frequently appears on the screen after selecting a command from a pull-down menu. It is used to specify additional command options.

Dial-up connection: Method of accessing the Internet using a high-speed modem and standard telephone lines.

Digital audiotape (DAT) drive: Backup technology that uses 2- by 3-inch cassettes that store 1.3 gigabytes or more.

Digital signal: Signal that represents the presence or absence of an electronic pulse.

Digitizer: Device that can be used to trace or copy a drawing or photograph. The shape is converted to digital data that can be represented on a screen or printed on paper.

Digitizing tablet: Device that enables the user to create images using a special stylus.

Direct access storage: Form of storage that allows the user to directly access information.

Direct entry: Form of input that does not require data to be keyed by someone sitting at a keyboard. Direct-entry devices create machine-readable data on paper or magnetic media or feed it directly into the CPU.

Direct file organization: File organization that makes use of key fields to go directly to the record being sought rather than reading records one after another.

Direct-image plotter: Plotter that creates images using heat-sensitive paper and electrically heated pins.

Directional arrow keys: Keys labeled with arrows that are used to move the cursor.

Discrete-word recognition system: Voice-recognition system that allows users to dictate directly into a microcomputer using a microphone.

Disk: *See* Floppy disk

Disk caching: Method of improving hard-disk performance by anticipating data needs. It requires a combination of hardware and software.

Disk drive: Input mechanism that obtains stored data and programs from a disk. It also stores data and programs on a disk.

Diskette: *See* Floppy disk

Display screen: *See* Monitor

Distributed database: Database that can be made accessible through a variety of communications networks, which allows portions of the database to be located in different places.

Document: Any kind of text material.

Document file: File created by a word processor to save documents such as letters, research papers, and memos.

Domain code: Last part of an Internet address, which identifies the geographical description or organizational identification.

Domain name: Part of an Internet address, separated from the domain code by a dot (.), that is a reference to a particular organization.

Domain name system (DNS): Internet addressing method that assigns names and numbers to people and computers.

DOS: The standard operating system for IBM and IBM-compatible microcomputers.

Dot-matrix printer: Printer that forms characters or images by using a matrix of pins that strike an inked ribbon.

Downloading: Process of transferring information from a remote computer to the computer one is using.

Drawing program: Program used to help create artwork for publications.

Drive gate: Door covering the slot in a disk drive into which a disk is inserted.

DDS: *See* Decision support system

Dumb terminal: Terminal that can be used to input and receive data but cannot process data independently.

Dynamic file link: Feature offered in some software that allows the user to link cells in one worksheet file to cells in other worksheet files.

EBCDIC (Extended Binary Coded Decimal Interchange Code): Binary coding scheme that is a standard for minicomputers and mainframe computers.

Edit: Word processing feature that makes revising and updating easy.

EISA: *See* Extended Industry Standard Architecture

Electronic bulletin board system (BBS): Electronically posted information on a computer that can be accessed by other computers using telephone lines.

Electronic mail (e-mail): Similar to an electronic bulletin board, but provides confidentiality and may use special communications rather than telephone lines.

Electronic spreadsheet: *See* Spreadsheet

Electronic town: Concept that helps us visualize the convergence of electronic resources that are available to members of a community.

Electrostatic plotter: Plotter that uses electrostatic charges to create images made up of tiny dots on specially treated paper.

E-mail: *See* Electronic mail

End user: Person who uses microcomputers or has access to larger computers.

Enter key: Key used to enter a command after it has been typed into the computer.

Enterprise computing: System in which a user on one network in an organization can access resources available throughout the organization.

EPROM: *See* Erasable programmable read-only memory

Erasable optical disc: Optical disc on which the disc drive can write information and also erase and rewrite information.

Erasable programmable read-only memory (EPROM): PROM chip that can be erased with a special ultraviolet light. New instructions can then be written on it.

Erase: Remove, as in removing obsolete electronic files from a disk.

Ethics: Standards of moral conduct.

Expanded memory: Special "island" of memory of up to 32MB that exists outside of the DOS 640K limit. Intended to help older microprocessors that cannot directly access memory over 1 MB.

Expansion board: Optional device that plugs into a slot inside the system unit. Ports on the board allow cables to be connected from the expansion board to devices outside the system unit.

Expert system: Computer program that provides advice to decision makers who would otherwise rely on human experts.

Extended Binary Coded Decimal Interchange Code: *See* EBCDIC

Extended Industry Standard Architecture (EISA): 32-bit bus standard developed by nine manufacturers of IBM-compatible microcomputers.

Extended memory: Directly accessible memory above 1 MB.

External modem: Modem that stands apart from the computer and is connected by a cable to the computer's serial port. Another cable connects the modem to the telephone wall jack.

Facsimile transmission machine: *See* Fax machine

Fax machine: Device that scans an image and sends it electronically over telephone lines to a receiving fax machine, which converts the electronic signals back to an image and recreates it on paper.

Fax modem: Special modem that enables the user to send and/or receive faxes.

Fax/modem board: Expansion board that provides the independent capabilities of a fax and a modem.

Fiber-optic cable: Special transmission cable made of glass tubes that are immune to electronic interference. Data is transmitted through fiber-optic cables in the form of pulses of light.

Field: Each column of information within a record is called a field. A field contains a set of related characters.

Find: In word processing, a command that allows the user to locate any character, word, or phrase in a document.

Firmware: Read-only memory.

Flat-panel monitor: Monitor that lies flat instead of standing upright.

Flexible disk: *See* Floppy disk

Floppy: *See* Floppy disk

Floppy disk: Flat, circular piece of magnetically treated mylar plastic that rotates within a jacket.

Formatting: Preparation of a disk so that it will accept data or programs in a computer. Also called initializing.

Form-letter feature: *See* Mail merge

Formula: Instructions for calculations in a spreadsheet.

Free-Net: Electronic community that is free not only for the members of the town but for others as well.

FTP (file transfer protocol): Internet service for transferring files.

FTP site: Computer on the Internet that allows copying of its files.

Full-duplex communication: Mode of communication in which data is transmitted back and forth at the same time.

Function: In a spreadsheet, a built-in formula that performs calculations automatically.

Function key: Key used for tasks that occur frequently, such as underlining in word processing.

Gantt chart: Chart using bars and lines to indicate the time scale of a series of tasks.

GB, G-byte: *See* Gigabyte

Gigabyte (GB, G-byte): Unit representing about 1 billion bytes.

Goal seeking tool: Program tool used to find the values needed to achieve a particular end result.

Gopher: Program that helps individuals on the Internet to access other computers on the Internet.

Gopher site: Internet computer that provides menus describing its available resources and direct links to the resources.

Grammar checker: In word processing, a tool that identifies poorly worded sentences and incorrect grammar.

Graphical user interface (GUI): Special screen that allows software commands to be issued through the use of graphic symbols (icons) or pull-down menus.

Groupware: Software that allows two or more people on a communications network to work on the same document at the same time.

GUI: *See* Graphical user interface

Half-duplex communication: Mode of communication in which data flows in both directions, but not simultaneously.

Hard copy: Images output on paper by a printer or plotter.

Hard disk: Enclosed disk drive that contains one or more metallic disks. A hard disk has many times the capacity of a floppy disk.

Hard-disk pack: Several platters aligned one above the other, thereby offering much greater storage capacity.

Hardware: Equipment that includes a keyboard, monitor, printer, the computer itself, and other devices.

Hashing: Program that uses mathematical operations to convert the key field's numeric value to a particular storage address.

Head crash: Occurs when the surface of the read-write head or particles on its surface contact the magnetic disk surface.

Help: A feature in most application software providing options that typically include an index, a glossary, and a search feature to locate reference information about specific commands.

Hierarchical database: Database in which fields or records are structured in nodes.

Hierarchical network: Network consisting of several computers linked to a central host computer. The computers linked to the host are themselves hosts to other computers or devices.

High-definition television (HDTV): All-digital television that delivers a much clearer and more detailed wide-screen picture.

Host computer: A large centralized computer. A common way of accessing the Internet. The host computer is connected to the Internet and provides a path or connection for individuals to access the Internet.

Hybrid network: *See* Hierarchical network

Hypermedia: *See* Multimedia

Hypermedia database: Database using object-oriented technology to store and link a wide range of data including graphics, animation, video, music, and voice.

Hypertext: Documents that have highlighted text that identifies links to other pages of information.

Hypertext link: On the World Wide Web, links that allow users to jump effortlessly from one computer's resources to another computer's resources.

Icon: Graphic symbol on a pull-down menu that represents a command.

Image scanner: Device that identifies images on a page and automatically converts them to electronic signals that can be stored in a computer.

Index sequential file organization: Compromise between sequential and direct file organization. Records are stored sequentially, but an index is used to access a group of records directly.

Individual database: Collection of integrated records useful mainly to just one person.

Industry Standard Architecture (ISA): Bus-line standard developed for the IBM Personal Computer. It first consisted of an 8-bit-wide data path, then a 16-bit-wide data path.

Information: Data that has been processed by a computer system.

Information superhighway: Term to describe the future of communication networks and computers. *See also* Internet

Initializing: *See* Formatting

Ink-jet plotter: Plotter that forms images by spraying droplets of ink onto paper.

Ink-jet printer: Printer that sprays small droplets of ink at high speed onto the surface of the paper.

Input device: Piece of equipment that puts data into a form a computer can process.

Insertion point: The cursor on the display screen. It shows the user where data can be entered next.

Integrated circuit: *See* Silicon chip

Integrated package: Collection of computer programs that work together and share information.

Intelligent terminal: Terminal that includes a processing unit, memory, secondary storage, communications software, and a telephone hookup or other communications link.

Interface card: *See* Expansion board

Interlaced monitor: Monitor that creates images by scanning down the screen, skipping every other line.

Internal hard disk: Storage device consisting of one or more metallic platters sealed inside a container. Internal hard disks are installed inside the system cabinet of a microcomputer.

Internal modem: Modem that is a plug-in circuit board located inside the system unit.

Internal storage: *See* Memory

Internet: A huge computer network available to nearly everyone with a microcomputer and a means to connect to it. It is a resource for information about an infinite number of topics.

ISA: *See* Industry Standard Architecture

ITV (interactive TV): Cable television service that provides videos on demand, video games, interactive shopping, and an array of entertainment and informational services.

Jacket: Protective outer covering for a floppy disk.

K, KB, K-byte: *See* Kilobyte

Keyboard: Input device that looks like a typewriter keyboard but has additional keys.

Key field: Group of logically related characters in a file record used for sorting purposes.

Kilobyte (K, KB, K-byte): Unit representing about 1000 bytes.

Label: Column or row heading in a spreadsheet.

LAN: *See* Local area network

Laptop: Portable computer that weighs between 10 and 16 pounds.

Laser printer: Printer that creates dotlike images on a drum, using a laser beam light source.

LCD: *See* Liquid crystal display

Light pen: Light-sensitive penlike device used with a special monitor to enter commands by touching the monitor with the pen.

Liquid crystal display (LCD): Display consisting of liquid crystal molecules whose optical properties can be altered by an applied electric field.

List address: Internet mailing list address. Members of a mailing list communicate by sending messages to the list address.

Local area network (LAN): Network consisting of computers and other devices that are physically near each other, such as within the same building.

Local bus: Bus combining the bus-width capabilities of MCA and EISA with the ability to send video instructions at speeds to match the microprocessor.

Lurking: Observing or reading communications from others on an Internet discussion group without participating.

Magnetic-ink character recognition (MICR): Direct-entry scanning device used in banks. This technology is used to automatically read the futuristic-looking numbers on the bottom of checks.

Magnetic tape drive: Device used to read data from and store data on magnetic tape.

Magnetic tape streamer: Device that allows duplication (backup) of the data stored on a microcomputer hard disk.

Magnetic tape unit: *See* Magnetic tape drive

Mailing list: Type of discussion group available on the Internet.

Mail merge: Feature that allows the merging of different names and addresses so the same form letter can be mailed to different people.

Mainframe: Computer that can process several million program instructions per second. Large organizations rely on these room-size systems to handle large programs with lots of data.

Main memory: *See* Memory

MAN: *See* Metropolitan area network

Mark sensing: *See* Optical-character recognition

Master file: Complete file containing all records current up to the last update.

MB, M-byte: *See* Megabyte

MCA: *See* Micro Channel Architecture

Medium band: Bandwidth of special leased lines, used mainly with minicomputers and mainframe computers.

Megabyte (MB, M-byte): Unit representing 1 million bytes.

Megahertz (MHZ): Unit representing 1 million beats (cycles) per second.

Memory: Part of the microcomputer that holds data for processing, instructions for processing the data, and information (processed data) waiting to be output or sent to secondary storage.

Memory manager: In Windows, extends the capabilities of DOS to access well beyond 640 kilobytes.

Memory-resident program: Program that stays in memory all the time, until the computer is turned off.

Menu: List of commands available for manipulating data.

Metropolitan area network (MAN): Network linking office buildings in a city.

MHZ: *See* Megahertz

MICR: *See* Magnetic-ink character recognition

Micro Channel Architecture (MCA): Bus-line standard developed to support IBM PS/2 microcomputers. MCA bus has a 32-bit-wide data path.

Microcomputer: Small, low-cost computer designed for individual users.

Microcomputer database: *See* Individual database

Microprocessor: The central processing unit of a microcomputer. The microprocessor is contained on a single integrated circuit chip.

Microprocessor chip: The single electronic component of a microcomputer that contains the central processing unit.

Microsecond: One-millionth of a second.

Microwave communication: Communication using high-frequency radio waves that travel in straight lines through the air.

Midrange computer: *See* Minicomputer

Minicomputer: Desk-sized machine falling in between microcomputers and mainframes in processing speed and data-storing capacity.

Modem: Communications device that translates the electronic signals from a computer into electronic signals that can travel over a telephone line.

Modulation: Process of converting digital signals to analog signals.

Monitor: Output device like a television screen that displays data processed by the computer.

Motherboard: *See* System board

Mouse: Device that typically rolls on the desktop and directs the cursor on the display screen.

Multimedia: Technology that can link all sorts of media into one form of presentation.

Multimedia PC: Powerful microcomputer system with a fast microprocessor and a large hard-disk drive. A multimedia system also has a soundboard, speakers, and a CD-ROM drive.

Multiprocessing: Operating system that can effectively subdivide the CPU into separate, independent parts. This allows several users to independently run programs at the same time.

Multiprogramming: Operating system that interrupts and switches rapidly back and forth between several programs while they are running. This allows several users to run different programs *seemingly* at the same time.

Multitasking: Operating system that allows a single user to run several application programs at the same time.

Multiuser: Refers to an environment in which two or more users can use a computer at the same time.

National Information Highway (NIH): Term used to describe the future of communication networks and computers. *See also* Internet

National Information Infrastructure (NII): *See* National Information Highway

Network architecture: Describes how a network is arranged and how the resources are shared.

Network database: Database with a hierarchical arrangement of nodes, except that each child node may have more than one parent node.

Network gateway: Connection by which a local area network may be linked to other local area networks or to larger networks.

Newsgroup: Most popular type of Internet discussion group. Newsgroups use a special network of computers called the UseNet. Each of these computers maintains the newsgroup listing. The newsgroups are organized into major topic areas that are further subdivided into hierarchies.

Node: Any device connected to a network. Also, points in a hierarchical database connected like the branches of an upside-down tree.

Noninterlaced monitor: Monitor that creates images by scanning each line down the screen.

Nonvolatile storage: Permanent storage used to preserve data and programs.

Notebook: Portable computer weighing between 5 and 10 pounds.

Numeric keypad: The keys 0 to 9, located on separate keys adjacent to the keyboard, used for tasks principally involving numbers.

Numeric keys: *See* Numeric keypad

OCR: *See* Optical-character recognition

OMR: *See* Optical-mark recognition

OOP: *See* Object-oriented programming

Open architecture: Microcomputer architecture allowing users to expand their systems by inserting optional devices known as expansion boards.

Operating environment: Program designed to extend the capabilities of DOS by creating an easy-to-use environment in which to work.

Operating system: Software that interacts between application software and the computer. The operating system handles such details as running programs, storing data and programs, and processing data.

Optical-character recognition (OCR): Scanning device that uses special preprinted characters, such as those printed on utility bills, that can be read by a light source and changed into machine-readable code.

Optical disc: Storage device that can hold 650 MB of data. Lasers are used to record and read data on the disc.

Optical-mark recognition (OMR): Device that senses the presence or absence of a mark, such as a pencil mark.

OS/2: The operating system developed for IBM's more powerful microcomputers.

Output device: Equipment that translates processed information from the central processing unit into a form that can be understood.

Packaged software: Programs prewritten by professional programmers that typically are offered for sale on a floppy disk.

Packet: Before a message is sent on the Internet, it is broken down into small parts called packets. Each packet is then sent separately over the Internet. At the receiving end, the packets are reassembled into the correct order.

Page: The linked information sources in a hypertext document. Any one page may contain many hypertext links to related information.

Page description language: Language that describes the shape and position of letters and graphics to the printer.

Parallel data transmission: Data transmission in which bits flow through separate lines simultaneously.

Parent node: Node one level above the node being considered in a hierarchical database or network.

Parity bit: Extra bit automatically added to a byte during keyboarding to test accuracy.

Passive-matrix monitor: Monitor that creates images by scanning the entire screen.

Password: Special sequence of numbers or letters that limits access to information, such as electronic mail.

Paste: In word processing, the command that reinserts highlighted text into a document.

PC card: *See* PCMCIA card

PCMCIA (Personal Computer Memory Card International Association) card: Credit card-sized expansion boards developed for portable computers.

PC/TV: The merger of microcomputers and television.

Peer-to-peer network system: Network in which nodes can act as both servers and clients. For example, one microcomputer can obtain files located on another microcomputer and can also provide files to other microcomputers.

Pen-based computer: Small computer that allows the user to use a stylus to write directly on the display screen.

Pen plotter: Plotter that creates plots by moving a pen or pencil over drafting paper.

Peripheral Component Interconnect (PCI): Bus architecture that combines the capabilities of MCA and EISA with the ability to send video instructions at speeds to match the microprocessor.

Peripheral device: Hardware that is outside of the system unit, such as a disk drive or a printer.

Personal computer: *See* Microcomputer

Personal digital assistant (PDA): A device that typically combines pen input, writing recognition, personal organizational tools, and communication capabilities in a very small package.

Personal information manager (PIM): Software designed to help maximize personal productivity. Typically includes electronic calendars, to-do lists, address books, and notepads.

Personal laser printer: Inexpensive laser printer widely used by single users to produce black-and-white documents.

PERT (Program Evaluation Review Technique) chart: Chart showing the timing of a project and the relationships among its tasks. The chart identifies which tasks must be completed before others can begin.

PIM: *See* Personal information manager

Pixel: Smallest unit on the screen that can be turned on and off or made different shades.

Platform scanner: Hand-held direct-entry device used to read special characters on price tags.

Plotter: Special-purpose output device for producing bar charts, maps, architectural drawings, and three-dimensional illustrations.

Plug and Play: Set of hardware and software standards developed to create operating systems, processing units, and expansion boards, as well as other devices, that are able to configure themselves.

Plug-in board: *See* Expansion board

Pointer: Additional connection between parent node and child node in a hierarchical database. *See* also Cursor

Point-of-sale (POS) terminal: Terminal that consists of a keyboard, screen, and printer. It is used like a cash register.

Polling: Process whereby a host computer or file server asks each connecting device whether it has a message to send and then allows the message to be sent.

Port: Connecting socket on the outside of the system unit. Used to connect input and output devices to the system unit.

Portable computer: Small computer that is easily carried around.

Portable operating system: Operating system that can be used with different types of computer systems.

POS terminal: *See* Point-of-sale (POS) terminal

PPP (point-to-point protocol): Software that allows your computer to become part of a client/server network. The provider or host computer is the server providing access to the Internet. Your computer is the client. Using special client software, your computer is able to communicate with server software running on the provider's computer and on other Internet computers.

Presentation graphics: Graphics used to communicate a message or to persuade other people.

Primary storage: Memory that holds data and program instructions for processing the data.

Printer: Device that produces printer paper output.

Procedures: Rules or guidelines to follow when using hardware, software, and data.

Processing rights: Refers to which people have access to what kind of data.

Processor: *See* Central processing unit

Program: List of instructions for the computer to follow to process data. *See also* Software

Programmable read-only memory (PROM): Refers to a chip that contains instructions that can be written but not changed.

Project: One-time operation composed of several tasks that must be completed during a stated period of time.

Project management software: Software that enables users to plan, schedule, and control the people, resources, and costs needed to complete a project on time.

PROM: *See* Programmable read-only memory

Proprietary database: Enormous database an organization develops to cover certain particular objects. Access to this type of database is usually offered for a fee.

Protocol: Rules for exchanging data between computers.

Provider: *See* Host computer

Public gopher: Internet software that allows free access to its facilities.

RAIDs: *See* Redundant arrays of inexpensive disks

RAM (random access memory): Volatile storage that holds the program and data the CPU is presently processing.

Random access memory (RAM): *See* RAM (random access memory)

Read: *See* Reading data

Reader/sorter: Special-purpose machine that reads characters made of ink containing magnetized particles.

Reading data: For floppy disks, the process of taking the magnetized spots from the disk, converting them to electronic signals, and transmitting them to primary storage inside the computer.

Read-only: Refers to a disk that cannot be written on or erased by the user.

Read-only memory (ROM): *See* ROM (read-only memory)

Read-write head: Electronic head that can read data from and write data onto a disk.

Real-time processing: Processing that occurs when data is processed at the same time the transaction occurs.

Recalculation: Process of recomputing values in electronic spreadsheets automatically.

Record: Each line of information in a database is a record. A record is a collection of related fields.

Redundant arrays of inexpensive disks (RAIDs): Groups of inexpensive hard-disk drives related or grouped together using networks and special software. They improve performance by expanding external storage.

Register: High-speed staging area that holds data and instructions temporarily during processing.

Relation: Table in a relational database in which data elements are stored.

Relational database: Most flexible database organization, where data elements are stored in tables and no hierarchical structure is imposed.

Release: The number after the period in a software package. Changes in releases refer to minor changes.

Rename: Give new filename to file on a disk.

Replace: In word processing, command that enables the user to search for a word and replace it with another.

Rewriteable optical disc: Similar to CD-Rs except that they can be written to many times. That is, a disc that has been written on can be erased and used over and over again.

Ring network: Network in which each device is connected to two other devices, forming a ring. There is no host computer, and messages are passed around the ring until they reach the correct destination.

RISC (reduced instruction set computer) chip: Powerful microprocessor chip found in workstations.

Robot: Machine used in factories and elsewhere that can be reprogrammed to do more than one task.

Robotics: Field of study concerned with developing and using robots.

ROM (read-only memory): Refers to chips that have programs built into them at the factory. The contents of such chips cannot be changed by the user.

Row headings: The labels down the left side of the worksheet area of a spreadsheet.

RPG (Report Program Generator): Procedural language that enables people to prepare business reports quickly and easily.

RS-232C connector: Serial port, a port set up for serial data transmission.

RSI: *See* Repetitive strain injury

Satellite communication: Communication using satellites as microwave relay stations.

Scenario tool: Program tool that allows the user to test the effect of different combinations of data.

Screen resolution: Measure of the crispness of images and characters on a screen, usually specified in terms of the number of pixels in a row or column.

Scroll bar: Bar usually located on the right and/or bottom of the screen. It enables the user to display additional information not currently visible on the screen.

SCSI card: Small computer interface card. This card uses only one slot and can connect as many as seven devices to the system unit.

Search: In word processing, command that enables the user to find a particular term in a document.

Search operation: Activity in which a disk drive rotates a floppy disk to proper position so the read-write head can find the appropriate data on the disk.

Secondary storage: Permanent storage used to preserve programs and data, including floppy disks, hard disks, and magnetic tape.

Sector: Section shaped like a pie wedge that divides the tracks on a disk.

Seek operation: Activity in which the access arm in a disk drive moves back and forth over the floppy disk to read data from or write data to the disk.

Semiconductor: Silicon chip through which electricity flows with some resistance.

Sequential access storage: Method of storage where information is stored in sequence, and all information preceding the desired information must be read first.

Sequential file organization: File organization in which records are stored physically one after another in predetermined order.

Serial data transmission: Method of transmission in which bits flow in a series, one after another.

Shared laser printer: More expensive laser printer used by a group of users to produce black-and-white documents.

Shell: Special-purpose program that allows a person to custom-build a particular kind of expert system.

Shortcut key: Key in applications for a frequently used command. They make it easier and faster to select certain commands.

Silicon chip: Tiny circuit board etched on a small square of sandlike material called silicon. Chips are mounted on carrier packages, which then plug into sockets on the system board.

Simplex communication: Mode of communication in which data travels in one direction only.

SLIP (serial line internet protocol): Internet protocol that enables your computer to become part of a client/server network. The provider or host computer is the server providing access to the Internet. Your computer is the client.

Smart card: Card about the size of a credit card containing a tiny built-in microprocessor. It can be used to hold such information as frequent flier miles.

Smart terminal: Terminal that has some memory and allows users to perform some data editing or verification before the data is sent to the host computer.

Soft copy: Images or characters output on a monitor screen.

Soft-sectored disk: Floppy disk that must be initialized (formatted) to place tracks and sectors on the surface.

Software: Computer program.

Software suite: Individual Windows application programs that are sold together as a group.

Solver tool: Program tool that allows the user to find the values needed to achieve a particular end result.

Source document: Original version of a document before any processing has been performed on it.

Spelling checker: Program used with a word processor to check the spelling of typed text against an electronic dictionary.

Spreadsheet: Spreadsheet based on the traditional accounting worksheet that has rows and columns that can be used to present and analyze data.

Star network: Network of computers or peripheral devices linked to a central computer through which all communications pass. Control is maintained by polling.

Structured query language (SQL): A database programming control language that allows direct communication to specialized mainframe databases.

Style sheet: In desktop publishing, a feature that enables the user to determine the basic appearance of single or multiple pages.

Subnotebook: Hand-held or pocket-size portable computer.

Subscription address: Mailing list address. To participate in a mailing list, you must first subscribe by sending an e-mail request to the mailing list subscription address.

Supercomputer: Fastest calculating devices ever invented, processing billions of program instructions per second.

Super VGA, SVGA: Refers to a very high resolution standard that displays up to 256 colors.

Synchronous transmission: Method whereby data is transmitted several bytes or a block at a time.

System 7.5: Apple Macintosh operating system designed for the Motorola PowerPC microprocessor.

System board: Flat board that usually contains the CPU and some memory chips.

System clock: Clock that controls how fast all the operations within a computer take place.

System software: "Background" software that enables the application software to interact with the computer. It includes programs that help the computer manage its own internal resources.

System unit: Part of a microcomputer that contains the CPU.

Table: The list of records in a database.

TB, T-byte: *See* Terabyte

TCP/IP (transmission control protocol/Internet protocol): The two standard protocols for all communications on the Internet.

Telnet: Internet service that allows you to connect to a host computer, log on to that computer, and run programs from that computer. Your microcomputer acts as a terminal.

Terabyte (TB, T-byte): Unit representing about 1 trillion bytes.

Terminal: Form of input (and output) device that consists of a keyboard, a monitor, and a communications link.

Terminal connection: Method of accessing the Internet using a high-speed modem and standard telephone lines.

Terminal network system: Network system in which processing power is centralized in one large computer, usually a mainframe. The nodes connected to this host computer are terminals with little or no processing capabilities.

Thermal printer: Printer that uses heat elements to produce images on heat-sensitive paper.

Thesaurus: Program that enables the user to quickly find the right word or an alternative word by presenting an on-screen thesaurus.

Time-sharing system: System that allows several users to share resources in the host computer.

Tool bar: Bar located typically below the menu bar. It contains icons or graphical representations for commonly used commands.

Topology: The configuration of a network.

Touch screen: Monitor screen that allows actions or commands to be entered by the touch of a finger.

Track: Closed, concentric ring on a disk on which data is recorded.

Tractor feed: Printer mechanism with sprockets that advance the printer paper, using holes on edges of continuous-form paper.

Transaction file: File containing recent changes to records that will be used to update the master file.

TSR (terminate stay resident): Refers to a program that stays in the computer's memory all the time, until the computer is turned off.

Twisted pair: Copper-wire telephone line.

Typewriter keys: Keys on a keyboard that resemble the regular letters, numbers, punctuation marks, and so on, on a typewriter.

Undo: Program feature that allows the user to restore work to the way it was before the last command was selected.

Unicode: Sixteen-bit code designed to support international languages like Chinese and Japanese.

Unix: An operating system originally developed for minicomputers. It is now important because it can run on many of the more powerful microcomputers.

Uploading: Process of transferring information from the computer the user is operating to a remote computer.

Upper memory: Memory located between 640K and 1MB of RAM. Although DOS uses this area to store information about the microcomputer's hardware, it is frequently underused and can be used by application programs.

User name: Special sequence of numbers or letters that limits access to electronic mail.

Utility program: Program that performs common repetitious tasks, such as keeping files orderly, merging, and sorting.

UseNet: Special network of computers that support newsgroups.

Value: Number contained in a cell in a spreadsheet.

Veronica: Software application typically available from a gopher menu that makes searching for information with gophers much more efficient.

Version: The number before the period in a software package. Changes in version number indicate major changes.

VESA local bus (VL-bus): A bus architecture that combines the capabilities of MCA and EISA with the ability to send video instructions at speeds to match the microprocessor.

VGA (video graphics array): Circuit board that may be inserted into a microcomputer and offers up to 256 colors.

Video display: *See* Monitor

Video display terminal (VDT): *See* Monitor

Virtual environment: *See* Virtual reality

Virtual memory: Feature of an operating system that increases the amount of memory available to run programs.

Virtual reality: Interactive sensory equipment (headgear and gloves) that allows users to experience alternative realities to the physical world.

Virus: *See* Computer virus

Voiceband: Bandwidth of a standard telephone line.

Voice-input device: Direct-entry device that converts speech into a numeric code that can be processed by a computer.

Voice-messaging system: Computer system linked to telephones that converts human voice into digital bits and stores telephone messages in "voice mailboxes" for later retrieval.

Voice-output device: Device that makes sounds resembling human speech that are actually prerecorded vocalized sounds.

Voice-recognition system: *See* Voice-input device

Volatile storage: Temporary storage that destroys the current data when power is lost or new data is read.

WAIS (wide area information server): Internet search tool that extends the search capabilities of gopher and Veronica. A WAIS search on a topic is more thorough and provides more specific references.

WAN: *See* Wide area network

Wand reader: Special-purpose hand-held device used to read OCR characters.

What-if analysis: Spreadsheet feature in which changing one or more numbers results in the automatic recalculation of all related formulas.

Wide area network (WAN): Countrywide network that uses microwave relays and satellites to reach users over long distances.

Windows: An operating environment that extends the capability of DOS.

Windows 95: Advanced operating system designed for today's powerful microcomputers. It does not require DOS to run.

Windows NT: An operating system designed to run on a wide range of powerful computers and microprocessors.

Wireless modem: Modem that connects to the serial port but does not connect to telephone lines. It receives through the air.

Word: Unit that describes the number of bits in a common unit of information.

Word art: Graphics enhancement that enables the user to manipulate text into various shapes in a document.

Word processing: Use of a computer to create, edit, save, and print documents composed of text.

Word wrap: Feature of word processing that automatically moves the cursor from the end of one line to the beginning of the next.

Worksheet area: Area of a spreadsheet consisting of rows and columns that intersect in cells.

Worksheet file: File created by an electronic spreadsheet.

Workstation: More sophisticated microcomputer that can communicate with more powerful computers and sources of information.

World Wide Web (WWW, W3, the Web): Internet search tool that uses hypertext to jump from document to document and from computer to computer. The Web is accessed by browsers.

WORM (write once, read many): Form of optical disc that allows data to be written only once but read many times without deterioration.

Write: *See* Writing data

Write once: Refers to an optical disc on which data is recorded by lasers and cannot be erased by the user.

Write-protect notch: Notch on a floppy disk used to prevent the computer from destroying data or information on the disk.

Writing data: For floppy disks, the process of taking the electronic information processed by the computer and recording it magnetically onto the disk.

WYSIWYG: Stands for "What You See Is What You Get." That is, the image on the screen display resembles the image of the final document that will appear when printed out on paper.

XGA (extended graphics array): Circuit board that can be inserted into a microcomputer and offers up to 256 colors under normal circumstances and more than 65,000 colors with special equipment.

Index

Illustration Credits

West Stock, Zephyr Picture #991106: 1-1; 1-8, 1-10, 4-1, 8-1 (*insets*)

Courtesy of Gateway 2000: 1-3

Courtesy of IBM Corporation: 1-4, 1-6, 1-9 (*left*), 3-11, 4-2 (*left*), 5-11, 6-10, 6-15, 7-17

Courtesy of Motorola and Cunningham Communication: 1-5

Courtesy of Cray Research, Inc.: 1-7

Courtesy of Apple Computer, Inc.: 1-9 (*right*), 1-14, 4-2 (*right*), 4-10, 5-10, 6-5, 7-1

Courtesy of Microsoft Corporation: 1-11 (*inset*), 2-5, 2-15, 3-5, 3-6, 6-3, 6-4, 8-3

Courtesy of Dell Creative Services: 1-12, 5-1

Fredrik D. Bodin: 1-13, 3-8

Courtesy of BASF: 1-16

Courtesy of QMS, Inc.: 1-17

Courtesy of Hayes Microcomputer Products: 1-18

Courtesy of Bank of America: 1-20

Courtesy of Aldus Corporation: 2-11

Courtesy of The Software Toolworks: 3-10

Courtesy of AimTech Corporation and Brodeur & Partners: 3-13

TSW/Andrew Sachs: 3-15

Courtesy of Trinzic Corporation: 3-16

Courtesy of SRI International: 3-18

Courtesy of Sun Microsystems, Inc.: 4-11

Courtesy of Intel: 5-7, 8-10

Courtesy of Xircom: 5-14

Mark Richards/Photo Edit: 6-1

Courtesy of Epson America, Inc.: 6-6, 6-20

Courtesy of Ford Motor Company: 6-7

Courtesy of H.E.I.: 6-8

Courtesy of Caterpillar Inc.: 6-9

Courtesy of Hewlett-Packard: 6-11, 6-17, 6-21, 6-22 (*inset*), 6-26

Courtesy of Lanier Worldwide, Inc.: 6-12

Courtesy of NCR: 6-13, 6-14

Courtesy of Toshiba America: 6-18

Courtesy of Tektronix, Inc.: 6-23

Courtesy of CalComp: 6-25

Courtesy of Bose Corporation: 6-27

Courtesy of Seagate Technologies: 7-7

Courtesy of SyQuest Technology, Inc.: 7-8

Courtesy of Stac Electronics: 7-11

Scott R. Goodwin, Inc.: 7-19

Richard Laird/FPG International: 8-2

Spencer Grant/Stock Boston: 9-12